Tribe and Society in Rural Morocco

Books of Related Interest

Technology, Tradition and Survival: Aspects of Material Culture in the Middle East and Central Asia
Richard Tapper and Keith McLachlan

Tribalism and Rural Society in the Islamic World
David M. Hart

French Military Rule in Morocco: Colonialism and its Consequences
Moshe Gershovich

Morocco Under Colonial Rule: French Administration of Tribal Areas
Robin Bidwell

An Account of the Empire of Morocco and the Districts of Suse and Tafilelt
James Grey Jackson

Tribe and Society in Rural Morocco

David M. Hart

FRANK CASS
LONDON • PORTLAND, OR

First published in 2000 in Great Britain by
FRANK CASS PUBLISHERS
Newbury House, 900 Eastern Avenue
London IG2 7HH

and in the United States of America by
FRANK CASS PUBLISHERS
c/o ISBS
5804 N.E. Hassalo Street
Portland, Oregon 97213-3644

Website: www.frankcass.com

British Library Cataloguing in Publication Data

Hart, David M.
Tribe and society in rural Morocco
1. Tribes – Morocco 2. Berbers – Morocco – Social life
    and customs 3. Morocco – Rural conditions. 4. Morocco
    – Social conditions
I. Title
307.7′72′0964

ISBN 0 7146 5016 1 (cloth)
ISBN 0 7146 8073 7 (paper)

Library of Congress Cataloging-in-Publication Data

A catalog record for this book is available from the Library of Congress

This group of studies first appeared in a Special Issue on 'Tribe and Society
in Rural Morocco' of The Journal of North African Studies (ISSN 1362-9387)
4/2 (Summer 1999).

Printed in Great Britain by Antony Rowe Ltd., Chippenham, Wiltshire.

Contents

Introduction

This collection of articles, most of which have been written since 1985, represents, in point of elapsed time, the residue of 11 years, not all continuous, between 1953 and 1967, of residence and fieldwork in Berber-speaking areas of Morocco. The latter was conducted, in particular, among the Aith Waryaghar in the Rif mountains in the north and among the Ait 'Atta of the Central Atlas range, the Saghru massif and the pre-Saharan oases in the centre and south of the country. I have spent, as well, at least one full year in periodic return visits to both areas since then. The material assembled here also represents certain aspects of Berber tribal ethnography to which I felt I had not given adequate coverage in previous publications (as in Hart 1976, 1981 and 1984), but also to some extent a rethinking of certain problems that seemed to me to require further investigation and analysis, particularly in the light of more recent research by other scholars.

I should also add that the great majority of the articles in this volume were written after my disillusionment over the value, for Muslim societies in North Africa and the Middle East generally, of segmentary lineage theory as originally expounded by Evans-Pritchard for the Nuer of the southern Sudan and the Bedouins of Cyrenaica (Evans-Pritchard 1940, 1949). My estrangement stemmed largely but by no means entirely from my debate on this subject with Henry Munson, Jr., with respect to my work on the Rif, in the pages of the *American Anthropologist* for 1989 (Munson 1989; Hart 1989). It will probably be noticed that I make few if any references to it in these articles. I have not abandoned it completely, but I no longer give it the primacy that I did in my earlier work, which was also influenced by that of the late Ernest Gellner (1969), with whom Munson also had a subsequent debate, with respect to his own work, as well as, to a lesser extent, my own, on the Ait 'Atta (cf. Munson 1993, 1995; Gellner 1996; Hart 1996). For the value of segmentary lineage theory in terms of what it actually explains now seems to me to be slight at best, especially as it is far more restrictive than it is inclusive. I should also add that, in more general terms, I have now come to turn more frequently to social history than to social anthropology as a disciplinary medium of expression.

It will be noticed too that these articles fall into two discrete sections – the first dealing entirely with the Rif, where I did my initial fieldwork and where I spent the most time, and the larger second one both on the Rif and on the higher Atlas mountains and the Saharan fringe below it in the southern part of Morocco. In the latter I compare specific institutions and sociocultural landmarks among Rifians on the one hand, with those among the Ait 'Atta and other southern Berber-speaking groups on the other. It had occurred to me as early as the late 1960s that what has been termed the 'controlled comparison' in anthropology (i.e. the comparison of what is truly comparable between one human group or region and another, even though they may in fact be widely separated spatially) can produce worthwhile analytical results, particularly if the groups or regions concerned are also culturally and structurally comparable and compatible.

Furthermore, although all Moroccans are Sunni Muslims of the Maliki rite, irrespective of whether their native language or speech happens to be Arabic or Berber, I should stress that my own work (with the exception of a brief sojourn among the Arabic-speaking camel pastoralists of the Rgaybat in the Western Sahara) was conducted almost exclusively among tribal groups whose members speak, natally, dialects of Berber rather than Arabic. These dialects are, in general, not mutually intelligible owing to millennia, rather than merely centuries, in spatial separation and independent development from each other. It is also worth noting that Berber, although not yet granted official status by the national authorities of either Morocco or Algeria[1], is nonetheless the 'aboriginal' language, so to speak, of both countries, as it is, indeed of much of the remainder of the Maghrib, of North Africa. Thus a shared, and dual, linguistic heritage (as well as treble, if French is also included, as a legacy of colonialism) and a shared Islamic institutional outlook and value system have also helped greatly to facilitate the limited comparisons of the sort I have attempted to make here.

Finally, a word should be said about the concepts of 'tribe' and 'society' as embodied in the book's title. The latter, as used here in the singular, is generally intended to refer to the national Moroccan society at large, while although there are probably almost as many definitions of 'tribe' as there are anthropologists who have tried to make them, the term as employed here must remain flexible and loose. It refers merely to the named human group of maximum size within a given region which is generally perceived to be such, both by its own members and by others, its neighbours of equal status and which is therefore recognised by all of them as having a distinct name and a distinct territory. As it happens, common territoriality is often larger and more significant than descent from a common ancestor in the patriline. Its various subgroups, all equally named and located at one level or removed further down are referred to as 'sections', while at two or more levels further down, these become 'subsections'. On the other hand, 'agnatic lineage' or 'patrilineage' refers, here as elsewhere, to the largest and most widely embracing unilineal (and here, patrilineal) descent group in which descent from a common patrilineal or agnatic ancestor can actually be traced, genealogically and on a step-by-step basis, by its living members.

BIBLIOGRAPHY

Evans-Pritchard, E.E., *The Nuer* (Oxford: Clarendon Press 1940).
——, *The Sanusi of Cyrenaica* (Oxford: Clarendon Press 1949).
Gellner, Ernest, *Saints of the Atlas* (London: Weidenfeld & Nicholson 1969).
——, 'Segmentation: Reality or Myth?', *Journal of the Royal Anthropological Institute (n.s.)* 1/4 (1996) pp.821–32.
Hart, David M., *The Aith Waryaghar of the Moroccan Rif: An Ethnography and History*. Viking Fund Publications in Anthropology No. 55 (Tucson: University of Arizona Press 1976).
——, *Dadda 'Atta and His Forty Grandsons: The Socio-Political Organisation of the Ait 'Atta of Southern Morocco* (Wisbech, Cambridgeshire: MENAS Press 1981).
——, *The Ait 'Atta of Southern Morocco: Daily Life and Recent History* (Wisbech, Cambridgeshire: MENAS Press 1984).
——, 'Rejoinder to Henry Munson, Jr., "On the Irrelevance of the Segmentary Lineage Model in the Moroccan Rif"', *American Anthropologist* 91/3 (1989) pp.765–9.
——, 'Segmentary Models in Morocco', *Journal of the Royal Anthropological Institute (n.s.)* 2/4 (1996) pp.721–2.
Munson, Henry, Jr., 'On the Irrelevance of the Segmentary Lineage Model in the Moroccan Rif', *American Anthropologist* 91/2 (1989) pp.386–400.
——, 'Rethinking Gellner's Segmentary Analysis of Morocco's Ait 'Atta', *Man: Journal of the Royal Anthropological Institute* 28/2 (1993) pp.267–80.
——, Answer to Ernest Gellner, *Saints of the Atlas* (above), *Journal of the Royal Anthropological Institute (n.s.)* 1/4 (1995) pp.829–32.

NOTE

1. Berbes languages have now been granted official status in Morocco.

Part I

Tribalism and Berber Identity

Tribalism: The Backbone of the Moroccan Nation

One has often read statements, especially in the publications of political scientists and high-level journalists, to the effect that Morocco (or any other Third World nation) is a 'developing country'. It is really impossible not to agree, in general terms, with this assertion, for it implies that not only, in certain spheres, is the country struggling to break with its past and to 'modernise' itself through socioeconomic change – which, particularly since 1970, has been galloping at an ever faster pace – but, equally and conversely, to retain, selectively, certain of those social institutions which have been central to the maintenance of its Islamic tradition throughout its history. But, with all due apologies to the political scientists and journalists in question, few of them have provided adequate descriptions or analyses of the so-called 'zero point' or 'base level' of 'traditional', and especially precolonial, Muslim society and culture in Morocco. Such description and analysis is properly the job of the sociocultural anthropologist, for any discussion of modern Morocco (or of any other emerging nation today, for that matter) can hardly be taken out of its historical and sociological contexts. What must be stressed is that such contexts are much more than mere 'background material'. They are the contexts – and still in many important ways very much living contexts – out of which any and all social change must necessarily become manifest.

A great deal, too, has been written by anthropologists about social change in general, and it is not the purpose here to recapitulate any of their conclusions. Suffice it to say that a problem – indeed a headache – with which the governments of many recently independent countries have had to come to grips is that of tribalism, the existence within their national borders of substantial elements of their populations which are organised into tribes. The general tenor of the thinking of these governments about tribes is that they are an obsolete form of social grouping, that their existence is incompatible with the place of the country concerned in the modern world, and that tribalism is an impediment to 'progress'. In short, tribalism has been viewed as a skeleton in many national closets, and therefore tribalism must go. Modern Morocco provides ample evidence for this generally prevailing trend of thought among the Afro-Asian elite, even though Moroccan tribalism, as shall be argued here, does not indeed constitute the barrier to modernisation which it may be believed to do in certain other new nations.

modern gov't
- tribalism = bad
inhibiting progress

Although the situation has become considerably modified today, it is a central fact of Moroccan political sociology under colonialism that prior to 1912 (and again, with admittedly gross oversimplification, the pre-1912 years may be regarded, for present purposes, as the 'zero point' in question) and the establishment of protectorates (of unequal size) by France and Spain, the country was more or less divided up according to three basic axes: an Arab–Berber axis, an urban–tribal axis and, somewhat more tenuously, a *makhzan–siba* axis. While bearing in mind that this whole frame of reference happens to represent a colonialist viewpoint, it seems nonetheless pertinent to consider, briefly, each of these in turn.

The first axis, Arab–Berber, is essentially linguistic. Arabic is the national language of Morocco (and in the 1962 Constitution it became so officially), but it is only spoken as a native language by about 60 per cent of a total population of about 27.5 million (1996). Berber is another language (or cluster of closely related dialects) entirely, that or those of three different sets of tribal groups, which do not quite achieve the status of ethnic minorities: all of them (barring recent migrants to the cities) live in difficult, mountainous terrain, although only the two in the Atlas (Western High Atlas and Anti-Atlas in the Tashilhit case and Middle Atlas and Central High Atlas in the Tamazight one) are spatially contiguous, while that in the Rif (the Tharifith case) is territorially separate from both of them. 'Berber' and 'tribalism' are by no means completely coterminous, but they have nevertheless tended to become so in the minds of modern Moroccans. Berbers represent, in this sense, both the most autochthonous as well as, until very recently, the most change-resistant and conservative element of the population.

The second axis, urban–tribal (rather than merely urban–rural, because 'rural' and 'tribal' were virtually coterminous in Morocco before 1912), is a socioeconomic one. All the cities were Arabic-speaking, but the tribes were, roughly, half and half, with Arabic-speaking tribes tending to be nearer the urban centres (of which there was quite a network, the most important having been the traditional imperial capital cities of Fez, Meknes and Marrakesh) and Berber-speaking ones tending to be further removed from urban influences. From this it follows that tribal autarchy, loudly proclaimed by a number of earlier writers, is a fallacy, for all the tribes have not only always had economic relations with each other, but those nearby with the cities as well. The tribesman in town is a very old phenomenon indeed, no matter how much he may distrust city-dwellers.

The third axis, *makhzan–siba*, was primarily political. These terms need some contextual explanation, even though the concepts they stood for became badly overworked in French colonial sociology. The unifying thread throughout all of Morocco was religious: it was, and is, Sunni Islam

Maliki Rite

of the Maliki rite (aside from a small and essentially urban Jewish minority). Ever since 808 CE, political power has been dynastic and centred in the Sultan (now King), a direct descendant of the Prophet Muhammad, who was (and is) in theory the spiritual and temporal head of the whole Muslim community; while the present 'Alawid dynasty, currently headed by King Hasan II, has held the throne since the mid-seventeenth century. The Sultan was surrounded with the usual appendages that one might expect, including, among other things, a large court with numerous ministers in which a strong division of labour and a high degree of protocol were prominent, as well as a standing army which also served as a tax-collecting force. As the Sultan, in order to keep the peace in his domain, had to be on the move continuously, crossing tribal territory (indeed, often several different tribal territories) in order to get from one urban centre to another, the court and the army moved with him. All the urban centres, and the majority of the tribal lands surrounding them, were entirely under government control, and therefore became known as *bilad al-makhzan*, or 'government land'; and the inhabitants of the *bilad al-makhzan* did not fail to pay their taxes to the Sultan when called upon to do so.

In actual fact the lands that fell fully into the *bilad al-makhzan* category covered not much more than the Atlantic coastal plain and adjacent plains regions of Morocco, considerably less than half the total surface area of the country. Most of the rest of the country is either mountains or desert, and with some notable exceptions most of this was *bilad al-siba* ('land of abandonment', 'land of dissidence'). This was purely tribal land, most of it Berber in speech, in which, so the colonialists' sociological argument ran, the Sultan was acknowledged as spiritual head of the country only, and in which, despite numerous punitive expeditions (especially under some of the more vigorous Sultans, such as Mawlay Isma'il (1672–1727) or Mawlay al-Hasan I (1873–1894)) when they were undertaken almost on an annual basis, taxes were seldom if ever paid.

In other words, it may be inferred that the difference between *makhzan* and *siba* was in essence one of payment or non-payment of taxes. The dichotomy between *makhzan* and *siba* was considered by the French to have been the linchpin of the Moroccan political system prior to the protectorate, for the divide-and-rule assumptions which they made about it were one of the mainstays of their colonial ideology; but it has also, in the work of one Moroccan writer after independence, been presented as a kind of optional 'social contract' situation: one could opt to be within the pale or beyond it, a view which is both challenging and challengeable (cf. Lahbabi 1958).

Let us now consider the Moroccan tribes themselves. We have already seen that some of them are Arabic in speech: these are called *qaba'il* (sing. *qabila*); others are Berber and are called by this term's Berber equivalent, *tiqbilin* (sing. *taqbilt*). But what, apart from linguistic differences, do they have in common? The answer is: a very great deal. There are, in conformity with the language difference, corresponding differences in nomenclature. An Arabic-speaking tribe may refer to itself as *Ulad X* or *Bni X* (cl. Ar. *Awlad X* or *Banu X*), both meaning 'sons of X', whereas a Berber-speaking one will call itself *Ait X*, or 'people of X'; these are small differences and the ultimate result is the same. This means that X may refer either to a common ancestor in the patriline, whether or not he is actually traceable genealogically, or to a place, generally a point of common origin. In fact, the latter is by a large margin the commoner of the two forms.

Descent, as among most Muslims, is invariably reckoned agnatically (which is to say, in the male line only), for all practical purposes; and the majority of Muslim tribal groups known to anthropologists undergo a process of subdivision through time and space which is known to anthropologists as 'segmentation'. This is easily defined: each tribe, whether an Arabic *qabila* or a Berber *taqbilt*, and whether it bears the name of a putative common ancestor or the name of a putative point of common origin, is divided or segmented into X number of sections, or clans, or primary segments (in Morocco, as it happens, seldom more than five, the implications of which are examined elsewhere, and in detail: cf. Hart (1967) in Ahmed and Hart 1984). Each of these is in turn subdivided or subsegmented into Y number of subsections, or subclans, or secondary segments (and in the Atlas it is usually these last which are given the label of *tiqbilin*); and each of these is in its turn again subsegmented into Z number of patrilineages, which in turn may themselves segment again, and again, and even again, down to the level of the elementary or nuclear family of father, mother and unmarried children. (It should be added that this follows standard anthropological usage in employing such terms as 'section' and 'subsection', 'clan' and 'subclan' and 'lineage' or 'patrilineage'.) The first is simply a named group of any sort at the primary or maximal level within a tribe, and the second is another named group of any sort that is encapsulated within it. The third, which may well correspond to the first in a *de facto* sense, and which may be yet another named group at a lower level, may also be a wide unilineal, and here agnatic, descent group within the tribe in question whose members say that they have a common origin or that they are descended from a common ancestor, but who cannot actually trace such descent genealogically. The same applies to the fourth, although it is encapsulated within the third, just as the second is within the first; while members of the fifth and smallest unit, the lineage or (as here) patrilineage, are, by definition, capable of tracing such descent genealogically, and step by step, usually from four to six ascending generations in this case. It is precisely this capability of tracing descent which marks off the patrilineage from any of the larger groups just mentioned.

It is also a basic principle of segmentary lineage theory that such lineages be regarded as corporate in a pyramidal sense: although the descendants of two brothers, A and B, may fight against each other, they will generally join forces if attacked by the descendants of the brothers' cousin, C, because, although A, B and C all go back ultimately to the same common ancestor D, the sons of A and those of B are more closely related to each other than either of them is to the sons of C. This is in theory, although in the Rif in particular no less than seven instances have been pointed to – one of them discussed in great detail – where the theory was strikingly violated, and violated indeed to the point of invalidation (cf. Hart 1976 pp.324–38). Nonetheless, and again in theory – a theory which is not only anthropological but also one espoused by tribal informants themselves – A, B and C will similarly and normally all band together to fight any less closely related section or clan E; and the members of one tribe, by the same token, will fight those of another. But it should be added that the theory is only that, a theory, and that it can readily be shown to have been contravened or even contradicted quite often, in one respect or another, by historical fact.

Each tribe has a given name and a given territory; and each section or clan within the tribe also has its own corresponding name and subterritory, so that the overall system of tribal land ownership is, again in theory, little more than the segmentary system flopped down spatially upon the ground. The linguistic axis of Arabic–Berber cuts across certain features of the tribal system which have already been referred to above. A few Arabic-speaking tribes, for instance, conceive of themselves as descended from common ancestors, but many if not most others, particularly the Arabo-Berber groups in the northwestern hills of the Jbala, are built up much more on the toponymy principle, with heterogeneous sections merely having come in and occupied territory which eventually became that of the tribe in question. The same is true of Berber tribes: those in the northern Rif and in the Western Atlas, the Sus and the Anti-Atlas regions in the southwestern part of the country, both tend to be organised on the toponymical and/or heterogeneous section principle, while at least some of those in the Middle, Central and Eastern High Atlases tend to be more aligned on the common ancestor principle.

One can also make, in general terms, an economic correlation here: the bulk, if not all, of the tribes, whether Arabic- or Berber-speaking, which are structured along the principle of heterogeneous sections are sedentary agriculturalists who live the year round in fixed houses, while most of those which claim the principle of common ancestorship are either sheep transhumants, as in the case of the Berber tribes of the Middle and Central High Atlases, or, among the Arabic-speaking Bedouins of the Western Sahara, full-scale pastoral camel nomads. And even here, in both cases, there are exceptions. (By 'transhumants', it is meant that the people concerned make two well-defined moves per year: up into the mountains in spring to pasture their sheep and to live in black goat-hair tents, and back down into the lower valleys in the autumn, where their permanent and several-storeyed mud-and-stone houses are located.)

Another feature common to most, though not all, Moroccan tribal groups is the existence, in their midst, of resident holy men (most not only claiming descent from the Prophet Muhammad, but possessing genealogical evidence, either written in Arabic or in their heads, to support this claim) who form lineages or even whole sections or clans within but somewhat apart from the rest of the tribal community. During the precolonial period their job was the arbitration of conflicts, both inside and outside the tribe. Such conflicts, in pre-protectorate Morocco, were very much the order of the day. It can be, and has been, argued that feuds and wars, far from promoting disintegration of the tribal system, provided in fact the main force and impetus which kept it going. This state of affairs, of 'peace in the feud', led French and Spanish investigators in the years between World Wars I and II to categorise tribal systems as 'systems of organised anarchy' (cf. Montagne 1931, translated into English by Seddon 1973; Blanco Izaga 1939; and same work, with others by the same author, translated into English by the present writer in Hart and Blanco Izaga 1975, and republished in Spanish in Hart and Blanco Izaga 1995). This is not, of course, quite the right label, for anarchy implies a total lack of government; but they were nonetheless on the right track, as tribal societies were not only strikingly egalitarian but were controlled internally by systems of superimposed representative councils.

Again, a generalisation can be made here: nomad and transhumant tribes tended to engage in intertribal warfare, while among sedentary agricultural tribes feuds were generally intratribal in character. In the Rif, for example, each tribe thought of itself as split almost literally in half (although in fact one such 'half' was invariably bigger than the other), and according to our own informants, when the two such factional alliance groups or *liff*-s (for 'moiety' is a singularly inappropriate label) were not fighting against each other, feuding continued just as intensively on a lower level, among the lineages of a given section or local community (Hart 1976 pp.313–24). Indeed, things did not stop here, and the much touted corporate unity of the agnatic lineage was often, in the Rif, rent asunder by vendettas between brothers and their sons, as noted above, generally because of deep-seated cleavages over partible inheritance (ibid. pp.324–38; Munson 1989; Hart

1989). Not only this, but among Rifians only the holier of the holy men abstained from fighting: the rank and file, who constituted 90 per cent of the total, fought among themselves, although not as a rule with outsiders. The holier holy men (the remaining and elite 10 per cent), in their white robes and with the *baraka* emanating from their persons (the 'blessing' God gave them to endow them with their ability as miracle-workers, an ability the lesser ones did not possess), lived up to the prestigious status and role assigned them by the community at large. They did this by seeing to it that feuds were interrupted by seasonal truces for plowing and harvesting, while at the same time they received helpful 'perks' through annual offerings from their constituents, as well as a 'cut off the top' when fines for murder were imposed by the sectional or tribal council.

For murder, under certain controllable circumstances, was indeed punished. In this connection, another feature of tribal organisation all over Morocco is the existence, in almost every tribe, of a weekly market, called *suq* of so-and-so, the word *suq* ('market') being followed by the name of the day of the week on which it is held and then generally by the name of the tribe in whose territory it is located. Market day is not only a day of economic exchange, but of social intercourse, when people (both of the tribe concerned and, often, of its neighbours also) see their friends and exchange news; and above all, it is a day of peace. The tribal council, furthermore, met in or just off the market precincts precisely to see that this peace was kept, as well as to deliberate on other issues which might have arisen during the course of the week. In the Rif, again, any man who murdered another on any of the paths leading to or from the market, not only on market day, but on the day preceding and the day following it as well, had not only to pay bloodmoney, in theory, to his victim's agnates (which the latter generally refused to accept, preferring to take vengeance on the person of the murderer himself or on that of any of his patrilateral kinsmen), but in addition a prohibitively heavy fine – significantly called *haqq* ('right' or 'due'), also in money (which has always been known in the region), to the council. If the murder had been committed in the market itself, this fine was doubled because the peace of the market had been 'broken', as Berbers say; and if under these circumstances the murderer was caught, he was shot outright. If he escaped but was unable to pay the fine, the council members descended upon his agnates in a body, burning their houses, cutting down their trees and confiscating their livestock. Not only this, but he himself had to flee to another section or another tribe entirely, and to remain in exile for at least a year, generally more, and often permanently, in order to escape the wrath of his victim's agnatic kinsmen. He could only return home when and if bloodmoney negotiations had been successfully concluded (for details, cf. Hart 1976 pp.283–309).

Woundings, too, were fined accordingly, and the council also imposed fines for the theft of larger livestock. In the Rif, however, theft of animals was as uncommon as murder was common; it is far more current in the Central Atlas, where fines were levied in sheep as much as in money and where, too, the mode of proof or tribal by collective oath reached its greatest development, as will become apparent shortly. The council, among Rifians and Western Atlas Berbers, was the body politic, and before the advent of bin 'Abd al-Krim, who led the Rifians in their two-front war against Spain and France (1921–26), and before 1912, when the French awarded Hajj Tahami al-Glawi the pashaship of Marrakesh while at the same time underwriting his overlordship not only of his own tribe, but of much of the Western Atlas, decision-making had never rested in the hands of a single individual. Political power tended to be decentralised, and the councils to be acephalous, in all the sedentary tribal regions; generally speaking, it was only among certain rural Arab groups that a greedy *qa'id* could 'eat' a whole tribe.

Among the Berber transhumants of the Middle, Central and Eastern High Atlases, a very different system prevailed: that of annual election of chiefs in which the section whose turn it was to provide the chief that year would remove itself from the other sections, whose members did the electing for it. Thus, if it was Section A's turn to provide the chief, Sections B, C, D and E elected, or selected, the appropriate individual from it; the following year, it was B's turn, and A, C, D and E did the electing in the same manner, and so on. A member of a holy lineage was usually on hand to solemnise the occasion, and the principal ritual feature of the election was that the outgoing chief stuck a blade of grass in the turban of the incoming one in order to ensure a fertile year. This system, peculiar to the region in question, was discovered by Ernest Gellner and labelled by him 'rotation and complementarity', the concept having been followed up by the present writer in the course of subsequent fieldwork among another large tribal group in the same general area (cf. Gellner 1969 p.81; Hart 1981 pp.76–93). But even here a chief whose 'luck' (Berbers refer to it as *aduku*, lit. 'slipper') was not good was easily impeached by the council before his year was up; conversely, if the year proved a good one and he himself proved to be a successful leader in war, he might last two or even three years before the next election.

We have already begun to note certain institutional differences between Arabic- and Berber-speakers: it is relevant to consider a few more. In cases of suspected theft, an Arabic-speaking tribesman had to take oath in the mosque, on a Friday, and on a copy of the Qur'an in order to attest his innocence. A Berber from the Rif also took (and takes) oath in the mosque, on Friday, and on the Qur'an, in the same way; but prior to the time of bin

'Abd al-Krim (who was responsible for changing a great deal of Rifian customary law: cf. Hart 1976 pp.381–94), he did so with five of his close agnatic kinsmen (making six in all) for minor matters, and with 11 agnates (making 12 in all) in a murder case. If, however, the homicide involved men of different tribes, the party under suspicion had to produce 49 co-jurors (50 in all, including himself). In this instance, however, fellow tribesmen rather than agnates would suffice, for it was a rare bird indeed who had as many as 49 living patrilineage-mates (ibid. pp.309–12).

A Berber from the Central Atlas, however, had to produce ten co-jurors (nine agnates plus himself) in cases of theft of animals, and 40 (39 agnates, or, in default, members of closely related lineages, plus himself) in case of murder. His nine most closely related agnates also accompanied him in his ritual flight to a neighbouring tribe after he committed a murder, but they returned home three days later to set about starting up bloodwealth and peace negotiations. In this region, however, oaths were always sworn at saints' shrines in front of a lay oath administrator, never in the mosque and never in the Qur'an: for Central Atlas Berbers argue that oaths taken in mosques and on the Holy Book are in fact 'too easy', particularly in terms of the possibility of perjury – which was punished by divine sanction, which usually meant the death or blindness of the perjurer. Oath-takings were very public affairs, by their very nature, and onlookers often heckled the co-jurors in order to trip them up. If the defendant or any of his agnates failed to repeat the oath correctly, it was as 'broken' as the Rifian markets mentioned above, and he had to pay the plaintiff. Some tribes in this area even had supreme courts of appeal; and two further refinements of the collective oath complex were (1) the existence in some tribes of accusing as well as of denying oaths, and (2) that a man who became angry with his own lineage-mates could change over to another co-juring group by sacrificing a sheep to them, and without losing his property rights in his lineage of origin. The same technique, exactly, was resorted to if a man were unable to supply the full quota of co-jurors that he might need (for details, cf. Hart 1981 pp.157–79).

The Moroccan tribal world was and still is very definitely a man's world in which women took and take little or no part, at least externally or overtly. Nonetheless, they often have a great deal of influence behind the scenes, although it should also be stated that the division of labour by sex is very unequal, as women tend to work far harder and longer hours than men do. In structural terms, however, and in the Rifian view of the situation, women, handed around in marriage from one lineage to the next within a given community or section, or, more rarely, to another section or another tribe, provided crucial links of alliance in which they themselves, being passive instruments of policy, had little or no choice or voice. Such links, too, were continually reinforced through subsequent marriages over time. The Qur'an stipulates that daughters must inherit half of what sons inherit, and it forbids, absolutely, a wife to divorce her husband, unless he is impotent. He, on the other hand, can divorce her with ease, although even in the Rif divorce is not in fact as common as might be expected. Neither are polygynous marriages: the great bulk of Moroccan tribesmen are monogamous, largely for economic reasons if for no other, although they are permitted up to and including four wives at a time by religious law.

But the Berbers in the Central Atlas show two variants here, which in the long run actually balance each other out: wives in some tribes were able, until independence, to divorce their husbands – though the latter might well have forbidden them to remarry a set number of men with whom they suspected their ex-wives of having carried on; and the balance occurred in inheritance, as daughters in a *de facto* sense got nothing at all. In fact, if there were no sons, the brothers of the deceased took over his daughters lock, stock and barrel, for this is one region, unlike the Rif, in which marriage with one's father's brother's daughter has always been held up as the ideal pattern, even though actual practice in some tribes shows considerable deviation from it. The double standard has always prevailed, and a cuckolded husband has always had the right to kill both his wife and her lover, especially in the Rif, where women have been more secluded, perhaps, than in any other rural area of the country. In one major Rifian tribe which the writer knows well, there were even in the early 1960s several murders per year resulting from adultery cases (Hart 1976 p.126).

Such, in general, was the fabric of tribal society in Morocco prior to 1912. It is now useful to bring the picture up to date. In the Rifian north, because bin 'Abd al-Krim, who because of his heroic resistance war against both the colonial powers was later to become a nationalist hero, had already introduced major changes among his Rifian constituents – by outlawing feuds and vendettas and destroying the feuding pillboxes which used to stand near every house, and by decollectivising oaths which in their previous plural form were repugnant to him as a judge of Muslim Law – the Spanish, after his surrender (to the French) in 1926, merely took over where he left off.

The French, however, in their very much larger zone, magnified the differences between Arabs and Berbers to the point where, in 1930 and the promulgation of the infamous 'Berber Dahir' (decree of autonomy in the administration of customary law, as opposed to Muslim Law, in Berber regions), divide-and-rule became official policy. This decree stated, in effect, that Berbers were 'noble savages' whose customary law – which, as stated above, shows some significant differences from Qur'anic norms, although in most respects they resemble two sides of a coin – had to be underwritten by France as a protectoral duty. It also implied, analogously, that Arabs were 'no-goods' who had to be watched. Thus the Berber Dahir and what it stood for – and at the time of its promulgation, it raised storms of protest all over the Islamic world – triggered Arab nationalism in Morocco. This nationalism, over the next 20 years, became increasingly articulate in the cities, while French Army captains in the heart of the Atlas mountains carefully saw to it that Berber Custom was kept in the deep freeze, and that Berbers themselves, through their *qa'id*-s or tribal leaders – at the top of the tribal political ladder (while the captains, both French and Spanish, who were their opposite numbers, were at the bottom of their own administrative ladders whose tops reached back to Rabat and Tetuan, the respective French and Spanish protectorate capitals) – were kept in political quarantine.

The storm broke in the cities in the early 1950s, led by the Istiqlal Party with the support of a large, detribalising urban proletariat. It did not spread to the countryside until mid-1955; the French, right up until the very end, and even beyond, believed in the myth that the Berbers, who were all mistakenly assumed to be under the Glawi's dictatorial command, would remain loyal to them: for the poachers of the years before 1933, the final year of 'pacification' of the Central Atlas by French arms, had nominally been turned into the game-wardens of the protectorate. The French regime fell at least in part as a victim of its own myth-making and self-deceptions: for it was Berbers, too, in the Moroccan Army of Liberation in the Rif who attacked simultaneously three French outposts and brought the resistance to the rural and tribal level. Not long afterward, the Glawi himself, the all-powerful Pasha of Marrakesh under the French, about-faced and declared his loyalty to King Muhammad V, newly returned from French-imposed exile in Madagascar; and this was the ageing Glawi's last act before his death, early in 1956. On the other hand, bin 'Abd al-Krim died in Cairo in 1963 after a very much longer exile which was, on Reunion Island, at first French-dictated, but which after his Cairene sojourn dating from 1947, when he jumped a ship that was to take him to France, eventually became self-imposed.

With independence in 1956, one of the first things that happened was that the Berber Dahir was rescinded. The title of *qa'id* was still retained in the tribal areas, but the young man who now held the position was a Moroccan government employee of the Ministry of Interior in Rabat. Aside from being, as a rule, not local to the tribe itself, he took over the position of tribal administrator which the French or Spanish army captain or civil controller had held before him. Thus the highest purely local official now, in this new single-stranded chain of command, was the *shaykh*. This was an important administrative change; and another development which was to have even more important repercussions in the tribal areas was the fact that everybody enthusiastically joined the Istiqlal Party which had been so instrumental in gaining Morocco's independence.

But the Istiqlal, the senior party, was not to retain an uncontested dominance. For various reasons, most of which centred around maladministration and insufficient representation at court, a disenchantment with the Istiqlal, which became particularly strong in Berber-speaking areas, was widespread by 1958. By the following year, two other major parties had emerged: the National Union of Popular Forces (UNFP) and the Popular Movement (MP). Both of these gained adherents among Berbers, the latter party (avowedly Berber-oriented) doing so in particular. In 1963, the MP merged with one or two lesser parties to form a right-wing coalition backing the monarchy and the 1962 Constitution, which were then being criticised both by the Istiqlal and the left-wing UNFP. As of 1964 (when the initial version of this article was first drafted), the latter party had virtually ceased to exist, and the monarchy was strongly supported by the Royal Army (FAR), in which, it is of interest to note, Berbers were particularly well represented, both as officers and enlisted men – something which was hardly the case in precolonial days, although it levelled out noticeably after the public execution for treason of ten high-ranking Berber officers in July 1971, directly following the unsuccessful army attempt on the life of King Hasan at Skhirat. There emerged a plethora of other political parties, as well as strong urban labour unionism. Some of these were more effective than others. The whole party structure is strongly redolent of Morocco's pluralistic society; and in the tribal areas in particular, party cleavages were quite often an index of older, pre-existing cleavages of a more traditional sort. This fact certainly represents a degree of continuity with the Moroccan past.

But the above is a digression from the present subject. The post-independence period also saw, as of 1958–60, the creation and implementation of the so-called 'rural communes', all over Morocco; and the avowed objective of these communes, a brainchild of the then Minister of Interior, Hasan Zimmuri, was to substitute the commune for the tribal section or even for the tribe itself (in the cases of small tribes) as a focus of local loyalty, and, ultimately, to render the whole tribal system obsolete by centring on purely territorial ties as opposed to ties of agnatic kinship. The scheme met, initially, at least, with only moderate success, greatest perhaps in the Atlantic coastal plains, very slight in the Rif and least of all in the Central Atlas, where Berber speech, Berber tribalism and Berber values still obtained in force, even though customary law and collective oath are today things of the past. These same Berbers, however, seemed very pleased, nonetheless, about wells, springs and irrigation-improvement schemes which the communes began to start in earnest in 1964, and out of which, for example, arose the DERRO development project in the Western Rif, although it was to founder in later years. Under the French, army officers in the *Affaires Indigènes* corps studied Berber in Rabat for so many hours per week as they did Arabic, while in Rabat for a good 20 years after independence 'Berber' was considered a dirty word. There are fairly clear signs today (as of 1997), however, that it is coming back into its own once more, albeit in more modern dress.

And last but by no means least, the immediate post-independence period was for its first four years characterised by a series of tribal revolts, all of them, significantly, in areas of Berber speech: in the Tafilalt in 1956–57, in the Rif (by far the most serious one) in 1958–59, and in the Central Atlas in 1960. There have been none since then which can in any way be labelled 'tribal', but early in 1984, for example, there were demonstrations in the Rif, again, over the high prices of staple foods, which were brutally suppressed. As Gellner observed in another context, these revolts were in some ways seemingly inexplicable, particularly since at least one of them (that of 1960) was proclaimed in favour of an individual who happened at the very time to be Prime Minister (cf. Gellner (1962) 1973). They were in no sense New Guinea-style nativistic movements, and although, as it happened, they occurred in just those areas characterised by *siba* before 1912, the post-independence pattern which they presented was, owing to the very unification of Morocco by the French during the protectorate, of quite a different character. They were certainly an assertion of tribal personality, but within a new and national framework. Through the channels of political parties, generally, most of the tribal leaders concerned gained pipelines into the capital city of Rabat; and as the real political struggle on the national level has not yet happened, now four decades after independence (again underscoring the 'transitional' and 'developmental' character of modern Morocco), these rebellions took on the aspect of local dress rehearsals. If and when it does come, no doubt whoever wins will sweep the board; but the extreme concentration of power in the hands of the monarchy and the army have provided grave deterrents to any attempted *coups d'état* since 1973.

Thus tribalism, and in particular Berber tribalism, still has its uses to the central government even today; and although official Rabat, in a very natural reaction against protectorate policy, has tended to soft-pedal any Arab–Berber distinctions, Berbers, as already indicated, have shown signs of re-emerging in a characteristically dissenting manner, albeit with more updated goals. Even though young and modernised Moroccans may dismiss the tribes as backward and overly pious, many of these same young men are themselves of tribal origins, rather than of urban ones, and they tend to be proud of the fact. The relative security of the protectorate period brought, among other things, a great influx of tribesmen into the cities as well as establishing patterns of labour migration which are now so well developed as to be taken, in certain cases (notably that of both wholesale and retail grocers from the Sus region), for granted. Tribe reinforces town; and in the strongly developed physical mobility of Moroccan tribesmen, who have always lived juxtaposed with their urban neighbours (just as Arabs and Berbers have always lived similarly juxtaposed), lies their awareness of the wider pluralistic society of which they form a numerically significant part.

It is for these reasons that the problem of tribalism in Morocco is not only a skeleton in the national closet (and one which showed strong signs of rattling in the immediate post-independence years), but it has also become one in many acculturated, urbanised, individual closets as well. It is, nonetheless, a skeleton which, though it will probably long preserve certain elements of its basic structure, shows definite adaptive potential in the evolving Morocco of today.

Update

This article, originally entitled *Tribalism: The Skeleton in the Moroccan Closet*, was first written as a public lecture in 1964, then cursorily revised in 1966, and then it lay fallow and forgotten in a desk drawer until further and more extensive revision, as well as the present update and change of title, were undertaken both in 1987 and again in 1997.

There seems to us to be no real need to go into anything like a full-scale résumé of Morocco's policies toward its formerly tribal and now merely largely rural inhabitants in the more than 30 years since the article was originally written, beyond noting that our own views on the whole question have in the interim merely undergone certain important modifications but not much basic change. In 1971, 1972 and 1973 Morocco went through three successive and unsuccessful *coups d'état*, staged by the military of one arm or another against the monarchy. The first two of these were highly publicised, especially through the televising of the execution of the rebellious generals after the initial one, while the demise of General Ufqir (Oufkir), the then Minister of Interior, came about as a result of his implication in both the first and, in particular, the second of these *coups manqués*. Although at the time the monarchy seemed shaky, King Hasan II was soon firmly in the driver's seat once again after they were over, and his power, popularity and charisma, furthermore, were greatly enhanced by the 'Green March' of 350,000 Moroccans to the edge of the then Spanish Sahara late in 1975. But although even today (1997) the support for the monarchy continues steadfastly in many if not most rural areas, the long Moroccan war in the Western Sahara against the so-called Frente Polisario

(Frente Popular para la Liberacion del Sahara Español y de Rio de Oro), now at last effectively over, had by the early 1980s begun to take its toll. In launching Morocco into this campaign, King Hasan adroitly played the card of irredentism: if there are troubles at home, keep them covered up by concentrating on a big external venture abroad – which is precisely what the Western Sahara conflict proved to be, despite the fact that the Moroccan historical claims to the region seem, if not airtight, to be certainly better than those of any other contender, least of all the local Saharan Bedouin nomads or former nomads who provided the Polisario with its main shock troops.

One may well ask: How does tribalism in Morocco, or its vestiges, fit into all this? In one sense, certainly, it no longer does so at all, in that it can now effectively be labelled as 'historical', simply because it has ceased to exist as such. It has, in fact, gone a couple of rungs further up the ladder to become regionalism instead – while the agnatic lineage has shown tendencies to disintegrate into a mere collection of related nuclear families. Regionalism is, indeed, a considerably bigger issue today than ethnicity, although members of the three major Berber dialect groups still tend, and strongly so, to see themselves as somewhat apart from the rest of the country, particularly in the Rif.

Nonetheless, another major factor in the economic development of Morocco as a whole after 1970 has been that of labour migration to the countries of the European Economic Community (particularly in France, Belgium and Holland), sparked by the Rifians, whose own previous experience of working for French farmers in colonial Algeria goes back to as early as the mid-nineteenth century. There is hardly a rural family anywhere today who does not have at least one member working in Europe. Rifian workers have returned from France and Holland to invest in agricultural enterprises in northern Morocco or in urban real estate in Tetuan and Tangier, while traditional agriculture has itself gone largely by the board. On the other hand, some Central Atlas workers seem to have developed a penchant for mining and metallurgy, winding up with good jobs at the Bureau of Mines in Rabat, and the Susis are still in full control of the wholesale and retail ends of the grocery trade throughout the country. These things can all be counted as plus signs.

But in answer to the last three questions posed at the end of the original essay, party politics in Morocco are currently at a low ebb and are securely controlled from Rabat; while the much-ballyhooed 'rural communes' still seem to have little real power and seemingly never enough money allotted to them to be able to finish up local irrigation and other projects once the latter get underway. (An example, from early 1987, is the Sidd Muhammad bin 'Abd al-Krim al-Khattabi, the dam set up on the Nkur River in the Rif, which still lay in a state of suspended animation while waiting for a royal inauguration visit from the king which only came in September of the same year; following it, the great bulk of the water flowing through it was directed straight to the provincial capital of al-Husayma, with very little left over for local farmer-irrigators.) The patronage system, too, is still present, and in force: it goes right back to Rabat, where the Great Patron himself sits in the Qsar al-Maliki, the Royal Palace. But since 1960, as noted, however, there has not been one single tribal revolt, totally contrary to what happened during the first four years after independence, which, now that decolonisation has also been fully attained, is very much a reality. In addition, we have noted, both with interest and with pleasure, that 'Berber' no longer seems to be quite the unspoken dirty word that it once was in the corridors of power in Rabat. Both 'Berber', *Amazigh* (pl. *Imazighen*), and possibly even 'tribe' (*qabila*), may conceptually, if only tacitly, come to occupy once again the front and centre positions which are rightfully theirs, along with that of Sunni and Maliki Islam, as the historical and sociological backbone of the Moroccan nation.

BIBLIOGRAPHY

Blanco Izaga, Col. Emilio, 'Conferencia sobre Derecho Consuetudinario Rifeño', ms. (1935).
——, *El Rif (2a. Parte) – La Ley Rifeña – II: Los Canones Rifeños Comentados* (Ceuta: Imprenta Imperio 1939).
Gellner, Ernest, *Saints of the Atlas* (London: Weidenfeld and Nicholson 1969).
——, 'Patterns of Rural Rebellion in Morocco During the Early Years of Independence' (1962), in Ernest Gellner and Charles Micaud (eds.), *Arabs and Berbers: From Tribe to Nation in North Africa* (London: Duckworth 1973) pp.361–74.
Hart, David M., 'The Tribe in Modern Morocco: Two Case Studies', in Gellner and Micaud (above) pp.25–58.
——, *The Aith Waryaghar of the Moroccan Rif: An Ethnography and History*. Viking Fund Publications in Anthropology No.55 (Tucson: University of Arizona Press 1976).
——, *Dadda 'Atta and his Forty Grandsons: The Socio-Political Organisation of the Ait 'Atta of Southern Morocco* (Wisbech, Cambridgeshire: MENAS Press 1981).
——, 'Segmentary Systems and the Role of "Five Fifths" in Tribal Morocco' (1967), in Akbar S. Ahmed and David M. Hart (eds.), *Islam in Tribal Societies: From the Atlas to the Indus* (London: Routledge and Kegan Paul 1984) pp.66–105.
——, 'Rejoinder to Henry Munson, Jr., "On the Irrelevance of the Segmentary Lineage Model in the Moroccan Rif"', *American Anthropologist* 91/3 (September 1989) pp.765–9.
—— (ed. and transl.), and Blanco Izaga, *Emilio Blanco Izaga: Colonel in the Rif*. Ethnography Series, HRAfLEX Books MX3-001 (2 vols., New Haven: Human Relations Area Files 1975).
——, *Emilio Blanco Izaga: Coronel en el Rif*. Biblioteca de Melilla No.8 (Melilla: Auyuntamiento Municipal de Melilla/Fundacion Municipal Sociovcultural/UNED-VCentro Asiociado de Melilla 1995).
Lahbabi, Mohammed, *Le Gouvernement Marocain à l'Aube du Vingtième Siècle* (Rabat: Editions Techniques Nord-Africains 1958).
Montagne, Robert, *Les Berbères et le Makhzen dans le Sud du Maroc: Essai sur la Transformation Politique des Berbères Sédentaires (Groupe Chleuh)* (Paris: Felix Alcan 1930).
——, *La Vie Sociale et Politique des Berbères* (Paris: Editions du Comité de l'Afrique Française 1931).
Munson, Henry, Jr., 'On the Irrelevance of the Segmentary Lineage Model in the Moroccan Rif', *American Anthropologist* 91/2 (1989) pp.386–400.
Seddon, David, *Translation of Montagne, Robert, The Berbers: Their Social and Political Organisation* (1931), (London: Frank Cass 1973).

Scratch a Moroccan, Find a Berber

Until the recent rise of the Berber linguistic and cultural movement in both Algeria and Morocco (in the former as of 1980 and in the latter as of only 1991) – a movement which has been given only the scantiest recognition, if that, by the governments of both countries, leery as they are of its possible political implications – it had been generally assumed by most observers, including the present writer, that the major criterion for defining the term 'Berber' was the linguistic one, and that Berber remains essentially an unwritten language. On this basis Berber-speakers in the Maghrib (i.e. those who speak one of several Berber dialects rather than Arabic, which is the national language of both countries, as their natal tongues) were held to have constituted about 30 per cent of the population of Algeria and about 40–45 per cent of that of Morocco.

Here it should be noted first that, in accordance with a prevailing trend in the Berber movement, Berbers today tend to refer to themselves as *Imazighen* (sing. *Amazigh*, lit. 'the (free) people'), to their language in general as *Tamazight* and to the Maghrib, to North Africa, as *Tamazgha*. Secondly, with respect to the 'traditional' percentage figures just cited, which stem largely from the French colonial dispensation, a number of views were expressed at a conference on Berber Culture held in August 1994 at Douarnenez, in Brittany, to the effect that these figures are too low. Indeed, one speaker, Ouzzine Ahardane, editor of the Tamazight weekly *Tidmi*, in Rabat, even voiced the opinion that in both colonial and independent Morocco the Berber-speaking percentage figure should read well over 50 per cent, and that in the precolonial period it would have been as much as 70–80 per cent.

These last amended estimates in particular must for the moment remain conjectural; but there is no question that Berber speech, as transmitted by Berberophone mothers to their offspring, far from dying out (as perhaps hoped for by Arab nationalists), is evidently on the increase, in both the rural and urban milieux of Morocco: for the latter had in fact become open to rural and tribally organised Berber-speakers once the French 'pacification' of both countries, which was completed in Morocco only as late as 1934 – 22 years after the establishment of the protectorate –, had been effected. The difference between the Berber situation as it was in 1934 and as it is today is that now the majority of Berber-speaking men, at least (though this would apply considerably less to women), are no longer monolingual, as many of them were even until the end of the protectorate in 1956. They are bilingual, in Moroccan Arabic, or even trilingual, in French, as well. (In the former Spanish and present North Zone, some still speak

Spanish, and even English has evidently become available, as well, as a second foreign language to those who are interested in learning it.)

It is worth mentioning, however, that in Morocco only two of the three major groups of Berber-speakers traditionally referred to themselves as *Imazighen*, namely the transhumant tribes of the Middle and Central/Eastern High Atlases, the Jbil Saghru and the pre-Saharan oases on the one hand, and the sedentary agricultural Rifian tribes in the north, along the Mediterranean littoral, on the other. The latter, although only since independence, however, have started to use the neologism *Irifiyen* (sing. *Arifi*) in order to differentiate themselves both in terms of dialect and of region inhabited from the former. The third group, in the Western Atlas, the Sus Valley and the Anti-Atlas, has always been known as *Ishilhayen* (sing. *Ashilhi*, also a neologism from Arabic *Shluh*, sing. *Shilh*) or *Isusiyen* (neologism from Arabic *Swasa*, sing. *Susi*, or inhabitant of the Sus), while in the Algerian Jurjura the Kabyle linguist Salem Chaker has noted that the term *amazigh* does not exist in *Thaqba'ilith* as traditionally spoken and that he never heard it until he started working in comparative Berber linguistics (Chaker 1987). Nonetheless, the terms *Amazigh/Imazighen* and its feminine form *Tamazight*, as authentically vernacular designations, seem now to have become completely accepted. Even so, we would also respectfully submit that there is nothing – at least today – which can be taken as pejorative about the term 'Berber', even though its original meaning in Roman times or earlier may have been that of 'barbarians, those who say "blah-blah-blah"'.

But there is much more than just the linguistic factor in north-west Africa that is authentically Berber, even though it is difficult to draw up a casual checklist. Such a list would indeed run the cultural, structural and institutional gamut from elements of material culture through certain features of economic and sociopolitical organisation and customary law to certain ways of looking at and interpreting Islam. Viewed both historically and regionally, these might include the collective storehouses or *igharman* (sing. *igharm*) and the collective pasturelands or *igudlan* (sing. *agudal*) of the Central Atlas; the collective oaths (*tigulla*, sing. *tagallit*) sworn at saints' tombs by accused individuals supported by a variable number of their agnates according to the gravity of the offence of which they were accused; the annual elections of the *amghar n-ufilla* (lit. 'big man on top'), the top tribal chief, by the twin processes of rotation and complementarity among participating tribal sections in the same area; the existence in the Rif of markets reserved exclusively for women; and the imposition in precolonial times of staggeringly heavy fines (*haqq* – lit. 'right, truth') for murder committed in the ordinary Rifian markets, fines which were collected by and distributed among the tribal councillors or *imgharen* (sing. *amghar*) as perquisites of office. In the same area too there was a general and chronic propensity toward both feud and vendetta and in both regions a disinclination to let women inherit, as well as an attitude toward Islam in which the saint's shrine (*siyyid*) has tended to play a bigger role than the Qur'an, although at the same time, also, religious orders (*turuq*, sing. *tariqa*) have tended to be dismissed as being of little account. Nonetheless, the existence of Berber-speaking *shurfa'* (sing. *sharif*) or descendants of the Prophet, on the other hand, settlements of whom are to be found in all the major areas of Berber speech, is undeniable, as is the genuineness of their genealogy: the Idrisids may have established the first officially Muslim dynasty in Morocco but they married local wives, who were nothing if not Berber. In the pre-Saharan oases south of the Atlas, too, there are, generally speaking, three endogamous social categories: the *shurfa'* (or, in Tamazight, *igurramen*, sing. *agurram*) at the top, who traditionally adjudicated disputes between and among the ordinary lay tribesmen. The latter, whether Berber or Arab, form the intermediate layer, while the bottom level consists of sedentary black date cultivators known as Haratin. – or Ismukha

It is tempting, too, for this foreign anthropologist to add a value judgement here, to the effect that the openness and frankness he has encountered in most Moroccan Berber informants, both among the Ait 'Atta of the Saghru and the Aith Waryaghar of the Rif, in the course of interviews, and their undeniable willingness and interest (despite an initial and understandable reserve on the part of some Rifians) in imparting both ethnographic and historical data and information about their societies and cultures contrasts notably with the extreme suspicion encountered, for example, among nomad Arabic-speaking Rgaybat informants in the Western Sahara, while the openness and frankness of the Berbers was only equalled by their own great sense of humour.

Throughout history most of what has been written about Berbers has been written by non-Berbers, almost all of whom have been prejudiced against their subjects into the bargain. Westermarck, who had a Moroccan Arabic proverb up his sleeve for every possible occasion, even cites one to the effect that '*l-'asil ma hiya sh-shham u l-bishna ma hiya ta'am u sh-shilha ma hiya klam*' ('Honey is not fat, sorghum is not food and Berber is not a language'; Westermarck 1930 p.135). Insofar as Berber was/is neither technically a written language nor the vehicle of a revealed religion, the reasoning went, it was thus regarded as culturally inferior to Arabic. Therefore, throughout the whole of the Islamic period the Berbers, conditioned to viewing Arabic as the linguistic and literary vehicle of a superior Islamic civilisation and culture, have also, for the most part, tended to imitate Arabs and denigrate themselves. But this attitude has now changed. They feel, rightly, that it now seems high time to redress the balance, although there is currently a debate within the Berber movement as to which script should be used, Roman, Arabic or Tifinagh (which until its resurrection by the movement had survived only among the Saharan Tuareg), each having its adherents, although those favouring the Roman script may be in the ascendancy. From a linguistic standpoint the latter might prove the most amenable, although adapting it to use by computer may pose problems through the necessity of special keys or some reorientation of existing ones.

In two earlier articles, one much earlier, published in 1960, and the other far more recent, published in 1992, I looked first at Arabic and Berber toponymy and anthroponymy, at tribal and place names, both in the Arabic-speaking region of the Jbala and Ghmara in north-western Morocco (Hart 1960) and, much later, at tribal and place names generally in Morocco and Algeria more or less as wholes (Hart 1992), with a view to accounting statistically for a good part of the Berber residue which is often very rich even in regions having populations which today speak only Arabic. But I must now admit that possibly I was, in so doing, looking through the wrong end of the telescope, and that perhaps I should have followed the simpler method of looking first at the Arab overlay to see just how much of the Berber substratum may have rubbed off upon it. Although Arabs and Berbers have lived in juxtaposition in the Maghrib for well over a millennium, it is quite apparent that the Berber element is very much more than just a residue. It is, indeed, the base of the whole North African edifice, and it is still very strongly so today, so much so that one can say: scratch a Moroccan, find a Berber.

In my view, there is nothing political, or nothing avowedly political, about the Berber linguistic and cultural movement, for it is also eminently peaceful in its intentions. Most recently, too, its stance has also become anti-fundamentalist, given the unprecedented rise of Islamism in Algeria and the current state of civil war between it and the government. What the movement wants and what in my opinion it should be accorded is official recognition in both countries, Algeria and Morocco, by virtue of being written into their respective constitutions. These would appear to be fully legitimate aspirations, and one can only hope that they will soon be realised.

BIBLIOGRAPHY

Chaker, Salem, art. 'Amazigh', *Encyclopédie Berbère* IV (Aix-en-Provence: Edisud 1987) pp.562–8.
Hart, David M., 'Tribal and Place Names among the Arabo-Berbers of North-western Morocco: A Preliminary Statistical Analysis', *Hesperis* I/3 (Rabat 1960) pp.457–511.
——, 'Arabic and Berber Names on the Tribal Map of North-west Africa: A Statistical Evaluation', *Awraq: Estudios sobre el Mundo Arabe e Islamico Contemporaneo* XIII (Madrid 1992) pp.157–204.
Westermarck, Edward, *Wit and Wisdom in Morocco: A Study of Native Proverbs* (London: George Routledge 1930).

Scission, Discontinuity and Reduplication of Agnatic Descent Groups in Precolonial Berber Societies in Morocco

In the context of Moroccan tribal ethnography a number of observers, including this author, have reported on the frequent presence of lineage, sectional or tribal names that are traditionally associated with a given section or tribe as existing also in another section or tribe entirely (e.g. Gellner 1969 pp.56–63; Maher 1974 p.29; Hart (1967) 1984*b*, 1970*a* p.47 n. 38, 1976 pp.264–70, 1981 and 1984*a*). This appears to have been particularly prevalent in the more mountainous, Berber-speaking parts of the country, especially in the Rif and in the Atlas, and our distinct impression is that it is considerably less so in the Arabic-speaking plains areas and in the cities.

It would appear desirable to provide this article with a solid historical base outlining the expansion of such groups, which in recent precolonial times at least seem on our evidence to have been more numerous among Berber-speaking communities or societies than among Arabic-speaking ones. Nonetheless, the large and loose Shawiya confederacy of the Casablanca hinterland, which is technically 'Arab', provides, through its original ethnographer Edouard Michaux-Bellaire, one such example of amalgamation which, if correctly reconstructed, might well have taken place somewhat before the big Berber push that began across the Atlas from south-east to north-west in search of greener pastures, starting in the mid-sixteenth century and ending abruptly in 1912 with the arrival of the French (cf. Hart 1993). The Shawiya case, too, seems fairly well documented: for the existence of groups which were originally Berber among this now linguistically totally Arabised group in that part of the Atlantic coastal region formerly known as the Tamsna seems well attested for the late medieval and early modern periods. These various Shawiya sections or groups were, for the most part, although not all, of Zanata Berber origin and affiliation, unlike the Berber groups in the Atlas; and the name Zanata still persisted as a group name in the Casablanca environs well into the time of the French protectorate, all of which comes to light through the investigations of Michaux-Bellaire (1915).

After noting that the descriptive term *shawiya*, referring to 'shepherds', began to be employed at some point between the time of Ibn Khaldun (fourteenth century) and that of Marmol del Carvajal (sixteenth century), Michaux-Bellaire sums up the overall ethnic composition of the Shawiya as follows: the sections or tribes of the Ulad Hariz, Ulad Sa'id and Ulad Ziyyan are of Hilalian Arab origin; those of the Sabbah, Ahlaf and Ulad 'Ali are, more specifically, of Ma'qil Arab origin; and that of the A'shash is of Sulaym Arab origin. This is to say that all the above groups go back to Bedouin origins in the eastern Maghrib and ultimately, we would assume, in the Mashriq.

On the other hand, the sections of the Zanata, Midyuna (which may once, Michaux-Bellaire informs us, have had Christian and Jewish elements) and Mzab are of Zanata Berber origin; that of the Mallila (which survives in the Berber toponym *Tit Mallil*, 'the spring of Mallil', not far from Casablanca) is of Huwwara Berber origin; those of the Ziyaida, Ulad Bu Ziri and Ulad Sidi bin Dawud are of Sinhaja Berber origin; and that of the Mzamza, from Amizmiz in the Western Atlas (whence their name), is of Masmuda Berber origin.

Also, according to a local legend, the Ulad Sabbah, the Ulad Hariz and the Mdakhra represent the last vestiges of a late medieval Berber heresy, that of the Barghwata, who maintained their own heterodox religious practices and a very free Berber version of the Qur'an until these were stamped out by the unitarian Almohads in the thirteenth century. Michaux-Bellaire notes, in addition, and perhaps tellingly, that even though all these Shawiya tribes or sections came to intermarry, with the usual resultant alliances and hostilities, they did not regard themselves, as Rifian and Susi Berbers do, as children of the region by imposing their own ethnonym on their territory. (This was left for the French to do.)

The above almost certainly represents an oversimplification of what actually happened; but the result is, as Michaux-Bellaire affirms, that the Tamsna/Shawiya region is now totally mixed in population, as its fertile plain probably always provoked the envy of other and purely Berber sheep transhumants to the south and east (ibid., Vol. I pp.111–16). In this particular instance, almost certainly, provocation came well before the great Berber passage to the north-west across the Atlas, which began from the Saghru and the desert in the late sixteenth century and which was brought to an enforced halt only with the establishment of the French protectorate, as described elsewhere (Hart 1993).

This Shawiya material is discussed in some detail purely to discern the kind of insights it might provide on the Berber evidence, which is obviously somewhat later in historical time. In the Berber cases (probably over 50 per cent of the total), the presence of scission, discontinuity and reduplication of agnatic or patrilineal descent groups certainly goes well back into precolonial times (i.e. well before the Franco-Spanish protectorate of 1912–56), and seems most often to have been the result of exile stemming from bloodfeud or tribal warfare inflicted on the perpetrating lineage or on its dissenter-founder in his new locality. Of course, other equally salient reasons have been adduced, such as poverty, bad harvests, flock failure, famine, drought and the like. As noted, it was brought to an end by the establishment of the Franco-Spanish colonial dispensation, although rural and tribal labour migration to the coastal and lowland cities began only after the French 'pacification' of the country had been achieved in 1934, with the concomitant cessation of the bloodfeud and the vendetta.

After independence in 1956, although the rates of urban labour migration greatly increased, the creation of the European Economic Community offered, by 1970, a major opportunity and outlet for Moroccan labour migration abroad. Questions of this sort, as well as problems which relate to them, are beyond the scope of this article, as is the perhaps related question of whether tribalism and the tribal condition have survived into the uncertainties of the present day.

In the context here at issue, however, scission, as opposed to simple lineage fission, involves the act of actual physical movement, of the ancestor or ancestors in question actually packing up and moving (which fission does not) – or, more likely, fleeing the consequences of a homicide, in order to escape the wrath of their victims' agnates – from one locality to another, often quite distant one (cf. Hart 1970a p.47 n.38; 1976 pp.265–7). Discontinuity and reduplication refer at once to the geographical factor of a given group name existing in more than one locality, indeed optimally in several localities which are non-contiguous with each other (Hart 1976 p.267; 1981 pp.18–63; 1984a pp.4–12).

In some cases, especially from the Rif, whole communities have been established outside the Rif itself in this fashion. Examples are Tangier and its Fahs, or outskirts (Hart 1957; 1976 pp.350–51; and pp.156–171 in this volume), where the whole community is composed of members originally stemming from all the tribes represented in Mawlay Isma'il's Rifian army or *gish ar-rifi*, installed after the English evacuation of the town in 1684, but in which the Thimsaman, Igzinnayen, Aith Waryaghar and Aith 'Ammarth came to predominate; Battiwa, near Arzew in the Algerian Oranie (Janier 1945; Hart, pp.156–171 in this volume), in which the founders came from the Aith Sa'id in the eighteenth century; Lamta outside Fez, in which the founders were from the Igzinnayen (Coon 1931 p.105, 1932 and 1962 p.316; Hart and Blanco Izaga 1975 Vol. I p.142); and in Mawlay Idris Zarhun, in which the founders were from the Axt Tuzin. There was also a large degree of similar movement within the Rif itself: an Aith 'Arus lineage in Aith Qamra of the lowland Aith Waryaghar, descended obviously from an exiled Aith 'Arus highlander, and the Dharwa Ufqir Azzugwagh branch of the Imjjat lineage today in l-'Ass in the Aith Turirth (another Aith Waryaghar highland section), whose founder was an exile from a feud in

Hibir of the Igzinnayen but who made good in his new locale and whose sons and grandsons became powerful men (Hart 1970a; 1976 pp.324–38). It may also, by the same token, be partially responsible for the names of *Imjjat* (Ar. *Mjjat*) and possibly *Iznagen* (Ar. *Znaga*), another Aith Turirth lineage which originated in the Igzinnayen (as well as a mountain, Adhrar Aznag, on the borderland between the Aith Waryaghar, the Axt Tuzin and the Igzinnayen) in widely different parts of Morocco: the former in the Meknes region, in the Ait Attab in the West-Central Atlas, in that of Imi n-Tanut in the Marrakesh Atlas, in the Anti-Atlas and in the Sagiyat al-Hamra; and the latter in the Axt Tuzin (also in the Rif), in the Ait Hadiddu of Tilmi, in the Central Atlas above Msimrir, and as a large *qsar* at Figig. These last instances may link the groups or localities bearing these names in the Rif with others bearing the same names elsewhere; but this is a purely nomenclature similarity from which, on an *ex post facto* basis, not much else, if anything, can be deduced. In the Imjjat case, the suggestion from one particular tradition that the members of this particular lineage group were forced to leave each of their previous points of occupation because of their obstreperous and lawless behaviour and the disturbances they created may have amusement value, but is structurally beside the point. Unaccounted for is the presence of a community called Bni Waryaghal in the Ta'ifa section of the Branis tribe in the south-eastern Jbala (Royaume du Maroc 1962 p.764), but as, on the evidence of Trenga, all of its four component lineages have purely Arab rather than Rifian names (Trenga 1916), it would seem probable that its ancestors may have come from the small Jbalan tribe of Bni Waryagil along the Wargha River to the west, rather than from the Aith Waryaghar of the Rif, who claim no kinship with the Bni Waryagil. The names are similar but not identical.

In the Anti-Atlas, the name of *Iguzzulen* or *Taguzzult* (Ar. *Guzzula* or *Jazula*) may still be famous as that of traditionally noble, warlike and victorious invaders from the south who headed a *liff* alliance, a tribal coalition against the autochthonous Ahuggwa or Tahuggwat, also known as Isuktan (Montagne 1930 pp.201–5, and map facing p.202). In itself, however, this fact does not explain the presence of a Wad Iguzzulen or Guzzula River about 60 km. south of as-Sawira (Essaouira) or that of a Saturday market, Suq s-Sibt Gzula, located about 15 km. outside Safi. Even less does it explain the existence of a village in southern Spain, al-Andalus, known as Alcala de los Gazules (al-Qal'at n-Iguzzulen, or 'Fortress of the Iguzzulen/Guzzula'), between Jerez de la Frontera and Algeciras, which is indeed overlooked by a thirteenth-century Muslim fortress, as indicated by its name. Perhaps the names of Ahuggwa and Isuktan, on the other hand, being more local and less illustrious, have not travelled so far, although that of Agadir, in its original sense in *tashilhit* of collective storehouse, seems to have done, as Alcala de Guadaira, near Sevilla, is derived from al-Qal'at n-Ugadir, 'the fortress of the collective storehouse'.

In the Central Atlas one of the most obvious and conspicuous examples is probably that of the discontinuous northern group of Ait 'Atta known as the Ait 'Atta n-Umalu – 'Ait 'Atta of the Shade' – located at Fum Udi near Wawizakht, near the present Bin al-Widan dam (Hart 1981 pp.100–102; 1984a p.51), in contradistinction to the main body of this very large tribe, on the southern slope of the Central Atlas, in the Saghru (at Ikniwn and Alnif), in the pre-Saharan oases of the Dadss (Bu Maln), Dra (Tazarin, Zagura, Tagunit and Mhamid), Tudgha (Tinghir), Farkla (Gulmima) and Tafilalt (Awfus), and in the Kamkam desert (Tawuz). The Ait 'Atta of the Shade probably became established in their present locale in the mid-seventeenth century as Ait 'Atta advance guard in their north-west push toward and even beyond their high pastures in the Central Atlas (Hart 1993).

In this instance the old tribal name has been integrally retained but with a new geographical suffix – 'of the shade' – added, the reference being to the northern or shaded slope of the Central Atlas which abuts the Middle Atlas on the south side of a watershed. Within it, however, out of some 29 recorded segment or descent group names, only four are recognisable as Ait 'Atta ones: Ait Unir, Ait 'Alwan (both sections of the same *khums* or 'fifth' in the home territory of 'Atta-land), Ait Wahlim (another *khums* name within the home territory of the main group), and Ait 'Attu (a small segment of the Ait Hassu section of the Ait Wahlim, also within the home territory). However, further south but still well to the north of the main body of this supertribe there are the equally discontinuous groups of the Ait Unir of Birnat and the Ait Bu Iknifen of Talmast (Hart 1981, 1984a), while at Msimrir, today populated entirely by Ait Bu Iknifen, there is an Igharm n-Ait Unir, or *qsar* of the Ait Unir, strongly suggesting that there were Ait Unir living there at some point in the past.

In exactly the same vein of thought, Michael Peyron has informed us that there is an Almu n-Ait Ndhir, or Ait Ndhir pasturage area, near the *qsar* of Luggagh in the Tagharghart valley close to the Jbil 'Ayyashi, far to the south-east of the present Ait Ndhir territorial holdings around l-Hajib, in the northern Middle Atlas south of Meknes (Michael Peyron, personal communication, 6 October 1994). There is also a community of the Ait Dawud w-'Ali, a major segment or section of the Ait Sukhman, presently located at Bu Miya among the Ait Imyill/Bni Mgild in the Midelt circle, Rashidiya province (Royaume du Maroc 1962 p.351), as well as both an (Ait) Idrasen, the name of a confederacy which ceased to exist as a functioning unit nearly two centuries ago, among the Marmusha at Almis, in the Bulman circle of the Sefrou province, and an Ait Khabbash, no doubt originally from that south-eastern most of Ait 'Atta sections at Tawuz, now at Bulman itself (ibid. p.276).

That this phenomenon is by no means restricted to the Ait 'Atta, the Ait Ndhir and the Ait Sukhman is also indicated by the evidently discontinuous Ait Murghad segment of Ait 'Atman u-Musa between the Tizi n-Tlaghamt Pass and Zibzat, south of Midelt, and at least 100 km. north of the main Ait Murghad bases of Tinjdad, Asul, Gulmima and (both to a lesser extent and a lesser distance) Rish (ibid. p.349; Maher 1974 p.29; Hart 1978). Indeed, it was the fact that the writer bumped into some of these people entirely by accident during a Moroccan trip in January 1994 which led to his inquiry into the matter and to writing this article as a result. Yet another example of extreme discontinuity is that afforded by the Ait Saghrushshn, with three small but separate groups in the Middle Atlas – those of Harira and Immuzar, and that of Sidi 'Ali in the Jbil Tishukt – and one large one considerably further south-east, at Talsint on the Upper Mulwiya. In this case, however, and curiously enough, it is one of the smaller northern groups, that of the Ait Saghrushshn n-Sidi 'Ali, of the Tishukt, which is held to have been the originating one, not the southerners at Talsint (cf. Destaing 1920 p.iv; Pellat 1955 p.i; Maroc 1962). This may indeed be the only case on record in which a southern group may have originated from a more northerly one.

It is a well-established fact that among most Moroccan tribes, irrespective of whether they are Arabic or Berber speakers, either individual sections of the tribe or even the whole tribe itself, far from claiming local or autochthonous origins, claim to have come from somewhere else, whether nearby or far away. Localism in origin traditions or myths tends to have little or no prestige value. Be this as it may, however, it can sometimes lead to embarrassing conclusions: Coon, for example, recorded in 1931 that the community of Thariwin ('springs') in the Asht 'Asim section of the Rifian tribe of the Igzinnayen claimed to have originated or come from the Aith 'Abdallah section of the equally Rifian and neighbouring tribe of the Aith Waryaghar (Coon 1931 p.19), but our own fieldnotes of 1953 from the same Aith 'Abdallah indicate precisely the reverse (cf. also Hart 1976 p.254).

It may be of interest, in this connection, to record our own findings with respect to autochthonous or 'homegrown' origin traditions with respect to internal units (lineages, local communities and sections) within the six tribal groups of the Central Rif as opposed to traditions of groups having originated elsewhere (and the list reads from the lowest to the highest percentage figures): Aith 'Ammarth (literally, 'people of the filling-up', with the logical inference that they all came from elsewhere to settle in this high and poor set of valleys, although this is not strictly true), 31 per cent; Igzinnayen, 32 per cent; Ibuqquyen, 42 per cent; Axt Tuzin, 55 per cent;

Aith Waryaghar, 58 per cent; and Thimsaman, 78 per cent (ibid. pp.235–6). Although the Thimsaman figure may well be too high and is possibly based on insufficient data, these figures, as well as the overall Central Rifian average, in this respect, of 49 per cent, are worth comparing and contrasting with the very much higher percentage of 85 per cent for autochthonous lineage groups, communities and sections among the Ait 'Atta (Hart 1981 p.122), which is probably one of the highest such figures in the country (also cf. Hart 1992).

There are, of course, contra-indications resulting in diminution and eventual elision of group names. Although Berque, citing al-Bakri from the eleventh century, tells us that in the latter's day the Masmuda were to be found in six localities in the Maghrib, the Sinhaja in 25, the Zanata in 14 and the Hawwara in 15 (Berque 1974 p.30), he is pointedly silent about trying to establish any ties between these localities other than those of onomastic equivalence or similarity. We can only deduce that by the present century this name distribution had changed or shrunk drastically: in Morocco, at least, as of the time the *Carte des Tribus* was drawn up by the French Residency-General in Rabat in 1933, there was only one Masmuda (in the Jbala near Wazzan), only three Sinhaja-s (Srir, Ghaddu and Musbah, all discontinuous from each other and located west and south of the Rif), and only one Zanata (section of the Shawiya near Casablanca). Furthermore, the idea that Sinhaja and Zanaga are basically derived from the same root, put forward by the French and perpetuated in an otherwise interesting paper by Sadki (1987), is difficult to accept *prima facie*. The names of Lamta, Lamtuna, Hawwara and Guzzula/Jazula (or Iguzzulen/Ijazulen) had also almost certainly shrunk from their one-time distribution on the Maghribi landscape by the immediate precolonial period.

Why was this so? The only plausible explanation would seem to be either that the original bearers of the names in question died out in the localities concerned or that their identities were subsumed and submerged into those of later occupants. In the Rif, especially among the Aith 'Ammarth, we have encountered traditions about lineages which died out entirely, and in the Aith Turirth section of the Aith Waryaghar, one of its oldest lineages, that of the Ihammuthen, was reduced to only three living members as of the 1950s. Hence the possibility of extinction cannot be ruled out. However, and we are entirely within the realm of conjecture here, what might have been more likely was accretion through clientage and intermarriage into newer and more dominant groups – exactly in the manner of a normal fugitive from a bloodfeud at home. If he could not pay either the *haqq* fine to the councillors (in the event that he committed his murder in the market and then got away with it) or the *diyit* bloodmoney to his victim's agnates (and here we combine accepted precolonial procedures from both the Rif and the Central Atlas), he was exiled for life. As he had come to the new receiving group as a supplicant, it was under their shadow that he lived and, if anything, their group name which he took. For his own group name or *nisba* of origin generally died at his own death, unless for some special reason, like that of distinguishing between half-siblings from different mothers (especially if one of the latter was from another tribe) or even simply because he might have distinguished himself in some way in his new group of adoption, it was locally perpetuated. But in this respect the Imjjat case, in which the sons and grandsons of a fugitive from a feud in the Igzinnayen became powerful *imgharen* or council members in the Aith Turirth in their own right and then indulged in a knockdown, dragout, senseless vendetta, is certainly exceptional (cf. Hart 1976 pp.329–38; in preparation).

Thus for scission, discontinuity and reduplication of agnatic descent groups to be effective – or to have been effective, for today such opportunities are either completely lacking or drastically curtailed – we might invoke, albeit with considerable misgivings, Gellner's otherwise attractive theory of 'disposition and process' (Gellner 1969 pp.56–60) when dealing with large transhumant groups such as the Ait 'Atta if we are to account for the presence of a segment such as the Ait Bu Iknifen in no less than ten different localities within Ait 'Atta territory. But the difficulty with this theory is that it implies equal proliferation within each section as well as invoking sectional cooperation in the conquest and acquisition of new pasturelands plus the transfer or movement of only a part of the original community to the new locale. (It also fails to answer questions such as why these same Ait Bu Iknifen can be found in ten different locations and the Ait l-Firsi, for instance, in only one. A serviceable answer for this one, however, can be found on the ground: poverty and neglect, in the case of the Ait l-Firsi, who live in the most fly-blown part of the Saghru and there only.)

In the Rif, an area of sedentary agriculturalism and not at all one of transhumance, such a thing could not have happened, and scission, discontinuity and reduplication, even though of constant occurrence at the microlevel, involved only individuals or at best a very few members of any given descent group. Rifian colonies were indeed established, as noted, but only outside the Rif, and in all known cases the contributing factors to their continuation and development were multiple, and their population was by no means restricted to descendants of exiles from feuds at home, despite the possible original impetus provided by the latter. In our review of his book, now almost a quarter century ago, we voiced our principal objections to Gellner's disposition-and-process theory as far as the Ait 'Atta are concerned (Hart 1970*b*; also Hart 1981 pp.71–2). This is, in brief, that Ait 'Atta sectional representation at both the centre of their territory, at Igharm

Amazdar in the Saghru, and at its peripheries is only partial and by no means total: for total representation would have necessitated an awareness of and striving for an egalitarianism in the territorial distribution of sections which in fact never existed. Although agreeing with Gellner that in such cases involving transhumants, mutual pasturage rights tend to take precedence over mutual bride exchange or inheritance expectations (Gellner 1969 pp.58–9), we must nonetheless point out that built into his otherwise elegant theory is a *de facto* equality in the proliferation of segments which could never possibly have happened 'in real life' or on the ground. As Orwell's Law has it, we are all equal but some of us are more equal than others.

BIBLIOGRAPHY

Berque, Jacques, 'Qu'est-ce c'est une "Tribu" Nord-Africaine?', in idem, *Maghreb: Histoire et Sociétés* (Algiers: Société Nationale d'Edition et de Diffusion (SNED); Gembloux: Duculot 1974) pp.22–34.
Coon, Carleton S., *Tribes of the Rif*. Harvard African Studies IX (Cambridge MA: Peabody Museum 1931).
——, *Flesh of the Wild Ox: A Riffian Chronicle of High Valleys and Long Rifles* (New York: William Morrow 1932).
——, *Caravan: The Story of the Middle East* (2nd Ed., New York: Holt, Rinehart and Winston 1962).
Destaing, Edmond, *Etude sur le Dialecte Berbère des Ait Saghrouchen*. Publications de la Faculté des Lettres d'Alger LVI (Paris: Ernest Leroux 1920).
Gellner, Ernest, *Saints of the Atlas* (London: Weidenfeld and Nicholson 1969).
Hart, David M., 'Notes on the Rifian Community of Tangier', *Middle East Journal* XI/2 (1957) pp.153–62.
——, 'Segmentary Systems and the Role of "Five Fifths" in Tribal Morocco', *Revue de l'Occident Musulman et de la Méditerranée (ROMM)* III/1 (Aix-en-Provence 1967) pp.65–95; republished with introduction and addendum in Akbar S. Ahmed and David M. Hart (eds.), *Islam in Tribal Societies: From the Atlas to the Indus* (London: Routledge & Kegan Paul 1984*b*) pp.66–105.
——, 'Clan, Lineage, Local Community and the Feud in a Rifian Tribe', in Louise E. Sweet (ed.), *Peoples and Cultures of the Middle East: An Anthropological Reader* (2 vols., Garden City, NY: Natural History Press 1970*a*) Vol. II, pp.3–75.
——, Review of Ernest Gellner, *Saints of the Atlas*, *Middle East Journal* XXIV/4 (Washington DC 1970*b*) pp.531–6.
——, *The Aith Waryaghar of the Moroccan Rif: An Ethnography and History*. Viking Fund Publications in Anthropology, No.55 (Tucson: University of Arizona Press 1976).
——, 'Notes on the Sociopolitical Structure and Institutions of Two Tribes of the Ait Yafalman Confederacy: the Ait Murghad and the Ait Hadiddu', *ROMM* XXVI/2 (1978) pp.55–74.
——, *Dadda 'Atta and his Forty Grandsons: The Socio-Political Organisation of the Ait 'Atta of Southern Morocco* (Wisbech, Cambridgeshire: MENAS Press 1981).
——, *The Ait 'Atta of Southern Morocco: Daily Life and Recent History* (Wisbech, Cambridgeshire: MENAS Press, 1984*a*).
——, 'Arabic and Berber Names on the Tribal Map of North-west Africa: A Statistical Evaluation', *Awraq: Estudios sobre el Mundo Arabe e Islamico Contemporaneo* XIII (Madrid 1992) pp.159–204.
——, 'Four Centuries of History on the Hoof: The North-west Passage of Berber Sheep

Tranhumants Across the Moroccan Atlas, 1550–1912', *Morocco: The Journal of the Society for Moroccan Studies* No.3 (London: SOAS 1993) pp.21–55.

——, *Traditional Society and the Feud in the Moroccan Rif* (Wisbech, Cambridgeshire: MENAS Press; Tetouan: Université Abdelmalek Saadi, in preparation).

——, 'Precolonial Rifian Colonies Outside the Moroccan Rif: Battiwa and Tangier': see pp.156–71 of this volume.

—— (editor and translator), and Blanco Izaga, Emilio *Blanco Izaga: Colonel in the Rif*. Ethnography Series, HRAfLEX Books MX3-001 (2 vols., New Haven: Human Relations Area Files 1975).

——, *Emilio Blanco Izaga: Coronel en el Rif*. Biblioteca de Melilla No.8 (Melilla: Auyuntamiento Municipal de Melilla/Fundacion Municipal Sociovcultural/UNED-VCentro Asiociado de Melilla 1995).

Janier, Emile, 'Les Bettiova de Saint-Leu', *Revue Africaine* LXXXIX (89), 3–4 trim. (1945) pp.236–80.

Maher, Vanessa, *Women and Property in Morocco: Their Changing Relation to the Process of Social Stratification in the Middle Atlas*. Cambridge Studies in Social Anthropology No.10 (Cambridge: Cambridge University Press 1974).

Maroc, 1:500,000e, *Carte des Tribus* (1962).

Michaux-Bellaire, Edouard, *Casablanca et les Chaouia*, Vols. I–II, in idem (ed.), *Villes et Tribus du Maroc* (2 vols., Paris: Ernest Leroux 1915).

Montagne, Robert, *Les Berbères et le Makhzen dans le Sud du Maroc: Essai sur la Transformation Politique des Berbères Sédentaires (Groupe Chleuh)* (Paris: Felix Alcan 1930).

Pellat, Charles, *Textes Berbères dans le Parler des Ait Seghrouchen de la Moulouya*. Collection des Textes Berbères Marocains II, Institut des Hautes Etudes Marocaines (Paris: Larose 1955).

Résidence Générale de France au Maroc, Cabinet Militaire, *Carte des Tribus du Maroc*, Echelle 1:1,000,000e (1933).

Royaume du Maroc, Ministère de l'Economie Nationale, Division de la Coordination Economique et du Plan, *Récensement Démographique (Juin 1960): Population Rurale du Maroc* (Rabat: Service Central des Statistiques, Juin 1962).

Sadki, Ali, 'L'Interpretation Généalogique de l'Histoire Nord-Africaine Pourrait-Elle Etre Dépassée?', *Hesperis-Tamuda* XXV (Rabat 1987) pp.127–46.

Trenga, G., 'Les Branes', *Archives Berbères* I/3 (Paris 1916) pp.200–218; I/4 (Paris 1916) pp.293–330.

The Role of Goliath in Moroccan Berber Genealogies

Among most Berber-speaking tribal groups in Morocco the depth of the agnatic lineage, which usually coincides with one's informant's great-grandfather or great-great-grandfather in the patriline, is seldom more than four, and at the outside six or seven, generations, in which ancestors are actually remembered, named, and traceable on a step-by-step basis. Beyond this point they are not. This is the case for the Rifian *dharfiqth* or lineage group among the Aith Waryaghar in northern Morocco (Hart 1976 p.274), while among the Ait 'Atta in the South-Central Atlas, the Saghru massif and the Dra and Tafilalt oases, the lineage group in this region, and in the Tamazight dialect rather than in the Rifian one, usually known as *ighs* (lit. 'bone') never exceeds four generations, while for small lineages it is only three (Hart 1981 p.74). Yet, perhaps paradoxically, the Ait 'Atta can claim to have a corporate lineage system whereas the Rifians cannot.

The Ait 'Atta case is reflected in the naming system current among the Berber tribes in the Central Atlas, collectively known as Imazighen, according to which a man is named as both the son of his father and as a member of the lineage of his patrilateral grandfather or great-grandfather (i.e. Muha u-Sa'id n-Ait Mhand u-Brahim, 'Muha son of Sa'id of the people of Mhand u-Brahim': here the ultimate referent Mhand u-Brahim may be either the true patrilateral grandfather or the great-grandfather).

A very marked exception to this, however, is provided by the much less frequent but infinitely deeper genealogies, which is to say, between 25 and 40 or more generations, of the members of holy lineages – who are known in Rifian as *imrabdhen*, with a whole tribal section of the Aith Waryaghar bearing this name, and in Tamazight as *igurramen* –, part of whose stock-in-trade is their ability to trace their descent from the Prophet Muhammad (Gellner 1969; Hart 1976 pp.256–60, 481–97). Such an ability or such a claim is emphatically not shared by the mass of lay tribesmen. Indeed, like the wearing of white robes, the adjudication of disputes between lay tribesmen and the possession of the miracle-working power known as *baraka*, it is a hallmark of the members of such lineages who are also, almost invariably, recognised as *shurfa'* (sing. *sharif*) or descendants of the Prophet.

At any rate, genealogies of the *shajara* or 'tree-like' variety which are written in Arabic, which apply most often to *shurfa'* and which encompass units at any level above that of the agnatic lineage as provided verbally by informants, are few and far between. In this article, however, we discuss the implications of one that does so, and one which in fact purports to account for whole tribes and even whole regions. This is the claim, mentioned or discussed by at least two previous investigators, Sanchez Perez for the Rif and by Guennoun, and much more recently by the present writer, for the Imazighen region of the Middle, Central and Eastern Atlases (Sanchez Perez 1950 p.61; Guennoun 1939–40 pp.17–218; Hart 1978 pp.55–6), of a possibly generalised Moroccan Berber descent from Jalut or Jallut. This figure, Jalut, corresponds to that of Goliath in the Biblical Old Testament, well known to adherents of all three monotheistic 'religions of the book', Judaism, Christianity and Islam, because he was killed by David. We might add here that it seems ironic that Sanchez Perez makes this claim for the Rifians in an article about their leader bin 'Abd al-Krim, who as a *qadi* and as a *sharif* or descendant of the Prophet, albeit one of a minor and latent line, would himself almost certainly have been most distressed by it (Sanchez Perez 1950).

Such a claim, that Berbers in general are descended from a semi-mythical Palestinian who lived circa. 1200 BC, may seem, on the face of it, patently absurd. But the Qur'an and Muslim tradition accord rather more importance to Goliath than the Bible does, while the eminent early Arab historian al-Mas'udi (circa. 893–956) has gone so far as to say that Palestine was originally inhabited by Berbers who were descended from one of the sons of Canaan and that *Jalut* was the name or title borne by their kings down to the one who was killed by David, while the place name 'Ayn Jalut, 'Goliath's spring', persists in Jordan to this day (Carra de Vaux 1953 pp.84–5). For his part, a second and slightly earlier Arab historian, al-Tabari (839–923), cited by the nineteenth century Moroccan historian el-Nasiri es-Slaoui (1923 p.148), has the ancestral Berbers leaving Palestine and becoming dispersed through North Africa after the death of their leader who was slain by David (ibid.). Shatzmiller, after noting that a third and still earlier historian, ibn Qutayba (907), added to this the information that Jalut's 'real name' was Wannur ibn Harmal, then postulates that this first 'eastern' period terminates what she has referred to as the 'first stage' of Berber origin myths, while the 'second stage', in which mentions of Jalut or Goliath evidently become less frequent, begins with the Almohads (Shatzmiller 1983 p.147).

This at least seems a fairly complete representation of the Arab view, which, as Brett and Fentress have commented in a recent general study, gave genealogical precision to the perception of the Arab conquerors of the Maghrib that the Berbers not only formed a nation but that they were divided into two distinct groups, the Butr and the Baranis, possibly based on distinctive clothing worn by the members of each one (Bulliet 1981; Brett and Fentress 1996 p.131). These groups were subsequently to give way to what we have labelled elsewhere as a 'three-ring circus' classification (Hart 1982), the triangular medieval conflict of the Masmuda, Sinhaja and Zanata – which became binary when the Masmuda dropped out. This classification was made famous by an earlier generation of French interpreters of ibn Khaldun (transl. by de Slane, 4 vols., 1925–56; Gautier 1952), but it has also long ceased to correspond to any present-day reality. This is so despite, for example, a recent (and evidently somewhat tongue-in-cheek) asseveration by the Moroccan ex-minister Mahjoubi Aherdan that the three original Berber brothers Amasmud, Azanath and Asinhaj were the sons of no less a man than Amazigh and his wife Tamazight (Aherdan 1991 p.35). It is worth recalling here that to date, as Berber is essentially an unwritten language despite the *tifinagh* alphabet and writing which survives today only among the Saharan Tuareg, Berber history has been written almost exclusively by non-Berbers.

Even so, and given also the fact that Berber and Arabic are both member languages of the same Hamito-Semitic (or Afro-Asiatic) family, it seems probable, as Camps has stressed, that the term *jalut* or *jallut* is related to or is even a direct cognate of Berber (Tamazight) *agallid*, 'king, paramount chief' (Rif. variant *ajiddjidh*), the term by which the pre-Islamic Berber ruler Massinissa was designated (Camps 1980 pp.25–6). This fact or bit of intuition has come to us via a Punico-Libyan/Berber inscription from Thugga in Tunisia, an inscription which may also possibly have indicated the origins of the modern practice of the Imazighen tribes of central Morocco of annually rotating chieftainship, which was the norm among the transhumant tribes in the Middle, Central and Eastern Atlases until Moroccan independence in 1956 (cf. Brett and Fentress 1996 pp.37–40; Gellner 1969 pp.81–104; Hart 1981 pp.76–93). Hence the genealogies which we are now about to examine and which point to Jalut or 'Goliath' as their apex or founder-ancestor show some genuinely Berber figures as points of fission below him, even though they are unquestionably modelled along Arabo-Islamic lines. Nonetheless, we can only agree with the assessment of Peyron, who also indicates, incidentally, that traditions concerning Jalut are by no means restricted to Morocco but are also to be found in the Sahara, to the effect that we are dealing here with a figure who has become, at the very least, semi-legendary (Peyron 1995).

Moving into early modern times, Peyron even cites a missive dated 1646 in which *Jalut* is used by the Moroccan sultan Mawlay Mhammad as a term of crowning insult, on top of 'bastards' and 'sons of prostitutes', to refer to the ancestry of the Middle Atlas Berber *agurram* Muhammad al-Hajj al-Dila'i, who was very much at odds with the ruling dynasty (en-Nasiri es-Slaoui 1906 p.24; Peyron 1995 p.2375). From al-Mas'udi in the tenth century to Moroccan sultans and their Berber opponents in the seventeenth is a long time for the Jalut legend or origin myth to have persisted. As we shall see, however, it has indeed persisted, with no doubt certain modifications and adjustments, right down to the present day, even if, in certain cases, like that just mentioned, the name of the unfortunate Jalut has been used as a term of opprobrium.

Although knowledge and citation of the Jalut tradition in the Rif, for example, seems purely residual today, it can still be discerned here and there: there is a local community named Ijaluthen or Ijalluthen, 'people/children of Jalut', in the Azghar section of the coastal tribe of the Ibuqquyen (Buqquya), while our own information agrees with that of Sanchez Perez (1950 p.61) in that the Aith Waryaghar (Bni Waryaghal), the tribe of bin 'Abd al-Krim, refer to their southern neighbours of the Igzinnayen (Gzinnaya) as *Dharwa n-Jalut/Jallut*, 'sons of Jalut/Jallut/Goliath' (rendered by Sanchez Perez in Arabic as *Ulad Jalut*: cf. ibid. p.61) and even, correspondingly and jokingly, as *r-'adhawth n-Sidna Dawud*, 'the enemies of our lord David'. Again, according to Sanchez Perez (1950 p.61), Coon would have envisioned Jalut, as the ancestor of all Rifians, wandering up the Iharrushen valley in the Igzinnayen in very early times (as per Coon 1931 p.19; 1932 pp.3–25); but here, as it happens, Sanchez Perez has confused Jalut with a local lineage ancestor named 'Abd r-Mumin.

But it is in the Central High Atlas region that the Jalut or Goliath origin tradition appears to have reached its apogee. Here we present, in fact, two versions of it, with the later and simpler one being given first. This one is not in the least residual as the Rifian ones are, but is, to the contrary, vibrant and all embracing: according to an aged informant from the Ait 'Ayyash interviewed in 1969, Jalut or Goliath had four sons. The eldest, Baibi, is otherwise unidentified but evidently died without issue and may therefore be discarded. The other three, however, were none other than Amazigh, Asusi and Arifi, in that order, the ancestors, respectively, of the Imazighen of the Middle and Central High Atlases, the Ishilhayen or Isusiyen of the Western Atlas and Anti-Atlas and the Irifiyen or Rifians of the northern Rif. In other words, it not only attempts to account in blanket fashion for the speakers of all three major Berber dialect groups in Morocco but it also postulates, as Peyron too has noted, either that Amazigh was a son of Jalut or possibly even that all three were actually one and the same individual (Peyron 1995 p.2376).

The other Central High Atlas tradition with respect to Jalut or Goliath is more detailed, more coherent and more fully genealogical in character, while at the same time narrowing the field down just to the transhumant Imazighen tribes of the Middle and Central Atlas region. It is attested by a *shajara* document in Arabic, unfortunately undated, which was discovered and translated by Captain. Roger Henry at the Zawiya of Sidi Bu Ya'qub in Asul in the territory of the Ait Murghad (now in the Province of Errachidia) in 1937. What follows, however, is not Henry's translation, which was inaccessible to me, but the commentary on it, in some detail, by Commandant Said Guennoun, himself an Algerian Kabyle (Guennoun 1939 pp.217–19), as well as our own comments, now third-hand, on Guennoun's reading of Henry's materials.

In this particular genealogy too Jalut had four sons, the first of whom, Baibi once again, was killed by Arabs (rendered as *I'araben*?) while still a child, thereby attesting to a long-standing hostility between Berbers and Arabs in this region. The other three sons, however, were not as all-embracing as Amazigh, Asusi and Arifi in the previous tradition but were named Malu, Midul and 'Atta. The eldest, Malu, had six sons, who themselves fathered most of the major tribes of the Middle Atlas: (1) Abu l-Qasim al-Zayyani, the ancestor of the Zayyan or Iziyyan; (2) al-Yazid Ishqirni, the ancestor of the Ishqiren; (3) Muhammad al-Yusi, ancestor of the Ait Yusi; (4) Brahim al-Sukhmani, ancestor of the Ait Sukhman; (5) Shaykh al-Mikki l-Mjildi, ancestor of the Ait Mgild/Mjild; and (6) Sadden Yimmur, ancestor of the Ait Sadden.

Midul, the second son, had five sons whose descendants came to form the bulk of the Ait Yafalman confederacy in the south-eastern Atlas during the first half of the seventeenth century, in about 1630–45, possibly at *makhzan* or Moroccan governmental instigation in order to combat the growing power and expansion of the Ait 'Atta (Hart 1978; Mezzine 1987 p.56 n.77, 96 nn.1–5): (1) Yahya/Yihya, ancestor of the Ait Yahya/Yihya of Kardus and Tunfit; (2) Agra, ancestor of the Igarwan, both of Sidi Bu Ya'qub and of the Meknes region; (3) Murghad, ancestor of the Ait Murghad; (4) Hadiddu, ancestor of the Ait Hadiddu; and (5) Immur/Yimmur, ancestor of the Ait Immur/Yimmur, today in the Marrakesh region.

Finally, and according to this genealogy, the third son, 'Atta, also had six sons, whose descendants make up the core groups of the supertribe of the Ait 'Atta, whose heartland is the Saghru but who extend north well into the Central High Atlas, to the south well into the Dra Valley and to the east as far as Tawuz, beyond the Tafilalt oasis (Hart 1981, 1984a): (1) Hlim/Halim, the ancestor of the Ait Wahlim, in the Saghru, the South-Central Atlas, the Ahsiya and the Dra Valley; (2) 'Azza, the ancestor of the Ait Y'azza, in the Saghru and the South-Central Atlas; (3) Khalifa, ancestor of the Ait Unibgi of the South-Central Atlas, Marrutsha and the Tafilalt – and here in fact we have an elision of two different Ait 'Atta sections, commented upon below; (4) Khabbash, ancestor of the Ait Khabbash of Tawuz – who in fact form part of the Ait Unibgi; (5) Isful, ancestor of the Ait Isful of Tabsbast and the

Dra Valley; and (6) Ndhir or Mtir, ancestor of the Ait/Bni Ndhir/Mtir, who are in fact not part of the Ait 'Atta at all but a northern Middle Atlas tribe, although one of their sections, the Ait Wallal, has a namesake section among the Ait 'Atta which is generally regarded as the oldest one in the supertribe. The document also evidently adds that the Ait 'Ayyash and the Ait Ufilla are of 'southern' (*qbala*) origin and that they are known jointly by the name of Ait Idrasen, whose ancestor may or may not also have been an ancestor of the Ait Yusi (Guennoun 1939 p.218). But the Ait Idrasen faded from the picture early in the nineteenth century, for Burke has demonstrated, in our view conclusively, that their power as a confederacy was broken forever after the Battle of Landa in 1819 (Burke 1991). Once this happened, the Ait Umalu tribes and behind them, those of both the Ait Yafalman confederacy and of course the Ait 'Atta as the latter's enemies, were freer to continue their own push to the north-west.

Such is the genealogy of Jalut and the transhumant Imazighen tribes as it stands, plus a certain amount of extrapolation on our part. It provides much ground for further comment. First of all, it is by no means all inclusive, as it does not refer to at least four major groups in the region at large – the Ait Sri, Ait Saghrushshn, Ait Massad and Ait Izdig – while the inclusion in it of the Ait 'Atta is, at least in our view, very much open to question, as my own Ait 'Atta informants never once mentioned any ancestor further back in time beyond their own Dadda 'Atta, who by my extrapolation lived in the latter half of the sixteenth century, who was also presumably killed in battle against Arabs, and who is buried at Taqqat n-Iliktawen near Tagunit in the Dra Valley (Hart 1981 pp.8–15; 1984*a* pp.39–51). Furthermore, none of our informants could provide the names of any of their actual sectional ancestors, although all, of course, knew the names of their sections *per se*, as *Ait X* or *Ait Y*. In addition, and as noted above, among the Ait 'Atta as listed in the above genealogy the Ait Khalifa and the Ait Unibgi sections are either elided or confused with each other, while those of the Ait Wallal, the Ait Unir, the Ait 'Alwan, the Ait l-Firsi and the Ait Khardi, even though the last two are very small, are not mentioned at all. There is no mention either of the superordinate organising concept of *khamsa khmas* or 'five fifths' which came to prevail both among them and, as it happens, among the Rifians of the Aith Waryaghar (Hart 1976 pp.248–60; 1981 pp.29–63; 1984*b*); but although the function of this institution was quite different in each case (cf. ibid. 1984*b*), we mention it here mainly to stress that it must only have been inaugurated at a later date.

Guennoun, who also has some trenchant comments to make about this genealogy, notes first that local oral traditions tend to diverge considerably from the genealogy itself as presented, although the question remains as to why the names of the sons of Malu are rendered in an Arabised form while the others are not. Possibly this might have been seen as a means of indicating greater prestige. The Ait Umalu, or 'sons of Malu' as alleged (falsely, as we shall see) in the genealogy, are made up of the Zayyan or Iziyyan, the Ait Mgild or Mjild, and the Ait Ishaq, as Guennoun also notes (Guennoun 1939 p.218), although the last-mentioned do not figure in the genealogy as it stands. Again, in our view the Ait Umalu should not necessarily include the Ait Sukhman, whose territory straddles the Middle and Central High Atlases and whose ancestor, whom our informants named as 'Ali u-Sukhman and not Brahim al-Sukhmani as the genealogy has it, was locally, and somewhat surprisingly (in that it is at considerable variance with other Berber oral traditions), held to have been a black slave (*ismakh*, and hence Sukhman) of Mawlay 'Abd al-Qadir al-Jilali. This was the case despite the fact that the great bulk of the Ait Sukhman do not look in the least negroid and appear to hold the same rather negative views about blacks that prevail among other Berber tribesmen (Hart 1984c).

Peyron takes the view that the term *Ait Umalu* was devised by Guennoun in an earlier work as merely a classificatory convenience (Peyron, personal communication, 1995; Guennoun 1929); but we think it may be somewhat more than this, for it does correspond to a certain geographical reality although not to a genealogical one. As we have indicated elsewhere and at length, the transhumant Imazighen tribes jostled with each other for almost four centuries, from about 1550 to the establishment of the French protectorate in 1912, in a slow but continual push from the Saghru to the north-west across the Atlas toward, eventually, the Atlantic coastal plains searching for grass for their sheep, and they were frozen into position only by the imposition of colonial rule (Hart 1993).

It is in this historico–geographical context, therefore, that Guennoun observes, tellingly, that Malu, the name assigned by the genealogy to Jalut's eldest surviving son, is not a personal name at all but is derived from *amalu* (Rif. cognate *maru*), meaning 'shade'. Hence these tribes are not 'sons of Malu' but 'people of the shade', which makes very much better sense, because the Middle Atlas, which they inhabit, represents the northern and shaded slope of the mountains, with abundant grass and covered here and there with stands of cedar and pine, while the Central High Atlas represents the southern slope, *asammar* (Rif. cognate *sammar*), which is much more barren and denuded owing to greater exposure to the sun, while the Saghru, the heartland of the Ait 'Atta, still further south, consists almost entirely of rocks virtually unrelieved by grass at all, to say nothing of trees. (Indeed, there is only one tree of any size at all in the Saghru, a gnarled and ancient terebinth, or *iggi*, which is locally held to be sacred.) These features can be observed almost at a glance, and they reflect the accuracy of the local terminology. However, Guennoun's assumption that the Ait Umalu came to form a confederacy as such after their component tribes were established in their present locality may be more questionable, for any such arrangements were usually entirely *ad hoc* and based on local needs in terms of alliance, defence and war (Guennoun 1939 p.218).

There is also no corresponding confederacy known as *Ait Usammar*, 'people of the sunny place/slope', on the southern or sunny slope – these terms rather resemble the Spanish use of *sol y sombra* in the bullring – but Midul, Jalut's second son, was, as we have confirmed independently, held to have been the ancestor of most of the tribes which came to form another confederacy, one which came to be known as the *Ait Yafalman* or 'people who have found peace' and which was hostile to the Ait 'Atta from the start, although Guennoun sees them as constituting a kind of buffer state between the Ait 'Atta and the *makhzan* (ibid. p.219). As he also points out, their collective name has nothing to do with that of their ancestor Midul, and is obviously more recent, stemming from an intertribal pact of mutual assistance among the contracting groups (ibid. p.218). However, the genealogy of the sons of Midul which we took down from an old Ait Hadiddu informant in 1961 shows one significant variation from that given above: the Ait Izdig were substituted for the Ait Murghad, who were designated as outsiders at whose instigation the confederacy was formed after, as the legend has it, one of their spokesmen had been grievously insulted and physically manhandled by the Ait 'Atta (Hart 1978 pp.55–6; 1981 pp.12–13; 1984a pp.45–6). Even so, and as it happens, the Ait Yafalman tribes were only able to check Ait 'Atta expansion in the north-east and not elsewhere, while the latter retain a series of oral traditions which justify that same expansion (Dunn 1973; Hart 1981, 1984a, 1993). The smaller group known as the Ait 'Atta n-Umalu, or 'Ait 'Atta of the Shade', for instance, located near Wawizaght athwart in the Middle-Central High Atlas divide, represents an early northern advance group of the supertribe in question. They are totally discontinuous in territorial terms from the main body of the latter and, as their name suggests, they are located on the threshold of the Middle Atlas as well as being complete outsiders both to any alleged Ait Umalu confederacy and, in our view, as noted, to the whole Jalut genealogy (Hart 1981, 1984a).

The two tribes which were able to maintain the Ait Yafalman confederacy as a going concern were the Ait Hadiddu and the outsiders of the Ait Murghad, both of them, like the Ait 'Atta, fierce fighters with excellent later combat records against the French, especially in the final 'pacification' by the latter of the Saghru (Ait 'Atta) and Central Atlas (Ait Murghad and Ait Hadiddu) regions which only ended in the summer of 1933. But the Ait Hadiddu show certain other peculiarities which are not shared by any of their neighbours, the foremost of which is their annual mass marriage ritual held every year in September at Imilshil (cf. Bousquet 1956; Hart 1978; Kasriel 1989; Kraus 1991). Guennoun notes that at the time of pacification this was because they were attributed a 'Christian' origin, no doubt by malicious neighbours (Guennoun 1939 p.232). This may not sit well with their alleged descent from Midul but, as should be apparent by now, Berber origin myths present us, oftener than not, with a mass of contradictions.

We hear much less of the Ait Izdig, located today at Rish and Karrando on the eastern peripheries of the region, while the other two tribes acknowledged by informants to have formerly been members, the Igarwan and the Ait Immur/Yimmur, were both early dropouts. In the case of the Igarwan, this was because, although they still retain a section near Midelt, their main body moved north to the Meknes region possibly as early as the late seventeenth century. The Ait Immur, on the other hand, were forcibly coopted by the energetic sultan Mawlay Isma'il, much of whose very long reign (1672–1727) was spent combating the tribes of the Imazighen region, into forming a *gish* or paramilitary corps at the service of the *makhzan* after they had revolted against him. He moved them first into garrison duty in the Tadla plain as of 1690; then about 1745, following a second revolt, they were moved again, this time north to the Gharb; and finally, about 1820, after yet another uprising, they were moved for a third time, now south to Marrakesh, to form part of a larger *gish* made up predominantly of tribes of West Saharan origin and located on the south-western outskirts of the city (LeCoz 1965; Hart 1993). This is where they are today, and according to reports they still retain their Tamazight speech.

In any event, the foregoing seems a reasonable summary of what is known or has been reconstructed about the semi-mythical figure of Goliath or Jalut and his role as an assigned apex in Berber genealogies. The genealogies themselves are incomplete, and certain individuals and groups have invariably been left out, either accidentally or by design, while their internal inconsistencies and contradictions are many. Although Jalut's undeniably Near Eastern but plainly non-Arab origins may have been a product of wishful thinking, they nonetheless provided the Berbers of North Africa with a certain respectability, which was often sneered at by Arabs, exactly as the Roman predecessors of the latter had sneered at the *barbari*. To both the Romans and the Arabs these same Berbers were often, indeed usually, subconsciously but vigorously opposed.

BIBLIOGRAPHY

Aherdan, Mahjoubi, *Un Poème pour Etendard* (Paris: Editions l'Harmattan 1991).
Bousquet, Georges-Henri, 'Le Droit Coutumier des Ait Haddidou des Assif Melloul et Isselaten',
    Annales de l'Institut d'Etudes Orientales XIV (Faculté des Lettres de l'Université d'Alger
    1956) pp.113–230.
Brett, Michael, and Elizabeth Fentress, *The Berbers* (Oxford: Blackwell 1996).
Bulliet, Richard W., 'Botr et Beranes: Hypothèse sur l'Histoire des Berbères', *Annales Economie-
    Société-Civilisations* 36/1 (1981) pp.104–16.
Burke, Edmund, III, 'Tribalism and Moroccan Resistance, 1890–1914: The Role of the Ait
    Ndhir', in E.G.H. Joffe and, C.R. Pennell (eds.), *Tribe and State: Essays in Honour of David
    Montgomery Hart* (Wisbech, Cambridgeshire: MENAS Press, 1991) pp.119–44.
Camps, Gabriel, *Berbères: Aux Marges de l'Histoire* (Toulouse: Editions Hesperides 1980).
Carra de Vaux, R., art. '*Djalut*', in H.A.D. Gibb and J.H. Kramers (eds.), *The Shorter
    Encyclopedia of Islam* (Leiden: E.J. Brill 1953) pp.84–5.
Coon, Carleton S., *Tribes of the Rif*. Harvard African Studies IX (Cambridge MA: Peabody
    Museum 1931).
——, *Flesh of the Wild Ox: A Riffian Chronicle of High Valleys and Long Rifles* (New York:
    William Morrow 1932).
Dunn, Ross E., 'Berber Imperialism: The Ait 'Atta Expansion in Southeast Morocco', in Ernest
    Gellner and Charles Micaud (eds.), *Arabs and Berbers: From Tribe to Nation in North Africa*
    (London: Duckworth 1973) pp.85–108.
el-Nasiri es-Slaoui, Ahmed ben Khaled, *Kitab el-Istiqsa* (transl. Fumey), *Archives Marocaines* IX
    (Paris: Leroux 1906).
——, *Kitab el-Istiqsa* (transl. de Graulle), *Archives Marocaines* XXX (Paris: Paul Geuthner
    1923).
Gautier, Emile-Felix, *Le Passe de l'Afrique du Nord* (Paris: Payot 1952).
Gellner, Ernest, *Saints of the Atlas* (London: Weidenfeld and Nicolson 1969).
Guennoun, Capt. Said, *La Montagne Berbère: Les Ait Oumalou et le Pays Zaian* (Paris: Editions
    du Comité de l'Afrique Francaise 1929).
——, Cmdt. Said, 'La Haute Moulouya', *Renseignements Coloniaux et Documents Publiés par
    le Comité de l'Afrique Française et le Comité du Maroc* (Oct.–Nov. 1939) pp.209–24; (Dec.
    1939) pp.225–40; (Jan. 1940) pp.25–32; (Feb. 1940) pp.42–8.
Hart, David M., *The Aith Waryaghar of the Moroccan Rif: An Ethnography and History*. Viking
    Fund Publications in Anthropology No. 55 (Tucson: University of Arizona Press 1976).
——, 'Notes on the Sociopolitical Structure and Institutions of Two Tribes of the Ait Yafalman
    Confederacy: the Ait Murghad and the Ait Hadiddu', *Revue de l'Occident Musulman et de la
    Mediterranée (ROMM)* XXVI/2 (1978) pp.55–74.
——, *Dadda 'Atta and His Forty Grandsons: The Socio-Political Organisation of the Ait 'Atta of
    Southern Morocco* (Wisbech, Cambridgeshire: MENAS Press 1981).
——, 'Masmuda, Sinhaja and Zanata: A Three-Ring Circus', *Revue d'Histoire Maghrebine*
    IX/27–8 (Tunis 1982) pp.361–5.
——, *The Ait 'Atta of Southern Morocco: Daily Life and Recent History* (Wisbech,
    Cambridgeshire: MENAS Press 1984a).
——, 'Segmentary Systems and the Role of "Five Fifths" in Tribal Morocco', in Akbar S. Ahmed
    and David M. Hart (eds.), *Islam in Tribal Societies: From the Atlas to the Indus* (London:
    Routledge and Kegan Paul,1984b) pp.66–105. Originally published in 1965.
——, 'The Ait Sukhman of the Moroccan Central Atlas: An Ethnographic Survey and a Case
    Study in Structural Anomaly', *ROMM* XXX/2 (1984c) pp.137–52.
——, 'Four Centuries of History on the Hoof: The Northwest Passage of Berber Sheep
    Transhumants across the Moroccan Atlas, 1550–1912', *Morocco: Journal of the Society for
    Moroccan Studies* 3 (London: School of Oriental and African Studies 1993) pp.21–55.
ibn Khaldun, *Histoire des Berbères et des Dynasties Musulmanes de l'Afrique Septentrionale*,
    (transl. by Baron de Slane, edited by Paul Casanova; 4 vols., Paris: Paul Geuthner 1925–56).

Kasriel, Michele, *Libres Femmes du Haut-Atlas? Dynamique d'une Micro-Société au Maroc* (Paris: Editions l'Harmattan 1989).

Kraus, Wolfgang, *Die Ayt Hdiddu: Wirtschaft und Gesellschaft im zentralen Hohen Atlas* (Veroeffentlichungen der ethnologischen Kommission, Bd. 7, Oesterreichische Akademie der Wissenschaften, Philosophisch-Historische Klasse, Sitzungsberichte, 574 Bd., Vienna: Verlag der oesterreichischen Akademie der Wissenschaften 1991).

Lecoz, Jean, 'Les Tribus Guich du Maroc', *Revue de Géographie du Maroc* 7 (1965) pp.1–52.

Mezzine, Larbi, *Le Tafilalt: Contribution à l'Histoire du Maroc aux XVIIe et XVIIIe Siècles*, Série Thèses 13, Publications de la Faculté des Lettres et des Sciences Humaines (Rabat: Université Mohammed V 1987).

Peyron, Michael, art., '*Djalout*', in Gabriel Camps (ed.), *Encyclopédie Berbère* XVI (1995) pp.2375–6.

Sanchez Perez, Andres, 'Abd-el-Krim', *Seleccion de Conferencias y Trabajos Realizados por la Academia de Interventores durante el Curso 1949–1950* (Tetuan: Alta Comisaria de España en Marruecos/Delegacion de Asuntos Indigenas/Imprenta del Majzen 1950) pp.59–76.

Shatzmiller, Maya, 'Le Mythe d'Origine Berbère: Aspects Historiques et Sociaux', *ROMM* XXXV (1983) pp.147–56.

The Role and the Modalities of Trial by Collective Oath in the Berber-speaking Highlands of Morocco

Islamic law, as embodied in the Shari'a – which in turn is based upon the Qur'an – has always been against oaths sworn collectively by any individual accused of a crime in the company and with the support of his agnatic kinsmen. It has done its best to individualise or decollectivise such oaths. But in one form or another, they have always been a feature of the customary law of many if not most Muslim tribal societies. By contrast, Shari'a law, the law of orthodox Islam, has generally been found in fact to apply most easily to urban conditions rather than to rural or, in particular, tribal ones. In this respect tribesmen, who are, normally speaking, more conservative, have tended to cling to older beliefs. Furthermore, as tribal societies in Islam have always regarded the agnatic lineage group as their major social unit, one such belief is that the support of a man by his agnatic kinsmen at an oath, in the event of an accusation against him by a member of another lineage group of any grave misdemeanour on his part, carries more weight than if, as the Shari'a stipulates, he were to swear to his innocence alone, on his own. This last is the case among the great majority, if not all, of the Arabic-speakers in Morocco, as elsewhere.

Given this fact, and despite or in the face of Shari'a injunctions, trial by collective oath, in one form or another, has been an outstanding jural feature not merely of Berber societies, but also of most other Muslim Middle Eastern tribal societies – such as, for example, the Bedouins in Israel and Jordan, the highland Yemenis (both are Arabs, to be sure, but tribesmen at the same time), the Somalis, the tribal Kurds and the Pukhtuns of Afghanistan and Pakistan. In the Berber case, as Marcy has cogently noted, the collective oath was the cornerstone of Berber customary law, which in Tamazight Berber is known as *izirf* ('way'), or *abrid* ('path'), while in Tashilhit and Tharifith (or Rifian) Berber, as well as in Moroccan Arabic, it is called *'urf* or *qa'ida*. Until Moroccan independence in 1956 it was the centrepiece of the Berber system of proof (Marcy 1954 p.150), a notion which is very clearly expressed in the proverb of the large tribe of the Ait 'Atta in southern Morocco to the effect that 'oaths are the roots of custom' (*tigulla ggant izuwran n-l- qa'ida*: cf. Hart 1981 p.158). Of equal relevance, as Ernest Gellner has also aptly observed, is the fact that not only was the legal decision procedure known as collective oath the most characteristic, as well as one of the most interesting, features of Berber customary law and of

Berber descent and social organisation – which are, respectively, patrilineal and, for want of a more appropriate term, quasi-segmentary – but that it was also, paraphrasing von Clausewitz, the continuation of the bloodfeud by other means (Gellner 1969 pp.104, 122). But Gellner's model, despite its usefulness, is based far more on theoretical considerations than it is on ethnographic ones, and it is not the one I propose to follow here.

This article examines the former heavy incidence of collective oath and compares the modalities of its regional variation among the three major Berber-speaking areas in the highlands of Morocco. In the Rif it lasted until approximately 1922, when the former *qa'di*, reformist and resistance leader bin 'Abd al-Krim, abolished and decollectvised it in favour of the individual oath as stipulated by the Shari'a, but in most of the Atlas it went on, as noted, with certain modifications, under French protectorate auspices until Moroccan independence in 1956. At this point Berber customary law was rescinded at a stroke in favour, once again, of the Shari'a and a national rather than a purely tribal law.

Although it was Westermarck in the early years of the present century, before the establishment of the Franco–Spanish protectorate over Morocco in 1912, who first set down for the ethnographic record the existence of collective oath – which he referred to as 'conditional self-imprecation' with respect to the oath itself and as 'compurgation' with respect to its collective character – among predominantly Berber-speaking groups (Westermarck 1926 Vol. I pp.492–517; cf. also Hart 1993), one gets the impression that he evidently did not fully understand the significance of its place in the overall pattern of Berber tribal sociopolitical organisation, despite the high quality of his illustrative material.

Hence we use as documentation for comparison in this article a number of more recent and more detailed sources: the materials from our own fieldwork among the sedentary Rifians or Irifiyen of northern Morocco, namely among the Aith Waryaghar (Hart 1976) on whom Westermarck's work in an earlier period also contains scattered but generally worthwhile data, and among whom the oath was referred to as *r-imin* or *thzaddjith*; those of Berque and Adam for the equally sedentary Ishilhayen tribes of the Western High Atlas, especially the Seksawa (Berque 1978), and the Ighshen, the Ait Wafqa and the Ait 'Abdallah u-Sa'id in the Anti-Atlas region contiguous to it (Adam 1948) in the south-western part of the country, who referred to the oath as *l-haqq* (Ar., lit. 'truth, right'); and for the transhumant Imazighen tribes of the large area encompassed by the Middle Atlas, the Central and Eastern High Atlases, the Saghru and the pre-Saharan oases of the Dra Valley and the Tafilalt, who referred to it as *tagallit* (pl. *tigulla*). By this, we refer, specifically, to the work of Marcy on the Zimmur on the north-western fringes of the Middle Atlas (Marcy 1949,

1954), and of Aspinion on the Iziyyan or Zayyan, also in the Middle Atlas properly speaking (Aspinion 1946). For the Central High Atlas, we will use our own material for the Ait Sukhman (Hart 1984*b*) and the Ait Murghad (ibid. 1978), that of both Bousquet and ourselves for the Ait Hadiddu (Bousquet 1956; Hart 1978), and that of Gellner for the holy lineages of the Ihansalen and some of their lay tribal neighbours (Gellner 1969). Finally, we also use our own data for the Ait 'Atta of the Jbil Saghru, the South-Central Atlas to the north of it and the pre-Saharan oases of the Dra Valley and the Tafilalt to the south (Hart 1981, 1984*a*).

In all these cases, oaths could be sworn at any time of year except during Ramadan, the Muslim month of fasting. In addition, the Ait 'Atta, among whom the *tagallit* oath was particularly highly developed, referred to the accused individual who was forced to swear it as *imikar* (lit. 'thief') and to his co-jurors and agnatic kinsmen, in such a context, either specifically as *imgillan* (sing. *imgilli*), or, in the context of the lineage group which they represent, as *ait 'ashra* (lit. 'people of ten'): for ten was, as we shall see, the normal number of co-jurors required (which included the accused individual and nine of his close agnatic kinsmen) for any oaths sworn over accusations of theft of livestock or over any cases having to do with property. For other cases, the number of co-jurors might be less or indeed be much more, and depended on a sliding scale based on the gravity of the offence. For more serious offences, as we shall see, the number of co-jurors required was increased accordingly. But starting at the near base level of ten, by which name the co-jurors were collectively known, it is directly relevant to the workings of the institution to note that these men were exactly the same agnates (*aitma, imkusa* or *imyisaten*) who would share both property rights and inheritance expectations with the accused individual and who would also be liable to vengeance and/or be forced to exact it in case of feud.

Therefore we begin the next section of this article by considering, in some detail, the different regional and tribal modalities and variations of collective oath. Note, first of all, as is natural, that if there were any witnesses (Rif. *shuhudh* (sing. *shahidh*); Tm. *iniyan* (sing. *iniyi*)) to a given crime, infraction or misdemeanour, their testimony of course overrode that of the accused and his co-jurors. Indeed, in such a case no oath was sworn, because the case was *ipso facto* open and shut.

There were essentially two main varieties of collective oath: in the Rif and the Anti-Atlas, as well as among the Kabyles of the Algerian Jurjura, oaths were generally sworn on Fridays, in the local mosque (*dhamzyidha*) and on a copy of the Qur'an. Among the transhumant Imazighen tribes of the Middle and Central Atlases, however, and as a major contrast to the situations prevailing in the Rif and in the Western Atlas, oaths were sworn at the shrines (*s-salihin* (sing. *s-salih*)) of local saints (*igurramen* (sing. *agurram*)) and administered by a neutral individual, known as *anahkam/ anahsham* or 'administrator', who was specially chosen for the occasion, with the time and site chosen by mutual consent. As Bousquet has noted, oaths assumed a position in the centre of the jural stage among these Imazighen tribes, while that which they assumed in the Algerian Jurjura, the Rif and the Sus was closer to the sidelines (Bousquet 1956 pp.116, 185; and for the Kabyles of the Jurjura, cf. Hanoteau and Letourneux 1893 Vol. III p.29). The Imazighen were well aware of the normal individual oath as prescribed by the Shari'a, but they felt it to provide too easy a way out for the defendant, for with no recusant co-jurors present there was no way open to 'break the oath' (*yirza tagallit*) if he were guilty.

It is well to point out here too that among these same transhumant tribes collective oaths were both more highly developed and their modalities were more complex than elsewhere, in particular because, as will be made clear, there was also a secondary system of oaths, those of accusation, called *ilkumen* (sing. *alkum*), which could be demanded by the plaintiff, who was known as *bab n-d-d'awt* (lit. 'summoner'), which went in precisely the opposite direction to that of the normal oath of denial, as sworn by the accused individual and his co-jurors. In such a case the plaintiff had to provide the latter because the burden of proof lay upon him. (It may be worth adding that a similar situation, with one slight difference, existed, it appears, among the Pukhtun tribes of the Pakistan North-West Frontier. In this society oaths were all of accusation and hence it was invariably the plaintiff who chose the co-jurors from among the agnates of the accused, although once again their number varied with the gravity of the offence. For example, prior to the formation of the state of Pakistan after India's independence from the British in 1947, ten co-jurors were required for a stolen rifle among the Mahsud of central Waziristan: cf. Hart 1985 p.69.)

An additional point of crucial importance must be stressed here, to the effect that perjury at oath was invariably held to be punished by supernatural sanctions, such as blindness or death, upon the person of the perjurer, while in the event that the oath was 'broken' it was incumbent upon either the accused individual and/or any of his co-jurors to pay, according to the circumstances of oath 'breakage', examined further on. Finally, and in order to clear up any possible misunderstanding, oath, whether individual or collective, is always terminologically and conceptually differentiated, in Morocco generally, from the two allied but nonetheless distinct notions of *'ar* and *'ahd*, the contents of both of which have been well examined by Westermarck (1926 Vol. I pp.518–64, 564–9; cf. also Hart 1993). Briefly defined, the former is an act of supplication, coercion or compulsion, through the sacrifice of an animal (generally a

sheep, goat or bull), by means of which the petitioner shames the person
whose help is desired into doing something against his will, while the latter
is a pact or vow (if between individuals) or a covenant (if between groups)
between parties of equal status. As indicated elsewhere (Hart 1976 p.309),
neither of these concepts, strictly speaking, is truly equivalent to that of
oath, but the strong interrelationship of all three of these factors will soon
emerge in the context of individual and regional examples.

We look first at collective oaths in the Rif, as exemplified by our
materials from the Aith Waryaghar tribe, and as reconstructed for the most
part from elderly informants in 1959–60, approximately 37 years after bin
'Abd al-Krim, himself a member of the same tribe, abolished them as
contrary to the regulations of the Shari'a (Hart 1976 pp.309–12). As noted,
the Aith Waryaghar and the Aith 'Ammarth generally referred to collective
oath as r-imin (from Ar. al-yamin, 'oath'), while their southern and eastern
neighbours, the Igzinnayen, the Axt Tuzin and the Thimsaman, normally
used the Berber term thzaddjith. Correspondingly, the designation for the
plaintiff was iziddjith, while the accused and his co-jurors were known as
yuxshin n-r-imin or izuddjen. It was also generally the plaintiff or plaintiffs
who stipulated how many co-jurors the accused had to produce.

It goes without saying that trial by collective oath stood/stands in
striking contrast to the norms of any Western jural system. But although,
generally speaking, collective oath in the Rif never reached the degrees
either of complexity or of sophistication that it attained among the Berber
tribes of the Central Atlas (Bousquet 1956 pp.116, 185), it was nonetheless
a linchpin of the jural organisation of the Aith Waryaghar during the period
known to them as ripublik or rifublik, which in Rifian parlance refers
specifically to the two-plus decades (1898–1921) before the advent of bin
'Abd al-Krim and the Rifian War with Spain and France (1921–26), even
though the roots of Rifian customary law, collective oaths, alliances,
feuding and vendetta were all very much older than this.

The two first points to be made about Rifian oaths, already alluded to
above, are the facts that co-jurors could in no way be confused with
witnesses, and that oaths had to be sworn in the Friday or congregational
mosque and on a copy of the Qur'an. In the first instance, it was noted that
the terminology for co-jurors and witnesses, who differ from each other
conceptually (an error often and inexplicably made by a number of French
writers on the subject), is also quite different, for in Rifian the latter are
shuhudh (sing. shahidh), as in Arabic. The Shari'a states explicitly that 12
ordinary witnesses – a number which happens to be just the same as that of
co-jurors required in a case of suspected murder – are equivalent to two
notaries, or 'adul (sing. 'adl), the testimony of one notary being worth that
of six ordinary witnesses. It goes without saying, furthermore, that if there

were witnesses to a crime, there was, automatically, no oath, for any accusation by an eye-witness automatically overrode the denial of the person accused, as well as, during the *ripublik*, those of his lineage-mates and co-jurors. Moreover, although the number of witnesses and the number of co-jurors in a murder case was exactly the same, 12, and apart from the fact that the function of the former was to accuse and that of the latter was to deny, witnesses were required not to be kinsmen, in any way, of the accused, whereas co-jurors, on the other hand, were invariably the latter's agnates and lineage-mates. The number 12 here may be, and probably is, an example of Custom imitating Canon Law.

Marcy has correctly noted that among Berbers generally, collective oath played a role that was, in theory, complementary to testimony, but that its importance arose from the general insufficiency of other means of proof (Marcy 1949 p.69): for if he can possibly help it, no man in any society is likely to commit a crime in front of witnesses. The distinction between trial by collective oath and testimony by witnesses is therefore of crucial importance, for witnesses and co-jurors are, conceptually speaking, at opposite poles.

Among the Aith Waryaghar, the number of co-jurors could in theory vary anywhere between six and 50, but in fact it was almost always either six (the accused and five co-jurors) or 12 (the accused and 11 co-jurors). The plaintiff always stipulated the number of co-jurors required, and the accused had to produce them. But given the very set rules of oath-taking, such stipulation was a mere formality. Six co-jurors were required for lesser offences, such as suspected damage to property or theft of livestock or irrigation water, while 12, as indicated, were needed for murder. However, while 12 was necessarily the maximum number of co-jurors and murder the maximum offence necessitating this number, it only applied within Aith Waryaghar territory. But in the event that an oath should involve the Aith Waryaghar with a neighbouring tribe, which was in fact not common, as for example over a large-scale land dispute or an intertribal homicide, then the number of co-jurors that the accused had to produce went up to 50. This meant the accused himself plus 49 classificatory agnates, who were fellow section members or fellow tribesmen. They were naturally far more ready to help out their own men in an extra-tribal crisis than in an intra-sectional or even an intra-tribal one.

Herewith we present such a case: in the Wednesday Market at Buridh, in the Igzinnayen tribe, a man from the neighbouring Marnisa wanted to kill his own tribal *qa'id*, 'Amar n-Hmidu. He had concealed a pistol in a handful of esparto grass, but someone else saw him do so and tipped the *qa'id* off. The would-be killer then threw the esparto grass and the pistol to a completely innocent dhu-Waryaghar man from the Timarzga section, who happened to be nearby. The Marnisa *qa'id* now accused the Timarzga man of having hired the other to kill him, but the latter protested his innocence. Even so, the *qa'id* then told the man that he had to bring 50 co-jurors to Marnisa territory in order to swear a collective oath. So the individual in question duly appeared there, with 49 fellow section members and other fellow tribesmen. By this time, however, Qa'id 'Amar n-Hmidu had realised that his accusation was probably wrong and had therefore cooled down, so instead of making the accused and his co-jurors take oath, he invited them all to dinner.

It is legitimate and natural to assume that it was sometimes stretching things to the limit for a defendant to find even 11 agnates to act as his co-jurors, so say nothing of 49. Hence it stands to reason that in the latter case the 'agnates' of necessity had to be fellow section members or fellow tribesmen. To qualify as a co-juror, a man had to be of age to fast during Ramadan, which is to say that he had at least to have reached the age of puberty. Although women may swear today (but only at home and not in the mosque), they were barred from doing so during the *ripublik*, a fact which clearly points up their jural status as minors. In the Rif, however, unlike in the Central Atlas, oaths were permitted during Ramadan but not on any of the Muslim feast days, such as the 'Aid s-Sghir, known in Rifian by its cognate *r-'aid amzzyan* (which immediately follows Ramadan) or the 'Aid l-Kbir, known in Rifian, again, as *r-'aid amqqran* (in the last month of the Muslim lunar year and calibrated to coincide with the last three days of the *hajj* to Mecca).

With respect to oath procedure, if one man accused another of some crime or misdeed, and the latter denied it, they would then agree to go to the local congregational mosque on the following Friday in time for the noon prayer, so that the accused could swear. Like an *'ahd* pact, the oath held equally for groups as for individuals, but otherwise the two phenomena were, as noted, very different. The plaintiff or plaintiffs had to be present at the mosque when the defendant and his co-jurors arrived. When all were assembled, they removed their footgear and weapons and went inside. The oath itself was generally deferred until after the *fqih* of the mosque had delivered his sermon to the congregation. When this was over, he would then ask the accused and his co-jurors the nature of the oath they were about to take; and then he made each one of them repeat it with his right hand on the Qur'an with the recitation in Arabic of the oath formula *bi-llahi alladhi la ilaha illa huwa* (lit. 'With God, aside from Whom there is no god other than He'). The accused himself swore first, followed by all his co-jurors individually. Note that there may possibly have been some instances in which the Qur'an was not employed as a vehicle for swearing, some informants opining that such cases were more the rule than the exception, and that in them the oath formula was reduced to *bi-llahi*, 'With God', only. Other informants, the majority, derided this practice, saying that it was only followed by the ignorant. In any event, it would seem that a copy of the Qur'an came into play more often than not, and that oaths were sworn at saints' tombs if there were no Friday mosque in the vicinity, a contingency which was most unlikely.

At any rate, after the oath had been taken, the *fqih*, who had witnessed it from the *mihrab*, the recess inside the mosque which indicates the direction of prayer, drew up a document in Arabic known simply as *tbriyith* or 'letter'. This certified that the accused, who was named, had sworn on such and such a date supported by such and such a number of co-jurors, also named, to the effect that he had not committed such and such a crime against the plaintiff, who was in turn also specified by name. Finally, he gave this document to the accused so that the latter could produce written evidence of his innocence.

As alluded to earlier, it was, and is, universally believed that anyone who perjured himself at oath would suffer the most dire consequences: either he, or some member of his family, or his livestock, would be struck dumb, blind or dead by God very shortly thereafter, or that some other equally horrendous calamity would befall him. A broken oath was termed *izuddj khaddakhs*, a phrase employed when, for example, a third party appeared after the oath was taken and announced that he had actually seen the accused commit the crime in question – although this should not be equated with the accusing oath of the Central Atlas, which had no Rifian equivalent. On one occasion, it appears that a sublineage of the Iznagen in the Aith Turirth section swore falsely at oath after one of their men had killed a member of another Iznagen sublineage. The result was that every single individual who had perjured himself sickened and died afterward, as an Act of God. Such an instance shows that, just as, culturally speaking, there is no separation between religion and politics in Islam and that the two are fused, there is also and equally no separation between the natural world and the supernatural.

This fact in itself would seem to me to cast considerable doubt on Gellner's implicitly more 'logical' theory behind perjury at oath – a theory which, incidentally, would not be acceptable to Muslims – as suggested in his otherwise most illuminating presentation of the institution as it was practised in the Central Atlas (Gellner 1969 pp.111–18). We should perhaps explain or qualify this view by saying that it seems to us that a central objective of ethnography is that of trying to make sense of any culture or social structure in its own terms and frame of reference before attempting to squeeze it into a procrustean Western model. In this respect, even though collective oath happens to be a major feature of Islamic customary law rather than of Islamic law *sensu stricto*, it is nonetheless far closer to the Muslim ethic than to any other.

Another important point is that if one of the accused's agnates did not want to swear for any reason, it was up to the accused to find a substitute for him. Furthermore, if the accused failed to turn up at the mosque in order to take oath at the stipulated time, he had to pay whatever damages were due. Any missing co-juror also had to pay if he did not have a valid excuse for his absence – such as illness, or a marriage or a death in the family. Thus, except in cases in which lineage groups were physically split into their component sublineages or extended families by vendetta (which was not at all uncommon), the burden of proof lay squarely upon the whole lineage group of the accused individual, the group which also, under normal circumstances, both took and was liable to vengeance during the course of a feud. Missing co-jurors were generally given until nightfall to appear. But after a certain time, the non-appearance of the accused, or his refusal to take oath, was considered sufficient proof of his guilt. He had, therefore, to pay whatever damages he had caused to the plaintiff, who had, of course, already assessed them. If, on the other hand, the plaintiff himself failed to appear, there was no oath at all. Any unavoidable detainment, of the kind mentioned above, on the part of the accused or of any of his co-jurors resulted in the postponement of the oath until the following Friday.

A final Aith Waryaghar case involving both the collective oath and the ubiquitous and prohibitively heavy fine, known as *haqq*, generally levied by the *imgharen* (sing. *amghar*), the members of the sectional or tribal council, on the person of any murderer who committed his murder in a market or *suq* and/or on market day, thereby disturbing a publicly recognised place and day of peace, involved men from the Timarzga section. A man of the Yinn 'Ari Mqaddim lineage lay in wait for two other individuals of the Yinn 'Abdallah who were passing through Aith Turirth territory on their way home from the Wednesday Market of Tawrirt (i.e., of the Aith Turirth). He shot them both and had, as a result, to pay a *haqq* fine of 2,000 duros (1,000 for each man) to the *imgharen*, as was customary. But the Yinn 'Abdallah were still not satisfied, and the following evening two of them killed the father of the Yinn 'Ari Mqaddim man on a path near his house. The men of the Yinn 'Ari Mqaddim then went to the adjudicator, a saintly descendant of the Prophet named Sidi Hmid n-Sidi r-Hajj Misa'ud, on the next market day in order to ask him to force 12 members of the Yinn 'Abdallah to swear an oath attesting to their innocence. There had been no witnesses to the last murder and, knowing this, the Yinn 'Abdallah men even volunteered to swear with double the necessary number (i.e. with 24 co-jurors. But Sidi Hmid, after consultation with the other council members, smelled a rat, vetoed the projected oath and made the Yinn 'Abdallah, in turn, pay 1,000 duros as *haqq*, which, as always, was distributed among the *imgharen* in equal shares. Thus a massive case of incipient perjury at oath was nipped in the bud as the notables of the tribal sections concerned got the upper hand.

Barring only one case that we know of, as recounted in a Spanish administrative report of April 1945 – in which the Aith Mhand u-Yihya w-Udhrar ('of the mountains') forced ten men from the Aith Ughridh to swear in the mosque of the Aith r-Qadi, in the centre of Aith Waryaghar territory, that they had a right to half the irrigation water emanating from a locality known as Dharmat, a right which had evidently been contested –, collective oath, completely abolished by bin 'Abd al-Krim, failed to become revived during the protectorate period, for the impress of this *qa'di* cum reformer on Rifian life and custom had been very great. Oaths may still be taken today, as before, at the Friday mosque and on the Qur'an, but they involve only the plaintiff and the accused. Co-jurors, that hallmark both of Berber oaths and of Berber lineage solidarity (which is in itself a deceptive issue), are today very much a feature of the Rifian past.

We turn next to how collective oath worked in the Western Atlas, in the Sus valley and in the Anti-Atlas. All things considered, in this general area it was practised very much as it had been practised in the Rif. On the evidence of Berque for the Western Atlas tribe of the Seksawa, the process and emphasis of oath seem to have been much the same: it was generally sworn on Fridays after the noon prayer in the local congregational mosque by the accused individual with a variable number of co-jurors, according, once again, to the gravity of the accusation (Berque 1978 pp.330–6). He also notes, interestingly, that neither might oaths be sworn nor marriage ceremonies be held before the beginning of May after the almond harvest was brought in, under threat of divine retribution (ibid. p.330).

But even though Berque's discussion of Seksawa oaths is restricted largely to the various pieces of documentary evidence for them in Arabic among various sections of the tribe in question from the late sixteenth century onwards, and even though he makes few specific ethnographic observations about the oath process or its structure and function, he lets us know, somewhat obliquely, that oaths were normally taken in the *timzgida*, the mosque (from Ar. *masjid*, with same meaning), on the Qur'an, that 12 co-jurors was probably the maximum number who could swear their innocence of any given accusation, and that the oath was generally recorded in Arabic and dated by the local *talib* or scribe. Berque also admits that collective oaths in the Western Atlas were far more threadbare in content from those in the Middle and Central High Atlases, which we examine further below. However, he also points up certain possible historical connections between Berber collective oaths – which in fact he terms both 'plural oaths' and 'ordeals', the latter of which underlines the threat of divine retribution in case of perjury, and 'plural oaths' on the one hand, and the notion, possibly Qur'anic, of afif (lit. 'crowd, multitude') or collective testimony which, again, citing a case dated as early as 1494 CE (899 AH), he refers to as 'plural testimony', on the other (idem pp.334–5). In this last instance the number of witnesses is or must be theoretically equal to the number of co-jurors required by the accused. He also notes but does not elaborate on the fact that under certain circumstances, it was the plaintiff who chose the defendant's co-jurors, who always turned out also to be the latter's agnates, precisely those men who under the laws of *fiqh* or standard Islamic jurisprudence would be forbidden to swear (ibid. p.331).

In support of this relationship between collective oath and *lafif*, Berque cites a case of perjury at an oath sworn at the mosque of Tifesfas over the theft of 12 dinars, which resulted in the deaths shortly thereafter not only of all 12 co-jurors but in those of all 12 of their adversaries as well (idem p.331). This reveals a decidedly different view of the question from that expressed by Gellner. Berque also mentions but does not analyse other similar cases. For the record, however, we are compelled to say that in our own work on collective oath both in the Rif and the Central Atlas, we have never run across the notion of *lafif*, which, judging from its root, at least (namely, that of *l-f-f* , 'to wrap, envelop'), may also possibly be related to that of *liff*, a term which refers to the large, factionally organised and impermanent blocs of Berber tribal or sectional alliance networks which were normally formed and broken up in the precolonial period both in the Rif and in the Western and Anti-Atlas presently under discussion (cf. Montagne 1930; Hart 1976 pp.312–38, 1996).

We now consider collective oaths in the Anti-Atlas region, and here the material provided by Adam (1948) is at once more lucid and more relevant than the suggestive but incomplete picture given us by Berque for the Seksawa. At the outset of his exposition, Adam makes the important point that although the Sus Valley and the Anti-Atlas mountains may seem far removed physically from the Arabic-speaking coastal plains and cities of Morocco, the Swasa, the Susi Berbers who are native to the region, are among the most devout Muslims in the country and have long been very strongly influenced by Shari'a law. Not only this, but most of them are literate enough in Arabic to have provided, traditionally, the largest number of *tulba'* (pl. of *talib*, 'student') of any region in the country and to have exported them as teachers of the Qur'an not only to the Arabic- speaking nomad tribes of the Western Sahara south of Morocco, but to virtually all the other regions of the country as well.

The Swasa were exporters of these *tulba'* long before the members of certain Anti-Atlas tribes also came to control the urban grocery trade, both wholesale and retail, in Morocco. The presence, the number and the influence of these literate men throughout Morocco has been sufficient to increase the number of written acts and documents in Arabic, and to give written contracts and modes of proof a degree of importance which the latter do not have in other Berber-speaking parts of the country, especially in those of the Middle and Central Atlas. The Ishilhayen Berbers of the Sus and Anti-Atlas regions have long had their own '*urf* or customary law, but the presence among them of such a large number of teachers of the Qur'an to educate their youth and inculcate it in Islamic tradition has resulted in giving them a major voice in the local councils and in orienting the people more toward the Shari'a than toward customary law – even though the persistence of the latter remained constant in the region until independence.

One result of this persistence of customary law was that of collective oath, never sworn by a single individual on his own, but supported by at least two of his agnatic kinsmen as co-jurors. The latter were, as elsewhere, increased in number according to the gravity of the offence, and the maximum number might run anywhere from 50 to as many as 100 co-jurors. As elsewhere, too, oath-taking was a public affair which also had a sacred character, and oaths were normally sworn either in a mosque or at a saint's shrine. As elsewhere, again, in Morocco, oath was resorted to only if there were no witnesses to the crime responsible for invoking it in the first place. Such cases Adam also reports as having been abnormally frequent and he observes, further, that the most original feature of Berber oaths in general was not so much the fact that they were ordeals which the accused had to undergo, but that they were always and obligatorily collective (ibid. p.301).

The three small Anti-Atlas tribes among whom Adam did his fieldwork on collective oath are located south of the Jbel Lkist and east of Kardus. They are the Ighshen, the Ait Wafqa and the Ait 'Abdallah u-Sa'id. These Swasa or Ishilhayen tribes all designated their collective oath as *l-haqq n-tigzdist*, rather than by the purely Berber labels of *tagallit* or *thzaddjith* employed by the Imazighen or the Rifians, respectively. The designation is of interest for two reasons. The first is because in the Susi context the Arabic term *haqq* (lit. 'right, truth') is that which refers to the oath itself (in the sense, presumably, that the accused individual who must swear it is obliged to tell the truth). This usage of *haqq* is different from that normally employed by Rifians to refer to the *haqq nj-suq*, the prohibitively heavy fine imposed by the tribal council members (as the council's 'right') on any man who killed another in the market place. It is also different from the Ait 'Atta concept embodied in the term *ait l-haqq*, 'people of the truth', referring to the six specialists in customary law from the localised tribal section of the Ait 'Aisa who made up the *istinaf*, the supreme court of appeal in the Ait 'Atta 'capital' of Igharm Amazdar in the Saghru, the court empowered to decide any issue brought to it by Ait 'Atta from other regions and whose members were changed in rotation with each new court case or session. The second point of interest is that in Tashilhit Berber the term *tigzdist*, meaning 'side', is generally employed to denote any objects which are ranged 'side by side'; and thus it refers to the accused individual and his co-jurors. Adam therefore translates *l-haqq n-tigzdist* as the 'oath of the lineage', in conformity with the general Berber tendency to identify social units and descent groups by labelling them as parts of the human body, such as *ikhs* ('bone') or *afus* ('hand'): for both these terms refer also to the agnatic lineage as a social group.

It follows therefore that in the *l-haqq n-tigzdist* the co-jurors of the accused individual are his agnates, from the closest one to him to the most distant genealogically. For after the accused man himself swore, his co-jurors then had to do so, in decreasing order of genealogical closeness, as follows: father, son, brother, father's brother, father's brother's son, etc. The major criterion was that of patrilineal kinship. If a married woman, however, should have had to swear, she normally chose as co-jurors either her own agnatic kinsmen or those of her husband; but she was forbidden to mix the two.

As among all Moroccan Berber societies, if one of the accused's co-jurors should refuse to swear during the course of the oath-taking, or should fail to turn up for it at the appointed time and place, the oath was 'broken' and the decision went against the accused. In such a society the individual exists, traditionally, only as a member of a social group. Lineage solidarity is in this context monolithic, while the *diyit* or bloodmoney which had to be paid by a murderer to the agnatic kinsmen of his victim was hence paid or received, as the case might have been, by the agnatic lineage as a unit. This is why the legal decision procedure which we here call collective oath was so frequently resorted to in these small-scale tribal societies. It is also why eye-witnesses to any crime, who ideally should have been members of lineages other than that of the man accused of it, were so rare, and why, in addition, perjury at oath on the part of any lineage mate and co-juror of the accused always carried the threat of divine retribution. Negative evidence for this state of affairs, at any rate, may be seen through the fact that, barring the numerous vendettas which occurred with even greater frequency even than bloodfeuds in the precolonial Rif and which we were able to reconstruct from interviews with elderly informants (Hart 1976 pp.313–38; 1989), very few incidences of fratricide have been reported for other parts of Berber Morocco.

However, the oath known in the Anti-Atlas as *l-haqq n-tigzdist* was not applicable in all cases, but only to those in which the plaintiff and the defendant were members of the same *taqbilt* or tribe. In the event that they were members of different tribes, a second type of oath, known as *l-haqq n-tiwizi* ('the oath of the working party') was invoked. In this one, an accused individual did not, or not necessarily, have to choose his co-jurors from among his closest agnatic kinsmen. He was given more leeway here, and could therefore call on his friends, uterine kinsmen or affines to help him organise a 'working party', as implied by the term *tiwizi*, such as might happen if he were to build his house, to plough his fields or to harvest his crops. This is so because *tiwizi* refers in Berber to any action involving mutual aid – such as obligatory hospitality to the village *fqih* or *talib*, which traditionally takes the form of every householder in the village taking turns to provide him with his dinner. Hence *l-haqq n-tiwizi* takes the form of a service rendered to any friend or kinsman, for kinsmen, whether patrilineal, uterine or affinal, always made up part of the personnel participating in a *haqq n-tiwizi*. But, as Adam tellingly observes, what better way is there to thank friends and relatives for services rendered than by inviting them to partake of a good meal? Here, as Adam also notes, the door may be open to all sorts of abuses, which are common enough to produce smiles on the faces of Berbers should the concept of *l-haqq n-tiwizi* crop up in the conversation.

Even so, the difference between these two types of oath are quite profound. In the neighbouring Anti-Atlas tribe of the Ammeln, among whom the *l-haqq n-tiwizi* oath was evidently not practised, the accused individual, if he were unable to fill his quota of co-jurors, as required by the type of oath he had to swear, from among his own agnatic kinsmen, could go to the next village, sacrifice an animal there and ask any of its residents to assist him by making up the required number. They could not refuse him, for sacrifice implies a sacred tie and a ritual obligation between the author and the recipient of the sacrifice. This last type of oath, called *l-haqq n-tigharsi*, implies not only its literal meaning of 'the oath of sacrifice', but also 'the oath of the tribal section' as well, for it also served to establish a ritual link between the accused individual and his co-jurors.

There are, however, instances in which, as Adam informs us, the lack of a prospective co-juror who failed to show up at oath did not necessarily break the oath. He himself knew of one such, which was sanctioned by the unanimous opinion of the *inflas* (sing. *anflus*), the tribal council. In this particular case the man who failed to appear was deliberately out to provoke his neighbour, even though the latter was from the same agnatic lineage. This prospective co-juror had slightly earlier accused the man about to swear of having poisoned his own son, and the man was freed from all suspicion. Then, in an affair involving inheritance, he had to swear a *l-haqq n-tigzdist* oath with 50 co-jurors and had to cede his place to his would-be ex-denouncer. The latter, of course, failed to swear. The tribunal admitted his replacement and hence the oath was not broken.

There is still more of interest here. For in such circumstances, there are certain individuals, well known in the region for their honesty and virtue, who did not necessarily have to swear collective oaths for they had become *igemmamem* (sing. *agemmam*), by virtue of the fact that no less than 50 persons attested to their right to bear this designation. Such a qualification was like a document in Arabic and was written up as it would have been in a specific act. Such a man was regarded as incapable of false testimony or perjury at oath. Although Adam never had the occasion to come across such a document, he claimed to have known two or three men from the Ait 'Abdallah u-Sa'id who qualified for *agemmam* status.

Nonetheless, the frequency of false testimony sometimes imposed a need for a less arbitrary procedure. As evidence for this Adam cites Emile Tyan (1938 Vol. I p.352) to the effect that toward the middle of the second century AH, a certain Ghawth ibn Sulayman, an Egyptian *qa'di*, obtained discretionary powers in order to institute a 'means of procedure destined to inform the judge on the morality of witnesses called upon to depose justice' (ibid.). This was the *tazkiya*, literally 'purification', a sort of inquiry into the soundness and morality of anyone who could qualify as a witness. At a later date a special functionary known as *muzakki* was placed in charge of proceeding with the inquiry and writing up a permanent list of 'trustworthy witnesses', *shuhud 'udul*, the forefathers of the modern *'adl*.

The quality of *shahid 'adl* was thus established by an act of *tazkiya*, in which several witnesses (12 or 20, according to the region and period under consideration) attested to the honour of the personage in question and his ability therefore to act as witness. This, then, is most probably the real origin of the *agemmam*. The analogy is evident, for we are dealing here with individuals whose veracity has been proclaimed officially and in advance by a certain number of witnesses and consigned to written form. Here we come back to the matter of law in Islam as opposed to custom among Berbers, for the institution of the *agemmam* is integral to the functioning of Berber law. Any man who benefits from this privilege becomes thereby abstracted from his lineage group and in his intrinsic quality as an individual he may be considered as a man apart from and independent of this group. His moral value is thereby recognised above and beyond the biological and structural principles of lineage solidarity and patrilineal descent. If indeed he has to submit to the ordeal of oath-taking, his course of action therefore lies in his own hands.

To recapitulate, the *l-haqq n-tigzdist* probably represents in this region the oldest modality of oath, expressing as it does in this region the solidarity of the lineage group, whether this be known either as *ighs* or as *afus*. However, in the Anti-Atlas we also find the magico-religious sanction behind the *l-haqq n-tigharsi* and the routine of pressing friends or kinsmen of any sort into doing service as co-jurors in the *l-haqq n-tiwizi*. Indeed, it is very possibly considerations of just this sort in favour of the Shari'a which have led it to replace Berber law in Morocco: for it may be argued in this context that personal conscience has appeared and substituted the Shari'a for archaic jural norms conditioned by agnatic lineage solidarity. As Adam appropriately notes, it must not be forgotten that to any of these Berbers, and perhaps most particularly to those of the Anti-Atlas, Islam represents the highest form of civilisation which is accessible to them (Adam 1948 p.309). But, it must be remembered, in the Sus it is not the *inflas* or tribal notables who form the intelligentsia; it is, rather, the *tulba'* who do so. This fact, impressed upon these Berber *tulba'* even more tellingly through their long-standing access to the Qur'an and hence to the written word as expressed in the Arabic documents which they draw up as scribes for their fellow tribesmen, is hence of great significance in any evaluation of the cultural and structural content to be found in the legal decision procedure as formerly resorted to and practised by these sedentary agriculturalists and *tulba'*. Of them a significant percentage have emigrated to the cities of the plain in recent years to turn into urban entrepreneurs in Casablanca and elsewhere (for details, cf. also Adam 1973; Waterbury 1972, 1973).

Long before this, however, the pious clerical forefathers of these men worked steadily toward the goal of bringing their *'urf* into alignment with the Shari'a. The degree of moral value which the Swasa placed upon the *agemmam* rendered him exempt from having to participate in collective oath, and this fact may be cited as a supporting example (Adam 1948 p.309). A further one is illustrated by the fact that in the Anti-Atlas any pact, alliance or agreement which is taken down, in Arabic and in writing, is given the designation in Tashilhit of *amsira*, literally 'writing' and referring to any written document (which is itself derived from the Berber verb 'to write'), and is therefore viewed as permanent by the contracting parties. This pair of facts also differentiates it from the temporary tribal alliances known as *liff*, both in the Rif and in the Anti-Atlas, which we have discussed elsewhere and, briefly, above (Hart 1976 pp.313–22; 1980). The notion of *'ar*, on the other hand, appears as a result to be somewhat downgraded by comparison, for it is viewed by the same Swasa or Ishilhayen tribes as being merely a request for help made through the act of sacrifice of an animal on the part of the petitionee to his protector-to-be. As such it is regarded as purely temporary.

As already mentioned, the institution of collective oath reached its greatest development and degrees of elaboration among the largely transhumant Imazighen tribes of the Middle and Central Atlas regions. We consider, first, oaths as they were sworn first in the Middle Atlas, among the

Zimmur (Marcy 1949) and the Zayyan or Iziyyan respectively (Aspinion 1946), and then move south into the Central Atlas to consider the modalities of oath among the Ait Sukhman (Hart 1984*b*), the Ihansalen (Gellner 1969), the Ait Hadiddu (Bousquet 1956; Hart 1978), the Ait Murghad (Hart 1978) and the Ait 'Atta (Hart 1981; 1984).

Marcy makes a crucial distinction, one valid not only for the Zimmur whom he studied personally, but for all Berber societies which practised collective oath, not only between testimony and oath, but also between objective and subjective proof. The first is furnished, whenever or wherever possible, by witnesses and the second by the accused individual and his co-jurors under the constraint of an essentially religious ceremonial which entails the apprehension of divine punishment in the event of perjury on the part of any one of them (Marcy 1949 p.66). This is an apt and succinct statement of the nature of collective oath, and not surprisingly, in view of the evidence here presented, Marcy informs us that in eight or nine cases out of any ten which appeared in front of the *jma'a* or *ajmu'*, the tribal council, oath had perforce to be resorted to given the almost invariable absence of witnesses. Testimony and oath thus constitute the two sides of a coin, each one closely dependent on the other, with the oath taking place only when testimony was either lacking entirely or insufficient. But Marcy also notes that in the latter instance, account was always taken at the beginning of the evidence, thereby constituted by a number of witnesses which was always less than the minimum number normally required by Berber customary law in any cases of importance – such as, among the Ait Saghrushshn, at least six witnesses with respect to matters involving movable property and 12 for matters involving real property or laws of personal status (ibid. p.69). It is also worth recalling here that the figures of six and 12 represented also the number of co-jurors – not of witnesses – in the precolonial Rif before the advent of bin 'Abd al-Krim, and might well be related to the fact that in Maliki law, the prevailing school of law in Morocco, one *'adl* or notary is equivalent to six ordinary witnesses.

The decision of whether any accusation was well-founded and whether an oath should be taken rested with the *jma'a*, the council, which also officially acknowledged the denunciation of his adversary made by the plaintiff. In the absence of any show of proof, however, the *jma'a* would never authorise an oath-taking unless a situation of fact existed which provided some ground for proof of the plaintiff's request. Marcy also noted, furthermore, that in matters of this kind, there were definite limitations imposed on the actions of the customary tribunals that the French protectorate administration set up in these Tamazight-speaking areas. The tribunals could only examine the claims of both parties, limit their extent, weigh their plausibility and only then could they judge whether an oath should be sworn (ibid. p.70).

Marcy goes on to summarise the collective oaths of these Imazighen tribes as the transition to a supernatural plane of any concrete litigation in which the plaintiff and the defendant stand opposed. It was based on a religious emotivity undergone by one of the parties under the control of the *jma'a* and within the limits of public order established by customary law; and the rules governing the way it worked were none other than the consequence of these principles (ibid. p.71).

First of all, in this region the oath was invariably sworn at the tomb of a local saint, who might have even been one not necessarily regarded as orthodox in terms of Islamic hagiography. The choice of the shrine in question was generally agreed upon by both parties to the oath; and if such agreement was not reached, either the accused individual had the right to choose the site unilaterally, or it was simply pre-established by custom. In the case of the northern Ait Saghrushshn depending on the *bureau* at Sefrou, this was the shrine of Sidi Mhand u-bil-Qasim above the village of Immuzar. Furthermore, if by any chance the accused came from an area where the Shari'a prevailed over customary law (as it evidently did among some of the northern-most Imazighen tribes closest to Meknes and Fez), he was allowed to swear on a copy of the Qur'an as consonant with Maliki law (ibid. p.71).

Furthermore, the essentially collective character of the oath was accentuated, in this region as in others, by the presence of a variable number of agnates of the accused individual who acted as his *ingilla* (the Zimmur term, or *imgillan* as among the Central Atlas tribes) or co-jurors, and if there were insufficient agnates to fill the quota, others were sought from a nearby village or encampment. If a stranger to the region was accused, it was incumbent upon his protector or *bab umur-ins* (*bab n-umur* in the Central Atlas) to find the necessary co-jurors for him (ibid. p.72).

But the number of co-jurors needed depended, as we have stressed, on the gravity of the offence. Marcy informs us that the maximum number among three of the major Middle Atlas tribes, the Zimmur, the Iziyyan and the Ait Mgild, might be as many as 100; the circumstances giving rise to such a large number are not indicated but one might infer that they involved disputes between members of any two of the three tribes in question. The number required for the murder of a fellow tribesman, on the other hand, was down to 40 among both the Iziyyan (Aspinion 1946 p.174) and the tribes of the Central Atlas, and from there it plummeted down to ten among the Ait Warayin and northern Ait Saghrushshn, among whom the influence and proximity of Fez and the Shari'a came to be strongly felt (Marcy 1949 p.72).

Disputes over property were the most common cause for collective oath among Imazighen tribes in general, and in these cases the minimum number of co-jurors required was five (i.e. the accused and four of his close agnates). Among the Zimmur a woman only needed three co-jurors (her own uterine brothers), as she had, among most of these tribes, no rights to inheritance in any event. In default of these, she had to swear with her mother although the oath had to be renewed on three successive Fridays to be considered effective, Friday being the recognised day for women to visit the local saint's shrine. But as women among the Ait Saghrushshn evidently inherit, a woman could take oath under the same conditions as a man (ibid. pp.72–3).

In all cases it was the absolute number of oaths, or the absolute number of co-jurors, that was the major factor, and questions of individual personality did not enter the picture. Minors could swear as well as adults provided they were assisted in doing so (especially if they were too young) by their guardians, while the formula of oath might be repeated several times by the same person if there were no possibility of supplying the requisite number of co-jurors. Form meant everything, for the oath was not only a legal trial but a religious one as well, given the fact that oath was a purgatory trial and given the threat of divine punishment for perjury. Nonetheless, under certain conditions the accused party might be able to reduce somewhat, through payment, the required number of co-jurors. On the other hand, the plaintiff then had to reduce the number of witnesses, if any, accordingly (ibid. pp.74–5).

Among the Zimmur, as Marcy notes, there were several standard formulas of oath, but all centred around the same set of themes. A typical example has the accused individual stating: *wa haqq had l-baraka* ('by the truth of the *baraka* of this saint, I will not eat, nor drink nor cohabit with my wife if what my adversary says is true!'). Then his co-jurors would support his allegation by saying something on the order of: *wa haqq had l-baraka, kikh ainna ikka gma* ('I pass where my brother has passed', meaning 'I accept the same responsibility as he does'). For fear of the curse of the saint and the mystical responsibility for sacrilege in the event of false oath rested on the heads of every member of the accused individual's lineage, those who paid or received blood compensation for him; and thus the sum total of possible maledictions, on a one-for-one basis, could be terrible. This fact was therefore an almost automatic guarantee of the sincerity of any individual taking oath. Herein lay the exceptional force of trial by collective oath, for, as noted, should the accused individual or any of his co-jurors fail to show up at the designated shrine at the time stipulated, the oath was regarded as 'broken' and the accused had to pay (ibid. pp.76–7) – although under certain circumstances in the Central Atlas it was, as we shall see, either the missing or the recusant co-juror who paid.

Another important feature of Zimmur oaths, as of those sworn by other tribes in the region, was the frequent presence among the co-jurors of a certain number of tribal notables, known as *nuqran* (from Ar. *nakira*, 'to deny'), whose independent testimony had more value. Such a tactic was particularly sought after in disputes involving neighbours holding contiguous plots of land, as it often happened that in fact each of the adversaries might swear an equally valid oath that the land in question was his own. Thus the *jma'a* was no more than a witness to the form the oath took, while the saint was the final judge of whether the accused had committed sacrilege. He could unleash terrible super-terrestrial calamities to strike the defendant down if he swore in bad faith. In this sense, Marcy concludes, Berber customary law met the Shari'a of mainstream Islam on common ground (ibid. pp.78–9).

To move on to the Iziyyan, Aspinion too has noted that if a stranger having no kinsman or protector in the tribal territory had to take oath, the *jma'a* would choose his co-jurors, impose the formula of oath, and pick the time and place for it to be sworn. Among these co-jurors, half of them would be *nuqran*, although the accused could request the substitution of others for any of them whom he thought might swear unfavourably, while an *amhars*, a term referring to a stranger, generally an Arab, who was under the protection and living in the tent of a powerful tribesman and was thus under certain obligations to him (*amhars* contracts being to this day particularly prevalent among the Iziyyan), could not support his protector or any of the latter's agnatic kin at oath (Aspinion 1946 p.173). As elsewhere, the refusal of any co-juror to swear rendered the oath ineffective. Any offence assessed at a payment running up to 100 old francs necessitated five co-jurors, of which two or three had to be *nuqran* and were decided upon by lot-drawing. The same amounts held for the theft of a sheep or a goat. Any offence assessed at over 100 francs required ten co-jurors, of whom five had to be *nuqran*, and the same amounts applied to the theft of any larger livestock (cow, mule, donkey, horse or camel).

The murder of a woman necessitated 20 co-jurors, of whom ten had to be *nuqran*, while the murder of a man necessitated double this amount, 40 co-jurors of whom 20 had to be *nuqran*. But whenever *nuqran* were involved, the stipulation was that only one of them could come from any given tent or lineage group. With respect to disputes over property, the number of co-jurors varied from 20 to 40, according to whether the dispute was between two individuals, two different lineage groups, two different sections or two different tribes (ibid. pp.174–5). As elsewhere, oaths were always sworn at the doors of saints' tombs, and invariably began with the formula *u haqqa n-barsha* ('I swear by the holiness of this saint'), with the co-jurors repeating, as above, *kkikh manis ikka uma* ('I pass where my brothers have passed'). If by any chance any co-juror was sick or otherwise unavoidably delayed, or if the oath should have been cancelled because of bad weather, it was delayed until all the necessary parties to it were assembled (ibid. p.174). There were, however, individuals who might refuse to let a whole lineage or tribal section take oath, in which case the *abarrah* or market crier would announce the fact in the *suq*. As elsewhere, any male who had not reached the age of fasting during Ramadan could not swear, while women might only swear if some accusation were levelled at them personally or in order to determine the doubtful paternity of a foetus or an *amgun*, a child regarded as 'sleeping' because of an arrested pregnancy (a condition which was held to be very common among the northern Imazighen).

One evident divergence from the Middle Atlas norm as exemplified by the Zimmur and the Iziyyan, above, was shown by those Imazighen tribes of the Central High Atlas both higher up and further south. This was the existence in all of them of an *anahkam* or *anahsham* (pl. *inahkamen* or *inahshamen*) or oath administrator who, when all were assembled at the shrine, called out the oath formula for the accused and his co-jurors to repeat. Among the Ait Bindaq (lit. 'people of the gun') and Ait 'Abdi sections of the Ait Sukhman, located at a height of over 3,000 metres on the Kusar plateau, the *anahkam* repeated the oath formula no less than six times, whereas he did so only three times for the other sections further downhill at Anargi, Taglift, Aghbala and Tagzirt, thus attesting to the proverbial hard-headedness of the former. In most of the Central Atlas, the *anahkam* was changed for each oath, but this was not the case among the Ait Bindaq. As always, the co-jurors were the agnates of the accused in order of inheritance, and their number varied with the gravity of the offence: among the Ait Bindaq, seven were required for the theft of a bull, 20 for the theft of a camel, and, as was normal everywhere in the region, the same for the rape or murder of a woman, which was then doubled to 40 for the murder of a man. This last was congruent with the fact that in terms of normal Islamic inheritance expectations one son counts the same as two daughters and that the *diyit* or blood compensation for a woman is, equally, half that for a man.

The penalty for theft of grain from an *igharm* or collective storehouse was 20 sheep for the main gate of the storehouse and ten sheep for any other gate, the idea being that the first 20 went to all those individuals who had cubicles (*tihuna* (sing. *tahanut*)) in the storehouse and the last ten to the individual *bu tahanut* or owner of the cubicle who had been robbed (Hart 1984*b* pp.147–8, 152 n.5). As among other Central Atlas tribes, too, the Ait Sukhman had both the *tagallit*, the normal oath of denial, and the *alkum*, the more special oath of accusation; and oaths could be sworn at all times of year except during Ramadan. Gellner has noted that when the Ait 'Abdi swore against their enemies of the Ait Hadiddu, they did so at Timzgida n-

Zagmuzen, while the latter, in swearing against the Ait 'Abdi, did so at Ait Tasiska in the Imdghas. Equally, the Ait 'Abdi swearing against the lay Ait Umzrai section of the Ihansalen did so at the Zawiya of Sidi Sa'id Ahansal, while the latter reciprocated at Sidi Bu Ishaq (Gellner 1969 p.109). Most other Central Atlas tribes, however, such as the Ait Is'hha, the Ihansalen and the northerly sections of the Ait 'Atta which are located outside the main body of the tribal territory, did not swear between October and April, during periods of heavy snowfall or rainfall, simply because a storm on one man's crops might have proved the oath of another to have been true through natural causes (Hart 1984b p.148).

Among the Ait Murghad above Msimrir, on the southern slope of the Central Atlas, five co-jurors (the accused and four of his agnates or *ait 'ashra*) were needed for theft of small articles or for theft inside a house; and the oath was sworn at the tomb of a female saint, Lalla ut-Tgidir. The thief had to pay 4 duros hasani for each door in the house: for a Berber house, *igharm* or *qsar*, is at least four storeys high and has many doors. As elsewhere, each infraction was sanctioned by a fine established by the council. Capt. Roger Henry noted, in two reports dated 1937 (Henry 1937a; 1937b), that when the maintenance of order required it, the *amghar* or local chief could dictate the amount, as it suited him, to recalcitrant adversaries. In such a case he would wet a stone with his finger: if calm had not been re-established when the stone dried, he pronounced his sanction. This judgment was known as *s-imi n-umghar* ('from the mouth of the *amghar*'), and the same procedure exactly was resorted to, but with more ritual and greater suspense, among the Ait 'Atta. Any litigation which did not fall under the *amghar*'s competence was handled by the *ajmu'*. An assembly might also be convoked which was empowered to judge without appeal, and this was known as the *ait l-haqq*, the 'people of the truth' and the guardians of custom.

Above and beyond this, and as elsewhere, ten co-jurors (the accused and nine agnates) were needed for theft of livestock, with the oath sworn at the shrine of Sidi Sa'id n-Imilwan, in the territory of the Ait Hadiddu (for the Ait Murghad and the Ait Hadiddu were technically allied tribes in the Ait Yafalman confederacy). Again as elsewhere, 40 co-jurors (the accused and 39 agnates, or at least the members of other related lineages to whom he had sacrificed a sheep) were required in the event of suspected murder, with the oath again sworn at Sidi Sa'id n-Imilwan. If, for example, only six out of ten co-jurors actually showed up, either the accused had to pay damages to the plaintiff, after which he went to the *amghar* and reclaimed against his missing agnates, or indeed the agnates in question had to pay, as they were in the minority. However, if the majority of agnates necessary to swear should still be missing at oath time, no oath was taken, the accused individual had to pay and the matter was considered closed (Hart 1978 pp.59–60, 73 n.14).

As everywhere, oaths were an integral part of customary law, which was underwritten by the French authorities during the protectorate period. To illustrate this fact, two elderly informants related the following story about themselves. A asked B to lend him 1,500 francs as against his threshing floor (*anrar*) as a *rahn*, or mortgage, for two months. When A finally got the money together he went to B to return it in order to redeem his threshing floor, but B replied in the negative, saying that A had sold him the threshing floor outright. This created a serious misunderstanding, and A denied B's asseverations of sale. The upshot was that B had to swear an oath with nine other co-jurors to the effect that he had bought the threshing floor and had not simply accepted it as security for his money. However, when they reached the tomb of Sidi Sa'id n-Imalwan to swear, the co-jurors decided not to support the accused because they realised that in fact he had not purchased the threshing floor. One of our informants was the co-juror delegated to tell B that they were not going to back him up at oath. The assembled co-jurors made a reclamation at the *bureau* at Msimrir, once the French *Affaires Indigènes* officer at the post had convoked them to ask why they did not want to swear. My informant told him that the reason for this was that B had not in fact bought the threshing floor. But at this point the other co-jurors changed their tune, telling my informant that he was misrepresenting them, and that they did want to swear after all. They even implied that he had been bribed to misrepresent them. For this the AI officer imprisoned my informant, but the latter was nonetheless determined to seek justice at the hands of the provincial customary law tribunal at Qsar s-Suq (now Rashidiya). When he went there, with all the co-jurors, and when he was asked why he did not swear, he replied that to have done so would have been unjust and that he would stick to his decision. The French now told him that he had to swear to the co-jurors that he had not received any money to swear against B – and that was the end of it, as the oath was now taken at Sidi Sa'id n-Imilwan (ibid. p.60).

Among the Ait Hadiddu, internal disputes were settled at the court or *istinaf* at Imilwan, in the Imdghas region, between Msimrir to the south and Igharm Aqdim n-Ait 'Attu w-Ikku to the north. This fact happens to be of considerable interest and shows some perspicacity on the part of the Ait Hadiddu, because the Imilwan people, who by trade are porters and ambulatory pedlars, are not true Ait Hadiddu at all but represent a dark-skinned (though non-negroid) relict population. They were chosen as *ti'aqqidin* (sing. *ta'aqqit*) or administrators of customary law precisely because they were neutral and outside the mainstream of Ait Hadiddu political life. Theoretically, at least, they had no political axe to grind. All documents (in Arabic) pertaining to customary law were kept in the house of the *akhatar n-ti'aqqidin*, the eldest member of the Imilwan, whose tenure as Keeper of Custom was for life. The normal procedure with respect to adjudication was for him to call in their respective lineage or section 'brothers' whenever it seemed appropriate in any dispute between two individuals, and, with the aid of the documents, to atempt to work out a solution based on precedent. Although in precolonial times a *fqih* at Sidi Bu Ya'qub (an important shrine in Ait Murghad territory, near Asul) handled any residual questions in which the Shari'a was also called into play, the Imilwan tribunal handled everything else (ibid. p.65).

Although the Ait Hadiddu admittedly show some singular sociocultural and institutional features which do not exist elsewhere in the region (such as the mass marriages which take place every year in late September at their annual *agdud* or feast of Sidi Hmad u-l-Mghanni near Imilshil), their oaths nonetheless conformed in all respects to the oath patterns of the region at large. Bousquet noted that the existence of material proof among them was extremely rare (Bousquet 1956 p.185). Forty co-jurors were required for murder (and bloodfeuding among the Ait Hadiddu was common), ten for theft inside a house or for theft of a mule, seven for theft of a cow, and five for theft outside a house. Theft inside a house was payable to the tune of 10 duros hasani for each door, as well as the sacrifice of a sheep by the thief in order to ask the pardon of the house owner. Oaths for murder were sworn at the tomb of Sidi Bu Ya'qub, and all other oaths (at least for the Ait Hadiddu of the Imdghas) were sworn at Imilwan. The *igurramen* or saints who normally served both the Ait Hadiddu and the Ait Murghad were all from the dissident, breakaway Ihansalen lineage of the Ait Sidi 'Ali u-Hsayn of Tamga. Sidi 'Ali u-Hsayn himself is buried among the Ait Dawud w-'Ali section of the Ait Sukhman dependent on Anargi (Gellner 1969 p.110); but three of his descendants are buried in Ait Murghad territory and two more in that of the Ait Hadiddu (Hart 1978 pp.65–6).

We now turn at last to the Ait 'Atta of the Jbil Saghru, the southern slope of the Central High Atlas, and the Dra and Tafilalt oases to the south and east, who had what was almost certainly the best developed and most elaborate system of oaths in Berber Morocco. It combined all the features of the Middle and Central Atlas oaths recounted above with a number of additional increments of its own. As elsewhere, the oath was a highly public affair, sworn on a predetermined day at a predetermined hour and at a predetermined saint's shrine, *s-salih*, with these choices made by the plaintiff. The *anahsham* or oath administrator had to come from a neutral lineage, although it was he, on occasion, who might designate the shrine where the oath was to be taken; and the oath-taking itself was performed in the doorway to the shrine. As elsewhere, the number of co-jurors, among whom the accused individual was counted first as *primus inter pares*, went from five for theft of livestock to 40 for murder.

The general ruling was that five co-jurors were required for theft of smaller livestock from fields or pastureland, but theft of camels among the nomad sections of the Ait Khabbash at Tawuz, in the Kamkam desert southeast of the Tafilalt oasis, and the Ait 'Alwan at Mhamid l-Ghuzlan in the Lower Dra Valley, necessitated ten co-jurors. Cattle theft among the Ait Y'azza section at Alnif, that of the Ait Unir at Bu Maln on the Dadss River and that of the Ait Khalifa at Marrutsha, required seven, while ten, again, were needed for litigation over land or for theft of a gun or from a house or an *igharm*. In the latter case, the fine levied was, as above, generally based on the number of doors in the *igharm* in question, at a rate of ten sheep per door. These were large sums indeed, and each sheep paid over had to be an *aguryan*, an unblemished year-old ram.

Regulations could, indeed, be even more stringent: among the Ait Y'azza of Alnif, once again, there was a fine of one sheep per furrow for ploughing somebody else's land, while if the thief of any animal were identified, the distance it had travelled to his house was measured by the number of its hoofprints. The fine exacted was 100 duros hasani per hoofprint plus an extra 100 duros for every night the animal spent in the thief's house. Among the northern and discontinuous section of the Ait 'Atta n-Umalu ('Ait 'Atta of the Shade') at Wawizaght along the Middle-Central Atlas watershed, any thief entering an *igharm* had to pay the same number of sheep as there were beams in the room (Hart 1981 pp.159–60).

As elsewhere, too, 20 co-jurors was the normal requirement for the rape or murder of a woman, as opposed to the usual 40 for the murder of a man. Among the Ait 'Atta of Usikis on the southern slope of the Central Atlas there was also a fine of 25 sheep for every hair on the woman's head, if she were unwilling or cried out; and if she were a virgin, the rapist had to marry her immediately. For the next four days he also had to invite 11 passers-by to dinner at his expense. If the girl wanted to divorce him afterward, she was quite free to do so (ibid. p.160).

With respect to procedure at oath, if it took place in the Ait 'Atta heartland of the Saghru, all parties concerned, if they had arrived at the appointed time at the shrine chosen, removed their footgear and their weapons, leaving them in a pile outside the *hurm*, the sacred precincts of the shrine itself. The plaintiff (*bab n-d-d'awt*) and the oath administrator (*anahsham*) now faced each other across the door of the shrine, and the defendant and his co-jurors lined up perpendicularly to them in front of the tomb. The *anahsham* then repeated to the accused and his co-jurors the words of the oath, generally three times. Slips were allowed during these first three repetitions of the oath, for they were trial runs, but when the oath was actually sworn any slip invalidated it. Then the accused himself would exclaim, '*Wullah! Wullah! Wullah! Di l-haqq n-Ullah! Aya dagh nakhfi tad'aid, miktusigh wa la tazrikh!*' ('By God! By God! By God! By God's truth! The thing/affair for which you have convoked me I have neither taken nor seen!'). After he swore he went over to stand by the *anahsham* facing the plaintiff. The first of his co-jurors would then repeat the first part of the formula ('*Wullah! Wullah! Wullah! Di l-haqq n-Ullah!*') and would then add, '*Aya dagh nakinna wa dagh arisha!*' ('By God! By God! By God! By God's truth! What this man has said is true!'). In a number of other Ait 'Atta communities, however, the co-jurors merely repeated the word *Skakht!* ('It is true').

The first co-juror, having finished, now walked around behind the tomb to stand behind the other co-jurors who had not yet sworn. Then the defendant, followed by the *anahsham*, circumambulated the shrine once more and the oath was over. Once it was finished each participant called all the others '*Aghyul!*' ('Donkey!'), after which he put on his sandals, picked up his weapons and went home. Generally, whichever party lost invited the *anahsham* for a meal, as he was not otherwise paid (ibid. pp.160–2).

The use of the insulting word 'donkey' in this context symbolized the fact that under certain circumstances, particularly with grave offences, the plaintiff and the spectators did their best to heckle and trip up the accused and his co-jurors. This would 'break' the oath, *irza tagallit* or *khsar tagallit*, and then the accused would have to pay. He could only avoid this sanction if the specified number of co-jurors had not arrived by the time the oath was scheduled. In such a case the missing men had to pay if they did not have valid excuses, such as illness or a long journey. Among the Ait Y'azza of Alnif they were even killed if they did not pay.

Also, if a missing co-juror were known to have been bribed by the plaintiff to stay away, he had to pay. If he were convinced of the defendant's guilt, he either told the plaintiff so, in which case the accused had to pay automatically, or he simply refused to participate. If so, he then had to obtain a substitute, usually through sacrifice, in order to make up the necessary quota.

Women and Haratin, the black date-palm cultivators who constitute much of the population of the southern Moroccan oases, were normally barred from participation in oath, although a woman of the accused man's lineage could take oath if she were nursing a baby son, a *tagunu̱nt* (diminutive of *agunun*, the hood of a jillaba or silham, worn entirely by men), who was over 40 days old and if she were carrying him on her back. This must have been exceptional, for normally, as noted, a man had to be old enough to fast before he was permitted to swear an oath. It might have occurred if the plaintiff had decreed that no *ifarqashen* or co-jurors from outside the defendant's lineage be allowed. Although, unlike *imluqten*, which implies mixed tribal ancestry, the term *ifarqashen* is not an insult, the concept only applied in incidents arising in markets, where any fellow Ait 'Atta could become co-jurors, thus underlining tribal solidarity in a wider context (ibid. p.162).

If either the accused or the plaintiff failed to show up, whichever one did appear would not fail to point this out to the *anahsham*. The latter now became a witness to the fact that the absentee had lost the case, but only when the fires were lit at nightfall, in order to give him every oppportunity to appeal. Should the *anahsham* himself fail to appear on time, the oath was simply deferred, for no oath could be held without an *anahsham*. Any excuse from swearing oath depended in the last analysis on the plaintiff's acceptance, even if the *anahsham* should disagree, as he, the plaintiff, was the injured party. This might well have been the case if, for instance, any of the co-jurors had had to travel a long distance: for such a readiness to participate was, in itself, a good indication that the accused was innocent (ibid. pp.162–3).

As noted, oaths were not sworn during Ramadan or on Fridays, and for obvious agricultural reasons they were generally deferred until the harvest was in. Oaths over smaller matters involving only five co-jurors or less were, reasonably enough, usually taken locally, at the tomb of a local saint of purely local importance, for there is at least one such in every local community. However, oaths over major disputes, involving Ait 'Atta of different sections or Ait 'Atta and other tribes, were sworn at major shrines.

Among the bigger shrines were that of Sidi Muhand w-'Ali, in the Wawizakht region, between the Ait 'Atta n-Umalu and the Ait Bu Zid; that of the Timzyida n-Tighighit, near Talmast above Zawiya Ahansal, where the localised section of resident Ait Bu Iknifen swore against their southern Ait Bu Iknifen brethren up on summer transhumance, owing to a perennial and still unresolved dispute between the two groups over pasturage; that of Sidi Sa'id Ahansal, at whose crucially important shrine any Ait 'Atta, resident or transhumant swore against the Ait Massad and the Ait 'Abdi section of the Ait Sukhman; that of Sidi Hmad u-l-Baghdad for disputes in the Dadss region between the local Ait Unir (Ait 'Atta) and the Haratin of the Ait Dadss; that of Sidi 'Ali u-Burk, the major saint of the Dadss region, where the Ait Bu Iknifen of Imidar swore; that of Sidi l-Hajj 'Amr at l-Hart n-Igurramen in the Tudgha region, where the Ait Isful (Ait 'Atta) of Tabsbast, the Ait Y'azza of Taghzut, the Ait l-Firsi of the Saghru and the Ait 'Atta of Taghbalt all swore; that of Sidi l-Huwwari, on the Ait 'Atta-Ait Murghad tribal frontier near Tinjdad, where the Ait Khalifa (Ait 'Atta) swore against the Ait Murghad; that of Sidi Salah in the Ktawa, for the southern Ait Isful and the Ait 'Alwan; and finally, in the Saghru itself, the core of Ait 'Atta territory as well as the tribal point of origin, the purely lay and inter-Ait 'Atta supreme court at Igharm Amazdar had ultimately the same function. By the same token the Ait Siddrat and the various tribes of the Ait Yafalman confederacy, including the Ait Murghad and the Ait Hadiddu, had their own saints, as we have seen. Hence, if any small group of Ait 'Atta were to escape as fugitives from a bloodfeud to the Ait Siddrat, the Ait Murghad or the Ait Hadiddu, or if the reverse had occurred, it meant that oath had escalated into war (ibid. p.163).

It may legitimately be asked at this point why no Ait 'Atta sections ever swore oaths at the tomb of their particular patron saint Mawlay 'Abdallah bin Hsayn (died between 1568 and 1592), who had a special relationship of friendship and protection with their own eponymous ancestor, Dadda ('Grandfather') 'Atta, who is buried at Taqqat n-Iliktawen in the Lower Dra Valley after having been killed in a battle against unidentified Arabs. This relationship transcended the deaths of both parties to continue through their descendants to the present day. But the *zawiya* and shrine of Mawlay 'Abdallah are located at Tamsluht, some 20 kilometres south-west of Marrakesh, nearly 300 kilometres to the west of Ait 'Atta territory. The latter normally visit his tomb with their *ziyara* offerings and donations to his descendants only once a year, in February or March, at a time very different from September when Mawlay 'Abdallah's annual pilgrimage or *musim*, to which only local people come, is held. The Ait 'Atta refrain deliberately from attending it, thus underlining their special relationship to him (ibid. pp.26–6; Hart 1984a pp.54–5). Hence those saints closer spatially to Ait 'Atta territory served as vehicles for collective oath, to which we now return.

The plaintiff could also stipulate the kind of oath that he wanted the accused and his co-jurors to swear. The fact is important because the Ait 'Atta had three different kinds of oath: the normal *tagallit*, as described above; the *tagallit n-nhah*, in which heckling by the plaintiff often turned the ceremony into a physical ordeal for the co-jurors; and the *alkum*, at which the plaintiff would produce his own co-jurors for a special kind of accusing oath (Hart 1981 pp.163–4).

The *tagallit n-nhah* was an ordinary collective oath with some special refinements. Usually it was only resorted to in grave cases, especially if the plaintiff wanted to make things as difficult as possible for the accused and his co-jurors. In fact, *nhah* was a technique which often rendered oath-taking full of pitfalls. After their 'pacification' of the Ait 'Atta at the final battle of Bu Gafr in the Saghru in February–March 1933, the French administration decided to abolish it for purely humanitarian reasons. *Nhah* was thus a major attribute of collective oath during the long precolonial period known to all Imazighen tribes as *siba* ('dissidence' – or 'organised anarchy').

The *nhah* ordeal was practised throughout Ait 'Atta territory with only a few exceptions, and was particularly prevalent in their core region of the Saghru. The *nhah* oath amounted to an obstacle course over which the accused and his co-jurors had to run. In the Saghru a circle of big stones was placed around the shrine where the oath was to be taken. The accused and his co-jurors had to march around this circle counter-clockwise, all of them blindfolded with the hoods of their jillabas or silhams covering their faces as well, and stepping either on each stone or around it. During the whole procedure the plaintiff and any and all spectators present would shout '*Hah! Hah! Hah!*' or ''*Aw! 'Aw! 'Aw!*' in order to distract and confuse the participants, for if any of them uttered a word or fell off a stone in the circle the oath was automatically 'broken' and the accused had to pay. Even though the French cut out the stepping-stones and the blindfolding, they could not prevent the plaintiff from yelling '*Hah! Hah! Hah!*'.

There were in any case still further refinements: in some localities co-jurors had to stand on one leg while swearing; in others they had to close one eye and/or stop up one ear; and in yet others they had to do both. In short, the *tagallit n-nhah* turned into a vindictive game of hopscotch amid the heckling, the raspberries, the cat-calling and other cries and gesticulations from the plaintiff and the onlookers. Yet the Ait Unir of Birnat just south of the Middle Atlas claimed that their *nhah* oath did not involve these extremes, while the Ait Khabbash denied having employed *nhah* techniques at all. It is clear that in collective oath, as in many other ways, the Saghru remained the Ait 'Atta heartland.

The *alkum* was in essence a reversal of the normal oath. It was sworn not by the accused but by the plaintiff and his own agnates to assert that the suspected individual had committed the crime in question. It was thus an oath of accusation and was practised throughout Ait 'Atta territory. Among the Ait Bu Iknifen of Imidar, for example, the *alkum* involved two sets of oaths: first a normal one of denial on the part of the defendant, and then one of accusation on the part of the plaintiff, each with the same number of co-jurors.

The *alkum* was most frequently resorted to with the full complement of 40 co-jurors when murder was suspected. It was the aggrieved party's ace in the hole, for where the accuser had a really strong case, the *alkum* put it to the test. The real point behind the *alkum* – and indeed behind the whole phenomenon of collective oath – is that *iniyan* (witnesses) normally overrode *imgillan* (co-jurors) and that accusation seldom occurred without reasonable foundation. Normally witnesses had to be neutral, but the mechanisms to insure that the accused did not escape scot-free were reinforced through the *alkum* (ibid. pp.164–5).

In order to follow up on the consequences of collective oath, it is now worth considering what would happen if the oath were 'broken'. Should this have been the case, then a concept known as *afanigg* came into play. It was roughly equivalent to the *izmaz*, the Tamazight term for the fines imposed by the chief or the council on any real or potential rule-breakers, particularly those trying to enforce their views against those of the majority. Typically, it was heavy precisely in order to hit any defendant who was dissatisfied with the verdict. Among the Ait Slillu (Ait Unir) of Nqub he had to feed 40 people for two days, while among the Ait Unir of Birnat the number rose to 100 and among the Ait 'Atta n-Umalu he had to provide 35 sheep, sugar and mint tea for everyone present. There is also the case of a particularly stubborn individual from the Ait Umzrai (Ihansalen) who had to pay *afanigg* to the councillors on no less than four occasions: he had clearly never learned from his mistakes and was poverty stricken as a result.

Such attitudes could also certainly involve co-jurors as well, as they had to support their kinsman morally during the oath, and also materially if he had to pay a fine, even though time lags of up to three months were normal and expected. Nonetheless, there were definite limits beyond which their help and protection could not extend. Incorrigible offenders who had already reduced their agnates to penury were either killed or, more usually, forced to seek safety elsewhere. If the new group to which the offender sought admission should refuse to accept him, his own agnates generally killed him, as he was now a liability and an embarrassment to his own *ait 'ashra*. This was not done, however, in case of murder, because in theory any murderer had to flee in exile to another tribe. Even if he were allowed to return home at a later date, and even if the *diyit* or bloodwealth were accepted by his victim's agnates, it meant in effect that he had to work for someone else as an *akhammas*, a sharecropper for one-fifth of the harvest, until such time as he had to some degree regained what he had lost. The average man could thus simply not afford to be a murderer twice over: once was enough.

Any accused individual understandably felt often that a prospective co-juror who had refused to participate in the oath had been bribed by the other side. Hence anyone who felt that he could legitimately complain about having been let down by his own agnates at oath could become a member of a new co-juring lineage group by sacrificing a ram, generally an unblemished one-year-old *aguryan*, to the members of the lineage concerned. He was then known as *u-tikhsi* (pl. *ait tiklhsi* – 'he of the sheep'), and the transfer of his allegiance was automatic as soon as the ram's throat had been cut.

Nonetheless, he apparently did not lose his *de facto* rights to land in his lineage group of origin, although he did forfeit his rights to a turn of irrigation water, to a cubicle or *tahanut* in the collective storehouse and to any *shfa'a* or pre-emption rights he may have had over either land or women. Indeed, it was usual for an *u-tikhsi* to take a new wife from his adopted co-juring group even if he still had another wife at home. The new marriage acted as a guarantee of the *u-tikhsi*'s participation in the jural affairs of his new group, such as contributions to or receipts from fines or bloodwealth paid by the group. He was also allotted a cubicle in the new group's storehouse and given a turn of irrigation water; but he could not inherit any land from them. It was his original lineage which inherited from him at his death, provided he had no children. Hence a shared stake in property cut across a shared legal responsibility: for an *u-tikhsi* lost his rights at home because of his absence, just as any long-term absentee did.

Nonetheless, an *u-tikhsi*, like a prodigal son, could return to his own lineage, section or tribe without any additional sacrifice. However, he had to do so before 40 years had passed or else his naturalisation would be deemed to be complete. But few *ait tikhsi* , if any, ever availed themselves of this opportunity.

The commonest *u-tikhsi* sacrifices seem to have occurred between different lineages within a given tribal section, rather than between sections. Extra-tribal sacrifices were very rare indeed. Theoretically an *u-tikhsi* suffered from no social or political disability as a result of his action and could even become chief of his new co-juring group. In reality, however, such an assertion was as hypothetical as the once celebrated claim that 'any American can become president'. The Ait 'Atta, perhaps even more than other Berbers in the region, subscribe to the idea that any man who cannot get along with his own agnates is a fool (Hart 1981 pp.165–6).

In Tamazight, divine punishment for perjury at oath is generally subsumed under the concept of *tunant* ('fate'). This term refers only to bad luck, unlike *aduku* (lit. 'slipper') which, like Arabic *l-fal*, refers both to good and bad luck indiscriminately. It is precisely the kind of bad luck embodied in the term *tunant* that befalls a perjurer: blindness, insanity, death, snake or scorpion bite, or drowning in a flood. Often the punishment in Ait 'Atta eyes seemed to be ideally suited to the crime.

A man of the Ait Usikis, for instance, who was still alive in 1960 and totally insane, once lost a mule of very poor quality. He and the man whom he had accused of stealing it both went to the tomb of Sidi Sa'id Ahansal to swear. Members of one of the resident holy lineages there showed him five or six good mules and asked him which one his own had resembled most closely. He picked the best of the lot, and when his turn came to make the accusation, his mouth became twisted up under his ears, he tore his clothes off, and began to eat grass. The price here was insanity: if you want a mule that badly, act like one!

In another case an Ait Y'azza man once fired his rifle within the precincts of the *hurm* or inviolate area of the Tafrawt n-Ait 'Atta in the

Saghru, where the community of Igharm Amazdar and the Ait 'Atta supreme court are located and where firearms were forbidden. He later lied about having done so, in a special oath, *ashiddad n-muhul*, taken without co-jurors, and as a result he became a hunchback.

The culprit should naturally be the first to be struck down, but, as Gellner has noted, disaster could come, say, in the form of a flood and devastate an entire region, with the loss of many lives (Gellner 1969 p.112): for he who swears falsely sins against God and hence against his agnates. This makes the central element very explicit, for collective oath as it existed in the Central Atlas could only exist in an egalitarian and patrilineage-based society, one in which the nodal point was represented by one's agnates (Hart 1981 p.167).

In order to finish up and round out this article, we now consider briefly the workings of the Ait 'Atta supreme court of appeal, the *istinaf* at their 'capital' (*l-'asimt*) at Igharm Amazdar in the Saghru, for they place great stress on its former political importance. Even though Igharm Amazdar evidently became the Ait 'Atta capital relatively late in time (about 1890), its symbolic value was twofold: as the site of the annual election of the top chief, or *amghar n-ufilla*, of this supertribe by a twin process known as rotation and complementarity which both Gellner and we ourselves have described elsewhere (Gellner 1969 pp.81–8; Hart 1981 pp.76–80), and as the site of the supreme court. The *istinaf* at Igharm Amazdar became, so to speak, the jural rock in the centre of what might, following Barnes, be termed the whole Ait 'Atta 'snowball state' (Barnes 1967 pp.29–63) – although in this case the 'snowball', as represented through systematic territorial conquest by the Ait 'Atta of large areas of land to the north, south and east of the Saghru, which started from the late sixteenth century and continued up until the establishment of the French protectorate, was of considerably greater significance than the 'state'.

Any consideration of the structure, function and organisation of the Ait 'Atta *istinaf* itself is limited by the fact that the bulk of the available material dates from the protectorate and does not go very far back into the long precolonial period known as *siba*. There is thus the distinct probability that the French administration froze the court into position. Nonetheless, all accounts of it are virtually identical, and the jural procedure involved, regardless of whether the French froze it or not, was simple, effective, based on majority rule and, in keeping with the whole tenor of Ait 'Atta sociopolitical life, highly egalitarian.

The guardians of Ait 'Atta customary law at Igharm Amazdar were known as *ait l-haqq* ('people of the truth') or, more often, as *ti'aqqidin n-Ait 'Aisa* ('the Ait 'Aisa specialists in customary law'): for those Ait 'Atta resident at Igharm Amazdar, who were known as Ait 'Aisa, acted as the *ait izirf*, the repositories of custom. For any given case, six *ti'aqqidin* (sing. *ta'aqqit*) were chosen: two from each of the three localised sections resident at Igharm Amazdar, which is to say the Ait Zimru (with one *ta'aqqit* each from the lineages of the resident Ait Bu Iknifen and Ait 'Aisa u-Brahim), the Ait Hassu and the Ait Y'azza. In no two consecutive cases were the *ti'aqqidin* the same individuals, as they were chosen afresh for each case. Thus everybody had a chance to become a juryman.

It is not entirely clear, however, just how the *ti'aqqidin* were chosen. Some informants said that they were simply nominated by the local *amghar n-tmazirt*, the local section or 'land' chief, or elected by the sections in question themselves according to the rotation and complementarity principle, or even just selected at random. At any rate, the turnover of *ti'aqqidin* was far greater than the annual turnover of chiefs. After all, in theory a chief lasted in office for a year, but a *ta'aqqit*, in his role of *anahsham*, lasted at most only a few hours, purely for the duration of his case. A second major difference between the two is that no *igurramen* or saints officiated either at the selection of the *ti'aqqidin* or at the meeting of the court, as they did when top or sectional chiefs were elected: for the court was entirely a lay tribal affair and the concept of *baraka* played no part in the proceedings.

But it is very clear, even so, that all the men of the Ait 'Aisa n-Igharm Amazdar had to have a thorough grounding in customary law, for at any time they might be called upon to act as *inahshamen*. Indeed, the *ti'aqqidin* were also *inahshamen*, specialist *inahshamen*, whose function was the adjudication of any jural issues which had remained unresolved in the home areas of disputants from any part of Ait 'Atta territory.

These six *ti'aqqidin n-Ait 'Aisa n-Igharm Amazdar* formed the *istinaf* under the *amghar n-tmazirt* – the 'land' or sectional chief of the Ait 'Aisa – who had the 'chairman's casting vote'. The procedure involved was very well thought out: if the court was tied on the verdict at three votes to three, six new *inahshamen* were selected from the same sections and in the same proportions. Then, if they too reached a three-to-three deadlock, a third set of *inahshamen* was chosen. If this third set should now also arrive at a draw, all 18 *inahshamen* were reconvoked: and if the verdict was still nine to nine, it was now up to the land chief's vote to decide the issue by a majority of one. The verdict was final and without appeal.

In French times the verdict of the court was arrived at in a little courthouse building, with the French *Affaires Indigènes* officer presiding, while the plaintiff and the accused waited outside. There was, however, no question here of any co-jurors. In precolonial *siba* times the members of the court deliberated in the open air and, according to an Ait Bu Dawud informant at Usikis, there were ten *ti'aqqidin* rather than six, chosen from all the 'five fifths' of the Ait 'Atta, the *khams khmas n-Ait 'Atta* (for definition and discussion thereof, cf. Hart 1984*c*), and they sat in a circle. Just outside it, on one side, were the *amghar n-ait l-haqq* and the *anahsham*, while on the other side stood the plaintiff and the accused. No co-jurors were allowed; and when all were present, the *amghar* picked up a stone and announced that anyone who spoke out of turn would pay a fine of 500 duros, and that first the plaintiff and then the defendant had the floor. Each spoke in turn and then left.

Now the *anahsham* asked each member of the *ait l-haqq* for his opinion in turn. A clear majority verdict obviously won, but if the votes were tied the *amghar* then asked the *anahsham* for his view on the matter. Again, there was the casting vote principle, to make the vote six to five, and whichever side the *anahsham* supported won the case. At this point the *amghar* would check the decision by asking the *anahsham* and the members of the court three times, '*Kasi tafanka?*' ('Are you sure?'). If there were no dissent this ended the matter. However, if the *anahsham* did not agree with either party or the members of the court, our informant said that the case had to revert back to a purely intermediate court at Tiraf n-Ait 'Alwan in the Lower Dra Valley near Mhamid l-Ghuzlan. This court was normally employed only for disputes between the local Ait 'Alwan and the Ait Isful, where the same procedure was repeated exactly and where the decision was now final.

Between these two accounts, there are, nonetheless, the following differences in detail:

(i) ten *ti'aqqidin* instead of six, allegedly chosen from all 'five fifths' of the Ait 'Atta (which seems dubious) instead of on a rotation-and-complementarity basis among the members of the Ait 'Aisa of Igharm Amazdar;

(ii) the *anahsham* or oath administrator rather than the land or sectional chief acting as chairman;

(iii) the lack of reference to the three separate bodies of *ti'aqqidin* who met, deliberated and rendered their verdicts in succession in the case of stalemate (which may have been a French contribution); and

(iv) the reversion to the court at Tiraf n-Ait 'Alwan if the vote at Igharm Amazdar had ended in a draw. This latter point is not mentioned in any French account (cf. de Monts de Savasse 1951; Thet 1951) and had possibly fallen into disuse by protectorate times. No doubt the Cartesian logic of the French would have led them to look with disfavour on the idea of two courts doing the work of one, even if the lower court acted only as a safety valve.

The members of the supreme court, whatever their ages, clearly had to have a knowledge of Ait 'Atta *izirf* which was greater than that of the average tribesman. In this particular tribal society in which virtually everyone had considerable knowledge of customary law, a fact aptly expressed by the Berber proverb to the effect that *ur iddjin imzggura mai tinin inngura* ('the old men have nothing more to say to the young ones'), and in which litigation, as elsewhere in Morocco, is regarded not only as a cheap pastime, but also as an agreeable one, such knowledge demanded a high degree of accuracy and sensitivity to local variations in *izirf* on the part of the *ti'aqqidin* of Igharm Amazdar. The judicial efficiency of this highly egalitarian political process, and indeed of the whole supertribal tribunal at Igharm Amazdar, was truly remarkable (Hart 1981 pp.169–72). It provided, as well, a case study of an exceptional jural procedure which may be regarded as the logical capstone and indeed outcome of the Berber legal decision procedure of collective oath, an outcome now raised, as it were, to a higher power. The fact that neither the collective oath nor the Ait 'Atta supreme court exist any longer today can, both in this writer's view and from a structural standpoint, only be regretted.

BIBLIOGRAPHY

Adam, André, 'Remarques sur les Modalités du Serment Collectif dans l'Anti-Atlas Occidental', *Hesperis* XXXY/3–4 (1948) pp.399–410.
——, 'Berber Migrants in Casablanca', in Ernest Gellner and Charles Micaud (eds.), *Arabs and Berbers: From Tribe to Nation in North Africa* (London: Duckworth 1973) pp.325–44.
Aspinion, Cmdt. Robert, *Contribution à l'Etude du Droit Coutumier Berbère Marocain: Etude sur les Coutumes des Tribus Zayanes* (2nd edn., Casablanca: Editions A. Moinier 1946).
Barnes, J.A., *Politics in a Changing Society: The Political History of the Fort Jameson Ngoni* (2nd edn., Manchester: Manchester University Press 1967).
Berque, Jacques, *Structures Sociales du Haut Atlas* (2nd edn., Paris: Presses Universitaires de France 1978). Originally published in 1955.
Bousquet, Georges-Henri, 'Le Droit Coutumier des Ait Haddidou des Assif Melloul et Isselaten', *Annales de l'Institut des Etudes Orientales*, Faculté des Lettres de l'Université d'Alger XIV (1956) pp.113–230.
de Monts de Savasse, Capt. R., 'Le Régime Foncier des Ait Atta du Sahara', ms., CHEAM No. 1815, 12 February 1951 (available for consultation at the Centre des Hautes Etudes de l'Afrique et l'Asie Modernes, or CHEAM, Rue du Four, Paris) pp. 59 plus 4 annexes.
Gellner, Ernest, *Saints of the Atlas* (London: Weidenfeld and Nicolson 1969).
Hanoteau, Gen. Adolphe, and Conseiller A. Letourneux, *La Kabylie et les Coutumes Kabyles* (2nd edn., 3 vols., Paris: Augustin Challamel 1893).
Hart, David M., *The Aith Waryaghar of the Moroccan Rif: An Ethnography and History*. Viking Fund Publications in Anthropology No. 55 (Tucson: University of Arizona Press 1976).
——, 'Notes on the Sociopolitical Structure and Institutions of Two Tribes of the Ait Yafalman Confederacy: the Ait Murghad and the Ait Hadiddu', *Revue de l'Occident Musulman et de la Mediterranée (ROMM)* XXVI/2 (1978) pp.55–74.
——, 'The Traditional Sociopolitical Organization of the Ammeln (Anti-Atlas); One Informant's View', *The Maghreb Review* V/5–6, Part 1 (1980) pp.134–9.

——, *Dadda 'Atta and His 40 Grandsons: The Socio-Political Organisation of the Ait 'Atta of Southern Morocco* (Wisbech, Cambridgeshire: MENAS Press 1981).

——, *The Ait 'Atta of Southern Morocco: Daily Life and Recent History* (Wisbech, Cambridgeshire: MENAS Press 1984a).

——, 'The Ait Sukhman of the Moroccan Central Atlas: An Ethnographic Survey and a Case Study in Sociocultural Anomaly', *ROMM* XXXVIII/2 (1984b) pp.137–52.

——, 'Segmentary Systems and the Role of "Five Fifths" in Tribal Morocco' (1967), in Akbar S. Ahmed and David M. Hart (Eds.), *Islam in Tribal Societies: From the Atlas to the Indus* (London: Routledge & Kegan Paul 1984c) pp.66–105.

——, *Guardians of the Khaibar Pass: The Social Organization and History of the Afridi of Pakistan* (Lahore: Vanguard Books 1985).

——, 'Rejoinder to Henry Munson, Jr., "On the Irrelevance of the Segmentary Lineage Model in the Moroccan Rif"', *American Anthropologist* 91/1 (1989) pp.765–9.

——, 'Oaths, Sponsorship, Protection, Alliance and the Feud in the Moroccan Berber Work of Edward Westermarck, in, Rahma Bourqia and Mokhtar Al Harras (Eds.), *Westermarck et la Société Marocaine*, Série: Colloques et Seminaires No. 27. Publications de la Faculté des Lettres et des Sciences Humaines (Rabat: Université Mohammed V 1993) pp. 131–57.

——, 'Berber Tribal Alliance Networks in Precolonial North Africa: The Algerian *Saff*, the Moroccan *Liff* and the Chessboard Model of Robert Montagne', *Journal of North African Studies* 1/2 (1996) pp.192–205.

Henry, Capt. Roger, 'Notes sur les Ait Sidi Bou Yacoub', CHEAM Report No. 45, January 1937a (available for consultation at CHEAM, Paris – see above) 31 pp.

——, 'Une Tribu de Transhumants du Grand Atlas: les Ait Morrhad', CHEAM Report No. 147, May 1937b (available for consultation at CHEAM, Paris – see above) 12 pp.

Marcy, Georges, *Le Droit Coutumier Zemmour*, Publications de l'Institut des Hautes Etudes Marocaines t. XL (Algiers: Jules Carbonel; Paris: Editions Larose 1949).

——, 'Le Problème du Droit Coutumier Berbère' (1939), *Revue Algerienne, Tunisienne et Marocaine de Legislation et de Jurisprudence* (1954) pp.127–70.

Montagne, Robert, *Les Berbères et le Makhzen dans le Sud du Maroc: Essai sur la Transformation Politique des Berbères Sédentaires (Groupe Chleuh)* (Paris: Felix Alcan 1930).

Thet, Lt., 'Le Tribunal Coutumier d'Appel des Ait Atta du Sahara a Irherm Amazdar dans le Sarhro', ms., CHEAM, Affaires Indigènes Memoires Fin de Stage No.94, 23 November 1951 (available for consultation at CHEAM, Paris – see above) 21 pp.

Tyan, Emile, *Histoire de l'Organisation Judiciaire en Pays d'Islam*, Vol. I (Paris 1938).

Waterbury, John, *North for the Trade: The Life and Times of a Berber Merchant* (Berkeley and Los Angeles: University of California Press 1972).

——, 'Tribalism, Trade and Politics: The Transformation of the Swasa of Morocco', in Ernest Gellner and Charles Micaud (eds.), *Arabs and Berbers: From Tribe to Nation in North Africa* (London: Duckworth 1973) pp.231–58.

Westermarck, Edward, *Ritual and Belief in Morocco* (2 vols., London: Macmillan 1926).

Rural and Tribal Uprisings in Post-colonial Morocco, 1957–60: An Overview and a Reappraisal

The object of this article is to examine – or perhaps in the light of an article by Gellner which is (at the time of writing) now over 30 years old (Gellner 1973, original 1962), to re-examine – a series of three rural and, to a large extent, tribal revolts which took place in Morocco in fairly rapid succession within the first half-decade after the country gained its independence in 1956. In that year Morocco emerged from the combined Franco–Spanish protectorate which had been established over it in 1912, and which had met with armed primary resistance, particularly on the part of Berber-speaking tribes in the Rif and the Atlas mountains, a resistance which the French were unable to 'pacify' – always in the name of the Moroccan sultan – until 1934. Thus the Moroccan rural, and especially tribal, record of resistance to colonialism is a formidable one.

However, since the last of the post-colonial tribal revolts in question was put down in the spring of 1960 there have been no others of this type, and now (at the time of writing), over three and one-half decades later, it seems reasonably safe to assume that no others will occur. The Casablanca student riots of 1965, the three successively attempted and failed *coups d'état* against the monarchy in 1971, 1972 and 1973, and further riots over food prices both in Casablanca and in the major towns and cities of the northern zone, Nador, al-Husayma and Tetuan, in 1981 and 1984 respectively, were not only essentially urban rather than rural, but their aims and the courses which they took were quite different from those considered here.

The three rural and tribal uprisings in question all took place in Berber-speaking regions. They were that of 'Addi u-Bihi, the Berber governor of the Qsar s-Suq (Ksar es Souk, and now Rashidiya/Rachidia) province in the south-eastern part of the country in 1957; that of the large Aith Waryaghar (Bni Waryaghal) tribe of the Central Rif, in the northern province of al-Husayma (El Hoceima) in 1958–59, which was also the most serious; and that of a recently appointed but rebellious *qa'id* who early in 1960, in an evident gesture against the political party then in power, the Union Nationale des Forces Populaires (UNFP, later USFP, or Union Socialiste des Forces Populaires), shot a local police chief in Bni Mallal and then took to the Central Atlas highlands of the same province, with the collusion of a Berber tribal leader of the Ait Sukhman in the Central Atlas who had also been an *amghar* under the French.

We first sketch in a background of the immediate pre-independence period, then look briefly at that in which power was transferred by the departing French and Spanish to the newly appointed Moroccan administration, and then, in somewhat greater detail, look at each of the three revolts in question. Our comments on the first of these are based principally upon a near-contemporary work by Zartman, the fullest account we have been able to find (Zartman 1964 pp.79–82); and on the other two they will be based largely on our own materials, both published as in the case of the Aith Waryaghar revolt of 1958–1959 (Hart 1973 pp.46–51; Hart 1976 pp.426–32) and unpublished as in the case of the Bni Mellal and Central Atlas episode of 1960. As the two latter cases show considerable variance with some of the arguments advanced by Gellner in his near-contemporary article (Gellner cited above), this is in part the reason behind this current reassessment. The chronological exposition, as we understand it, is then followed by an analytical commentary which attempts to answer the questions of why and how.

Local and nationalist resistance to the French presence in Morocco, the resistance which was to result in Moroccan independence four years later, began in earnest toward the end of 1952. But it did so then, and for the next three years, in a purely urban context – that of Casablanca first, then Fez, Rabat, Oujda, etc. – without touching the rural areas of the country – until the Wad Zam (Oued Zem)'massacre' of 20 August 1955 – after which, as it happens, a great many more Moroccans were killed in reprisal than there had been French settlers killed in the initial attack made on them by Sma'la tribesmen (cf. Blair 1970 p.185; Eickelman 1976 pp.174, 261; for overall casualty figures on both the French and the Moroccan sides throughout the resistance of 1953–56, in which the latter outnumbered the former by at least three to one, cf. Blair 1970 pp.176–7).

It was only just over a month later, as of 1 October of the same year, 1955, however, that the resistance moved fully into the 'bled', the countryside in the vicinity of the Franco–Spanish zonal border. Here units of the new Moroccan Army of Liberation, trained for at least a year previously in the eastern part of the Rif, in the Spanish zone and with the connivance of Gen. Garcia Valiño, the Spanish High Commissioner in Tetuan, co-ordinated to hit the French posts of Aknul, Buridh and Tizi Usli, all in the territory of the Rifian tribe of the Igzinnayen, originally scheduled to be in Spanish zonal territory but where the French had established a 'beachhead', so to speak, after the Rifian War of 1921–26, and one that they would not let go. Other units of the Army of Liberation at the same time, and under the leadership of Muhammad bin Miludi bin al-Ma'ati, attacked posts in the Marmusha or Imarmushen tribe in the north-eastern Middle Atlas south-east of Taza. (For an account of the activities of the Army of

Liberation in the Rif, cf. Hart 1976 pp.423–6; and for its role both there and elsewhere, cf. Blair 1970 pp.168–96; Waterbury 1970 pp.203–13; Ouardighi 1975; M'barek 1987.)

But the French had to let go when independence came in March 1956, for their zone, and in April of the same year the Spanish had to do so for theirs as well, when Franco, despite his colonialistic objections, was forced to give in gracefully to King Muhammad V. This, however, was one thing, and the Moroccan Army of Liberation or *jaysh at-tahrir* was another. By the end of June 1956 the Army of Liberation of the Rif, at least, had come in either to surrender to King Muhammad V in Rabat and to resume civilian status and activities or to be incorporated into the Royal Moroccan Armed Forces; and the life of its leader in the Rif, Si 'Abbas l-Msa'idi, who was not a Rifian himself but a native of the Ait Ishaq, a small Berber group south of Khanifra, came to a sudden end by gunshot in Fez on 27 June, probably at the instigation and behest of the nationalist leader Mehdi Ben Barka. But there were still other elements of it further south, particularly those which led the attack into the Spanish-held enclave of Ifni in October 1957 (while King Muhammad V was on a visit to the USA). Although the Army of Liberation was now to remain in the far south of Morocco, in the Tarfaya province and in the Western Sahara until 1959–60 before it was gradually disbanded, we are here concerned only with events in Morocco 'proper', so to speak. The existence of the Army of Liberation, although not absolutely crucial to the series of tribal revolts which was to begin within six months or so of its official termination, nonetheless provides a very convenient backdrop and starting point on which to comment upon and analyse them. We need only add here that by the 1980s many if not most of the former members of the Army of Liberation were drawing pensions from the Ministry of National Defence which were commensurate with their status as *anciens résistants*.[1]

We should note, furthermore, that in our considered opinion none of the post-independence tribal uprisings really threatened the Moroccan monarchy in any way, despite the fact that the last one may have been declared in the name of the populist UNFP (today USFP), the breakaway and leftist wing of the Istiqlal (Independence) Party established early in 1959 by Mehdi Ben Barka, who the following year was to become an exile from his country, who was to be condemned for treason *in absentia*, then conditionally amnestied by King Hasan II and who was eventually and finally to be assassinated in Paris in 1965 (cf. Ben Barka 1967). Indeed, our own materials suggest the contrary – and contrary to those of Gellner in the article cited above (Gellner 1973) – that this last revolt was staged not in favour of but against the UNFP precisely at a time when that party was in power. But we will cross this bridge when we come to it.

The first insurrection, in the Tafilalt region in mid-January 1957, was led by Brahim u-Sidqi n-Ait 'Addi u-Bihi. We infer this Berber rendition of his full name, comprising, as well as his own, the two names, respectively, of his grandfather and great-grandfather, which thereby formed the name of his agnatic lineage Ait 'Addi u-Bihi, in which both 'Addi and Bihi are also in fact Berber nicknames for the more Arabic and orthodox forms Sa'id and Brahim. 'Addi u-Bihi was an influential notable of the Ait Izdig tribe with his power base at Karrandu (Kerrando) and Rish, south of Midelt, as well as the governor of the Qsar s-Suq (now Rashidiya) province. He was in addition a man of unquestioned personal loyalty to King Muhammad V, and his uprising has been aptly characterised by Zartman both as a 'striking example of political intrigue and social adjustment in a country coming of age', from the tribal standpoint, and, from that of the new independent Moroccan government, as an 'effective show of force through a military operation' (Zartman 1964 pp.79–80).

But 'Addi u-Bihi, to call him by the name under which he has gone down in Moroccan history, took the very traditional view that he owed allegiance only to King Muhammad V, without benefit of any intermediaries. Hence he refused to recognise the jurisdiction of any officials appointed by either of the new Ministries of Interior or Justice – such as qa'id-s, police or judges – who were assigned to his province, which he regarded as his own personal fief. He was particularly irate about the all-encompassing pretensions of the Istiqlal Party, which under the then Minister of Interior, Dris Mhammdi, was doing its best to increase its hold and control over as many of the newly created ministries as it could. Indeed, it seems that he planned to arrest and hold Mhammdi and Justice Minister 'Abd al-Krim Binjillun when they came down to Midelt on an inspection tour of his province.

'Addi u-Bihi was a tribal and provincial Moroccan warlord in the style of the immediate precolonial period; and he behaved like one. When the king left the country on a Mediterranean cruise on 17 January, leaving his son Crown Prince Mawlay al-Hasan in charge, 'Addi u-Bihi announced that both His Majesty and the throne were in danger and immediately started to distribute some 7,000 rifles to his fellow tribesmen and to some of their neighbours. He then arrested and locked up the judge and the police chief of Midelt and took over the Post, Telegraph and Telephone building, while roadblocks were set up by his supporters to halt all traffic coming down from Fez on the only route to the north. That same night the Prime Minister ordered him to evacuate the Midelt post office, to reopen communication links and to proceed to Rabat at once in order to account for his extraordinary behaviour.

As acting commander-in-chief of the Forces Armées Royales, the Royal Moroccan Army, Crown Prince Mawlay al-Hasan ordered two battalions of less than full strength to move south from Fez on 19 February, following a cabinet meeting. One battalion waited at Bulman (Boulmane) after being forced to take the Sefrou–Bulman bypass because of snow, while the other marched on to meet the rebels' roadblock south of Idzar. The governor of the neighbouring Warzazat (Ouarzazate) province, Capt. Muhammad Midbuh (later killed in the 'garden-party putsch' against King Hasan at Skhirat in July 1971), tried to talk 'Addi u-Bihi into giving himself up, but to no avail, and then the king's aide, Col. Mawlay 'Abd al-Hafiz, also told the rebellious governor to let the army pass through, while the Crown Councillors Mawlay al-'Arbi al-'Alawi and Lahsin al-Yusi also tried to appease him – without result.

The prince therefore ordered 'Addi u-Bihi to be replaced by Maj. Muhammad bin al-'Arbi, the head of the king's military cabinet. In his statement, broadcasted by al-Yusi in Tamazight Berber and by Mawlay al-'Arbi in Arabic, Prince Hasan also offered amnesty to any of 'Addi u-Bihi's followers who might rally to the government. The army battalions pushed south next day, arriving almost without incident and with no combat at Midelt and Rish, where Maj. bin al-'Arbi and Capt. Midbuh disarmed the local population. By this time 'Addi u-Bihi had retreated to the family *qsar* at Karrandu (Kerrando), where he received the prince's envoys, Gen. Kittani and Muhammad 'Awad, the Director of the Royal Cabinet, and finally agreed to go to Rabat under conditions of *aman*, clemency, after which the prince made a tour through the Tafilalt province once its former governor had been replaced. In the end, after two years of waiting in jail in Rabat, 'Addi u- Bihi was finally put on trial, denied the *aman* because it had not been formally bestowed by the king and condemned to death. His final appeal was denied by the Supreme Court on 8 July 1960 and he died of dysentery in prison on 30 January 1961 (Zartman 1964 p.81 n.10).

Although there was little reported outcry or protest about 'Addi u-Bihi's imprisonment and death, most Imazighen Berbers in his own and the immediately adjoining provinces were very unhappy about it, a fact which Zartman failed to note in an otherwise clear and lucid account. And a real touch of irony comes through in Gen. Kittani's testimony at the trial with respect to the delicate position of the fledgling Royal Army (taken from ibid. pp.81–2, and *al-'Alam*, 23 January 1959):

> The mission of the Army is sacred, since it has the responsibility of defending Moroccan national territory and maintaining national security. His Majesty the King has not only advised us but ordered us not to spill a drop of blood unless it be in self-defense... I understood that if I did not promise ('Addi u-Bihi) the *aman*, it would have been difficult for us to eliminate the rebellion without bloodshed, and therefore the nation would have been exposed to danger.

The promise, of course, was not fulfilled and Zartman admits, albeit only in a footnote, that things might have been very different if the *aman* had not been offered. In his own testimony, 'Addi u-Bihi said that nobody arrested him and that if he was now in Rabat, it was only because he went there voluntarily on the promise of the *aman* by Gen. Kittani, and that neither he nor any of his followers would have been present if force had been employed (ibid. p.82 n.16). If this was an exercise in not shedding blood, the only blood that was shed was that of 'Addi u-Bihi himself, while the recently constituted Royal Army was to get considerably more practice in the next and much more serious tribal uprising, that of the Aith Waryaghar in the Rif, in October 1958.

The Aith Waryaghar, the tribe which had produced the Rifian leader bin 'Abd al-Krim, is located in the northern zone of Morocco which in colonial times had been under Spanish administration rather than under that of the French – unlike their southern neighbours of the Igzinnayen. The part that they played in the Independence Movement, too, was negligible compared to that played by the latter. During the Moroccan Army of Liberation campaign in late 1955, those Aith Waryaghar highland sections bordering Igzinnayen territory – and the Hispano–French zonal frontier – freely harboured both fugitives and combatants from the fighting area. As noted above, the Spanish administration turned a blind eye to this, just as they had turned a blind eye to the existence of Army of Liberation training camps near Nador all through 1954, when arms were being smuggled into the French zone. Active participation by the Aith Waryaghar in the fight against the French, however, was almost nil, although Spanish *interventor*-s or tribal administrators were warned by directives from Tetuan, the zonal capital, that the Aith Waryaghar territory could easily become a prize danger zone. Early in 1956 feeling arose against one particular *interventor*, who was removed from office for having fired on a group of people who had just come into a tribal market in order to kill the *qa'id*, Hajj Ahmad (or Hmid) Budra, who in the 1920s had also been bin 'Abd al-Krim's Minister of War. Apart from this incident, in which the Qa'id Budra was unhurt, the transfer of power in the region in general seems to have been accomplished fairly smoothly. In fact, the Aith 'Ammarth, neighbours of the Aith Waryaghar to the south-west and also in the Spanish zone, gave far more real assistance to the Army of Liberation than the Aith Waryaghar themselves did.

As elsewhere, and as soon as power had been effectively transferred, the Istiqlal Party was quick in establishing its foothold, and was welcomed enthusiastically throughout the region. Nonetheless, discontent soon set in when the Aith Waryaghar realised not only that none of their own people were being appointed to the new local and provincial administration, but that these posts were all, virtually without exception, from that of the provincial governor of al-Husayma down, being filled by south (ex-French) zone and French-speaking Istiqlal supporters. As another very tangible legacy of the Spanish administration had been that a considerable number of Aith Waryaghar had learned to speak passable or even fluent Spanish (for it goes without saying that the Spaniards did not bother to learn Rifian Berber), it galled them that French-speaking Arabs from the south zone, of whose existence they had previously been only dimly aware, had now come up from nowhere to fill the key positions. The fact that one of the first governors of the province was evidently a black from Casablanca did not help matters: for, as noted elsewhere (Hart 1976 pp.361–8), a major reason why the Aith Waryaghar, virtually alone in the Rif except for the help of the Aith 'Ammarth, had risen unanimously against the Moroccan *rugi* or pretender to the throne Bu Hmara in September 1908 and smashed his army on the banks of the Nkur River had been not so much that they had favoured the sultan of the day, Mawlay 'Abd al-Hafiz, as that the pretender's army was led by a black commander.

Furthermore, although Rifians generally had since the mid-nineteenth century formed a significant part of the labour force on the farms of French colons in the Oranie region of western Algeria, the Algerian border became effectively closed to Rifian and Moroccan labour migration with the coming of independence. Here was another source of discontent, as migrant labour had long been a source of considerable revenue to the region, whereas the result now was virtually total unemployment.

It was for these reasons that by 1957–58 most Rifians had become disenchanted with the Istiqlal Party and its officialdom, which had given them neither jobs nor adequate political representation. Specific examples are not far to seek. Among the Igzinnayen, one source of dissatisfaction was that the Istiqlal Party denounced their reburial in mid-1958 of the bodies of Si 'Abbas al-Msa'idi and of another important Army of Liberation leader, Si l-Hasan n-Hammush, a man of their own tribe, at the Thursday Market of Ajdir in their own territory. This caused a switch in their allegiance to the Popular Movement (MP, or *Haraka Sha'biya*), the Berber Party of Mahjub Ahardan, who had also been a prominent Army of Liberation leader. Among the Aith Waryaghar and the Aith 'Ammarth, dissatisfaction with the Istiqlal was just as high, and in the first instance one result was that the Democratic Independence Party (PDI, or *Hizb al-Shura*) began to gain a strong opposition foothold in the region, although Rabat officially ignored its existence there. A young and entirely unofficial spokesman from the ranks of the Aith Waryaghar now emerged in the person of Muhammad nj-Hajj Sillam n-Muh Amzzyan, from the large section of the Aith Bu 'Ayyash. He had been a minor sectional *mqaddim* under the Spanish, but like all the other tribal authorities installed by them, he had lost his job at independence. It was soon realised in retrospect that the Spanish had at least administered the tribe through its own people, which the new independent administration was most emphatically not doing; and Muhammad nj-Hajj Sillam was the *primus inter pares* in the ranks of the disgruntled, as well as the local head of the Democratic Independence Party.

The 18-point programme for the Rif which he and two other members of the Aith Waryaghar, 'Abd as-Sadaq Sharrat Khattabi and bin 'Abd al-Krim's own son Rashid, both of Ajdir in the section of the Aith Yusif w-'Ari, submitted to King Muhammad V in Rabat on 11 November 1958, is of considerable interest in retrospect, and parenthetical comments indicate clearly to what extent the programme had been achieved as of a decade later (cf. Hart 1973 pp.46–8; Hart 1976 pp.428–9).

1. Evacuation of all foreign troops from Morocco. (At the time, this did not effect the US bases in the country, but the objective was nonetheless realised within four years, by 1962, insofar as French and Spanish troops were concerned. As it happens, and to complete the record, the American airforce bases were also evacuated in 1962, but the naval bases were not turned over to the Moroccans until 1978.)

2. Formation of a popular government with a wide base. (The government in question was indeed formed, and many others have also been formed since, but how wide their bases are is open to question.)

3. Abolition of political parties and formation of a government of national union. (The first part was achieved forcibly through the occupation of al-Husayma province by the Royal Army for the next few years, but it was neither achieved nor desired at the national level; while the second has been achieved on at least one occasion since independence.)

4. Local recruitment of local civil servants. (By 1962, most lower-echelon civil servants were certainly locally recruited, but this was far less true of those on the upper echelons. Because of Rabat's basic and pervasive mistrust of Rifians in general and of the Aith Waryaghar in particular, the outlets for politically ambitious local men are still slim to this day, and prior to this time they had been nil.)

5. Freedom for all political prisoners. (Political prisoners from the Rif were numerous at the time the document was drafted, and the last ones were freed only in mid-1965.)

6. Return of bin 'Abd al-Krim to Morocco. (This was, at the time and in the eyes of those who drafted the document, its most important point, and the granting even of all the other requests except this one would have been deemed unacceptable. But bin 'Abd al-Krim himself, who had been imprisoned by the French on Reunion Island ever since his surrender in 1926, and then resident in Egypt ever since he jumped ship

there in 1947, on his way back to France, refused to return, and he died in Cairo in 1963.)

7. Guarantees to dissidents against reprisals. (This may have been responsible in part for the general leniency, apart from imprisonment, shown by the Moroccan government to tribal rebels since independence.)

8. Choice of capable judges. (By this was meant, obviously, Rifian ones.)

9. Reorganisation of the Ministry of Justice. (The judges from the south zone and the *qa'di*-s then in the Rif were locally considered to be notoriously inept.)

10. Bringing of criminals to justice. (It is here assumed that the 'criminals' concerned were in fact individuals in government service.)

11. A Rifian to be given an important post in the Moroccan government. (At the time of writing, no Rifian from the Aith Waryaghar, at least, has ever been awarded such a post. Although even as of 1958 there were several high-ranking Rifian officers in the Royal Army, none, again, were from the Aith Waryaghar.)

12. 'Operation Plough' (Operation Labour) to be extended to the Rif. (The name refers to an agricultural development scheme inaugurated in 1957, with King Muhammad V himself driving the first tractor; it was designed, over the course of three years, to bring 375,000 acres of land in the Gharb under cultivation. The programme never reached the Rif, where for the most part tractor ploughing is unfeasible, at least in the al-Husayma province; but as of 1966–1967, a DERRO project (Dévéloppement Economique de la Région du Rif Occidental) for planting sugar cane in the plain of al-Husayma was underway, as was a pine reforestation scheme in the Jbil Hmam. The DERRO project, however, ultimately foundered and proved a failure.)

13. Tax reductions for all of Morocco and especially for the Rif. (The *tartib* tax on agricultural produce and on animals was officially abolished by King Hasan II in April 1961, shortly after his accession to the throne on the sudden death of his father, King Muhammad V.)

14. Creation of an ambitious programme against unemployment. (Almost nothing has at the time of writing happened in this domain, but, highly aware of it, virtually every Rifian family has at least one male member working in Western Europe.)

15. Creation of scholarships for Rifian students. (As of 1967, when we left the field, this was only in a very incipient stage.)

16. Rapid Arabisation of education all over Morocco. (Rifians deplored, in 1967 just as much as in 1958, the administrative use of French by south zone civil servants in the former north or Spanish zone; but their protests were ignored, for French has become, willy-nilly, Morocco's

major foreign language, while locally it was only in 1994 that King Hasan recognised – unofficially – the existence of Berber. Such royal recognition, however, has yet to be written into the Moroccan constitution. There was no chance of the much smaller northern zone ever achieving ascendancy over the much larger southern one, but at the same time the achievement of anything resembling thoroughgoing Arabisation is still more of a hope – and an ambivalent one at that – than a reality.)

17. Creation of more rural schools. (Here the answer is, for once, a most emphatic affirmative, since King Hasan's drive toward 'Operation School' (Operation Ecole) all over rural Morocco in 1963.)

18. Reopening of the lycée or high school in al-Husayma. (It had been closed down earlier in 1958 and many students had been jailed.)

It is clear that this programme centred around dissatisfaction both with the prevailing political party and with the fact that no Rifians had been given government jobs, as well as a much more modern dissatisfaction with the underdevelopment of the region at large. But by the time it had been presented to King Muhammad, the Aith Waryaghar uprising had already been in progress for nearly three weeks, and Muhammad nj-Hajj Sillam had become its principal spokesman.

A traditional technique, that of using the market crier or *abarrah* to 'defy' the central government, or rather its prevailing political party, was employed at the outset; and Rifian tribesmen took to the hills, lit bonfires and it seemed as though a return to traditional dissidence was in the offing. After a few days and an appeal broadcast from Rabat the Igzinnayen, Aith 'Ammarth, Axt Tuzin and Thimsaman all came down from their hills, but the Aith Waryaghar did not. The first overt act of rebellion occurred on 27 October 1958, and all three of the Aith Waryaghar tribal administrative posts were equally involved: the Istiqlal Party office at the post of Bni Hadifa was stormed by irate tribesmen, who beat up the incumbent very badly, overpowered the paramilitary *mkhazni*-s at the 'bureau' and appropriated their rifles from the barracks. The same thing happened at the post of Imzuren, where one or two Aith Waryaghar were themselves killed, and at that of Suq l-Arba' Tawrirt there was a brawl inside the bureau as well, in which a *mkhazni* was badly wounded. The Aith Waryaghar markets were now all 'broken', in the traditional sense, and were to remain so for the next two months or more. The tribesmen themselves were up and acting more or less corporately for the first time since bin 'Abd al-Krim had surrendered in 1926, but they were hardly up in arms. The most extraordinary feature of this very serious uprising is, in fact, how poorly armed the Aith Waryaghar were. The Spanish authorities had confiscated all their rifles over the three-year period immediately following bin 'Abd al-Krim's surrender, and were incredulous at the time to find out the great amount of armament that they possessed. So apart from the confiscated rifles from the *mkhazni* barracks, they now had nothing save a few shotguns and fowling pieces owned by tribal authorities. Muhammad nj-Hajj Sillam had promised them arms in quantity, but failed completely to deliver when the time came (Waterbury 1970 pp.242–3). The rest were armed only with their billhooks (*hadida*-s) and with stones, which of course they could throw with remarkable accuracy, while a billhook at close quarters makes a formidable weapon (Hart 1976 pp.428–9).

It was only when the Aith Waryaghar took to the hills of the Jbil Hmam more or less *en masse*, after the 'breaking' of the markets, that the insurrection became a real rebellion. Even though their unofficial spokesmen reiterated that their only quarrel was with the Istiqlal Party, not in any way with the Royal Army and still less with the Monarchy (which they felt was in fact being undermined by the Istiqlal), it was clear that a show of force was necessary and the army was accordingly sent in (Zartman 1964 pp.86–90). The then Crown Prince Mawlay al-Hasan proved himself an able field commander after taking personal charge of the army in its encirclement of al-Husayma from the south. This bottling up of the area of insurrection was the consequence of the refusal of the Aith Waryaghar to heed King Muhammad's warning that a 'cruel punishment' would await them if they had not returned to their homes by 7 January 1959.

They did not return, and as a result they received the 'cruel punishment' in full measure. But at times they managed to give as good as they got: on one occasion the Crown Prince's personal plane, on attempting to land at Imzuren, was greeted with bursts of rifle fire from sharpshooters hidden at the edges of the airfield, and the late Gen. (then Col.) Muhammad Ufqir (Oufkir), later to become Moroccan Minister of Interior and killed after the Moroccan Air Force attack on King Hasan's Boeing 747 in 1972, himself took part on the army attack on the airstrip defenders, who were all killed. Royal Army troops attempting subsequently to clamber up into the fastnesses of the Jbil Hmam were greeted with volleys of rocks thrown at them by the furious Aith Waryaghar. But in the end – and January 1959 was the most difficult month of the campaign – they took a drubbing from the Royal Army that rankles to this day.

They came down from their mountains with displeasure and rancour, just as their fathers and grandfathers had done when bin 'Abd al-Krim surrendered; and the army and its commander, the Crown Prince, now became two more targets for their muttered opprobrium, while back in Rabat the Istiqlal Party cracked right in half on 26 January, with Mehdi Ben Barka leading its leftist and breakaway wing, the UNFP (*Muqawama*). It was never again to return to the uncontested dominance it had held in the immediate post-independence period.

However, before the Aith Waryaghar uprising came to an end in mid-February, Muhammad nj-Hajj Sillam, with some 60 other Aith Waryaghar notables, had slipped through the clutches of the Royal Army and fled through the Spanish-owned Melilla enclave to Spain itself. A price was put on his head, and this ex-*mqaddim* of the Upper Aith Bu 'Ayyash was condemned to death *in absentia*, by decree of the rarely severe King Muhammad V, a decree to which his son and successor King Hasan II was bound to adhere. Even here the situation was thoroughly traditional: the unpardoned murderer, unable to pay the *haqq* or fine for murder in the market to the *imgharen*, the assembled councillors, had to flee to another tribe, exiled for life on pain of death. Having previously been the most vociferous unofficial spokesman of the revolt, he was in no sense a charismatic leader and was sneered at by his fellows as just another impecunious tribesman escaping as an *adhrib*, an exile from a bloodfeud. He went to Spain and subsequently into Egypt; he died in 1996 in Holland, from whence his body was taken back to al-Husayma for burial.

The situation right after the quelling of the insurrection may have become somewhat eased when on 10 June 1959, King Muhammad V made his first state visit to al-Husayma, a visit greatly built up by the Moroccan press. The remaining notables of the Aith Waryaghar – those who had not fled to Spain or been imprisoned – wanted to sacrifice a bull to the king as *'ar*; but the latter refused, saying that an oath taken on the Qur'an would be quite sufficient.

For it must be noted that some 244 men of the Aith Waryaghar for whom escape was not possible stayed home and were jailed as political prisoners, though they were released a year and a half later in an amnesty granted by King Muhammad on the occasion of the Feast of the Throne (*'Ayd l-'Arsh*) on 18 November 1960. Two years after this, on 11 September 1962, all the escapees to Spain – save Muhammad nj-Hajj Sillam – were allowed to return after King Hasan, the son and successor of King Muhammad, granted a second amnesty on the occasion of his state visit to al-Husayma, when he also changed the military administration of the province back to civilian status and lifted the ban on political party membership – except in Aith Waryaghar territory, where these things came to pass only as of 1966. The atmosphere emanating from Rabat may have been one of forgiveness, but the implication was clear that the Palace 'had the number' of the Aith Waryaghar.

It will be recalled that the abolition of political parties had been one of the major Aith Waryaghar objectives as spelled out in the 18-point programme, and on this score the tribesmen and their military administrators were in full agreement. From the end of the uprising until the writer finished his fieldwork, the Aith Waryaghar were notable for their complete and totally voluntary abstention from political activity of any kind. But it was an abstention which was carried to extremes, to the point of complete lack of participation in other national issues with political overtones, particularly with respect to the series of elections at both the national and local levels, starting with that held for the members of the first Moroccan Parliament on 20 May 1960.

Fully congruent both with this political non-participation of the Aith Waryaghar and with their tremendous jealousy about the honour of their women was the fact that, although all over rural Morocco women were vigorously encouraged to vote in these elections (with the principle of 'one man, one vote' now being expanded to include women), the participation rate of the Aith Waryaghar women was nil. And the total tribal average for the first election in 1960 – that for the new 'rural commune' representatives – was only 43 per cent, the lowest figure for any part of rural Morocco (for even among the Ibuqquyen and the Aith 'Ammarth, participation was as high as 80 per cent). In the Aith Waryaghar view, the reason was simple, as well as conservative: they were not going to have their women stared at by a lot of strange Arabs – which was precisely what would happen, they thought, if they brought them to the polls.

They also gave what amounted to the same answer when first requested in that same year to provide girls for the regional Moroccan *folklorique*-style dances organised by the Ministry of Tourism for the folklore festivals held every year in Marrakesh. No Aith Waryaghar of either sex have participated in any such dance teams, although there was far less objection to the recording of Rifian rhymed couplets in song form, for here the performers were heard but not seen. It was in ways like this that the Aith Waryaghar were determined to dig their heels in and to refuse to cooperate with the central authorities. If their refusal on such matters was a question of *qa'ida*, of custom, nobody could contest it. It was yet another way for them to opt out, in part, of the wider system, a traditional response to a new situation (Hart 1976 pp.431–2).

This attitude of non-participation is nothing new. Rifians in general and those of the Aith Waryaghar in particular have always been aware of the *Gharb* – the 'Arab West' of Morocco – and have always distrusted it. Hence this attitude of partial rejection is still inherent in their wider terminal loyalties. They are proud to the point of arrogance of being Aith Waryaghar and of the reputation they had in the past for fighting, and they tend to be condescending in the extreme in their attitude toward all non-Rifian Moroccans, who are themselves quite aware of this sneering condescension, this seeming superiority complex on the part of poor tribesmen from a backward province;

and it irks them. The mistrust is mutual, and the kindest thing that military administrators from the south zone had to say about the Aith Waryaghar was that they are incredibly hard-headed (Hart 1973 pp.49–50).

It is no exaggeration to say that the only issue about which the Aith Waryaghar have shown marked enthusiasm since independence was the growing opportunity, during the 1960s, and particularly after 1970, to become labour migrants in Western Europe. Here, however, they have tended to be blocked, far more in the al-Husayma province than in that of Nador, by problems of administrative red tape over the acquisitions of passports, work permits and the like: for the authorities are well aware that the continuing wave of Rifian (and now Moroccan, in general) labour migration in Holland, Belgium and France, especially, is in its way another manifestation of the same partial rejection (Hart 1976 p.432). The spectre of the late Muhammad bin 'Abd al-Krim al-Khattabi, who in the view of the palace, although not at all in that of his own people sought the monarchy for himself, still haunts the 'Alawid dynasty. For the dynasty evidently still believes strongly that the North Zone tail must not be allowed to wag the South Zone dog (ibid. pp.435–6).

Just as in the Rif, at independence in 1956, most Berber tribesmen in the Central Atlas were solidly aligned with the Istiqlal Party of 'Allal al-Fasi. However, after the split within the Istiqlal early in 1959, and between the summer of that year and early 1960, a noticeable shift had come about in the political allegiances of at least some of the tribesmen in the region. As of late 1959, most of them were now divided between the UNFP, the new leftist wing of the Istiqlal, and the MP, the Berber Party of Mahjub Ahardan, even though some Istiqlal adherence was still maintained. In the Bni Mallal province, local government leaders favoured the UNFP, and kept telling the tribesmen that the people from Fez, the members of the old Istiqlal, had designs on them and would swallow them up.

There is a certain degree of conflict in information here, but our own understanding of the matter at the time was that many Central Atlas Berbers still supported the Istiqlal while their administrative (and predominantly Arab) qa'id-s and super-qa'id-s supported the UNFP – with the notable exception of one super-qa'id, Bashir bin Tahami, who on 17 March 1960 got into an altercation with the local police chief of Bni Mallal, Muhammad Aqibli, and shot him, after which he took to the mountains. Zartman, however, says that bin Tahami had previously been the leader of a cell of urban resistants and according both to him and to Waterbury he was also a member in good standing of the UNFP, whereas our own informant said that his sympathies were with the Istiqlal and that the quarrel between him and the police chief Aqibli was over a woman (cf. Zartman 1964 pp.90–91; Waterbury 1970 p.212).

Once bin Tahami escaped to the Central Atlas, his two strongest supporters were Haddu u-Mha n-Ait Tus, the *shaykh* or *amghar* of the 3,000-man Ait 'Abdi section of the Ait Sukhman located on the Kusar Plateau high above the mountain post of Zawiya Ahansal (and the only tribal leader in the region who had survived the transfer of power after independence) and another unspecified individual from Askar depending on the post of Taglaft. As soon as the Ait 'Abdi, in particular, heard that bin Tahami had escaped safely to the mountains, they attacked the posts at Anargi n-Ait Sukhman and Tillugwit n-Ait Is'hha. In both places they raided the barracks of the paramilitary *mkhazniya* and stole rifles (exactly as the Aith Waryaghar had done at their administrative posts in the Rif a year and some months earlier), and at the latter post they tied the authorities to trees. At Zawiya Ahansal their move on the post was unsuccessful, because Hasini, the *charge d'affaires*, a member in good standing of the UNFP, was able to telephone Bni Mallal and to order up three battalions of the Royal Army on the double.

Bin Tahami wanted to get in touch with Army of Liberation elements which were still operating further to the south, so he sent Muha u-Mha n-Ait Tus, the brother of Haddu u-Mha, to contact them. The Army of Liberation sent five men back with him to look the situation over, but by this time the Royal Army battalions had arrived, and they trudged up to the wall of the Kusar Plateau in heavy snow. Muha u-Mha escaped but the Royal Army caught the Army of Liberation men, including an officer whose leg had been broken by a bullet. They tried to make this officer, a Rifian, show them how to work the guns that his own men were carrying, but he refused.

At this point the Royal Army, now on top of and cordoning off the plateau, went after Haddu u-Mha after an ultimatum on 22 March, dividing all his property and burning his house – both time-honoured and traditional practices in the precolonial Rif. But Bin Tahami was captured first, near Taglaft, where he was found located in a cave, with a machine gun but virtually without food (cf. Zartman 1964 p.92). Haddu u-Mha himself was finally captured late in April in heavy snow in a forest on a mountain above Tillugwit. Three shots had been fired at him, all of which missed, at the time he had escaped from his house. He too had no food at the time of his capture, although he had been fed regularly by his fellow tribesmen and constituents. The *qa'id* at Zawiya Ahansal, a Susi, was also imprisoned because he had helped the Ait 'Abdi, and indeed it was only because a *mkhazni* had disobeyed orders that the rifles at the post there were not stolen as well.

Our informant observed that when the Royal Army told the people to plunder the house of Haddu u-Mha, a certain Muha w-'Arish of the Ait Umzrai section of the Ihansalen was among them, and old Bassu n-Ait Tus, the senior member of the Ait Tus lineage and the paternal uncle of the brothers Haddu u-Mha and Muha u-Mha, swore that if the government did not punish him for this, he would shave off his beard. Of the saintly or *igurramen* lineage of the Ihansalen, Sidi Ahmad (or Hmad) Amhadar was completely loyal to the army, and even went out with them on their hunts for the Ait 'Abdi culprits; he was, indeed, on one foray in which two Ait 'Abdi men were killed. So late in April Haddu u-Mha was captured and jailed in Qasba Tadla. Our informant thought at the time that he would remain in jail for life, because the government had evidently had a high degree of confidence in him while he was *shaykh* of his tribal section. As he had subsequently abused this confidence, his punishment was severe.

Nonetheless, he was, as it happens, released from jail five years later, in May 1965, in another general amnesty for political prisoners proclaimed by King Hasan II in that year during the feast of the 'Ayd al-Kabir. The capture of Haddu u-Mha ended the revolt, in which the Royal Army sent helicopters over Zawiya Ahansal for the first time. But Bashir bin Tahami was not even put on trial until the following year, and was then handed a life sentence. As of mid-1961, all political party activity was forbidden at Zawiya Ahansal, although permitted elsewhere in the Bni Mallal province.

It may be worth noting that at the time Bin Tahami escaped, and so did a certain Shafi'i, the head of the paramilitary *mkhazniya* or Forces Auxiliaires in Marrakesh, into the Western Atlas. He had evidently done nothing, but because after his escape he killed two of his army pursuers, he was caught and jailed.

Our informant also noted at the time that the goal of the Istiqlal Party was a Moroccan republic, with 'Allal al-Fasi as president, but he also averred that the UNFP, led by Mehdi Ben Barka, disagreed, and wanted to retain the monarchy and keep the king. Or such was the way that this particular passage was recorded in our notes. But it seems highly likely that what he meant was the precise opposite (i.e. that it was the UNFP under the aegis of Ben Barka that had a Moroccan republic in view and wanted to do away with the monarchy). This view is clearly revealed in Ben Barka's own writing, given the strongly Marxist 'revolutionary option' that he wanted for Morocco. His book on the subject was published posthumously, after his murder by the late Gen. Ufqir in Paris in 1965 where he had been in exile (cf. Ben Barka 1967).

On the other hand, and in complete opposition to the view taken by our informant, the accounts by Zartman, by Waterbury and even by Gellner maintain that bin Tahami was also a UNFP activist (cf. Zartman 1964 p.92; Waterbury 1970 p.212; Gellner 1973). The Istiqlal Party, as noted, had already split in January 1959; but since the 1960 revolt, as our own informant would maintain, was Istiqlal-sponsored and did not succeed, the party lost much ground, which was gained later not by the UNFP but by Ahardan's Popular Movement, which was, in effect, the Berber Party. Finally, Gellner also makes the cogent point, if only in a footnote, that most Moroccan tribesmen of the period had no real idea exactly what was/is meant by 'leftist' or 'rightist' political leanings; but the fact remains that in this instance they were loyal, as he also notes (Gellner 1973 p.362 n.1). But such loyalty becomes more understandable if our informant's explanation that they favoured the original wing, and not the breakaway (UNFP) one, of the Istiqlal Party, and hence the monarchy as well, is accepted.

The 1960 episode in Bni Mallal and the Central Atlas had a 'happy ending' nearly 20 years later, for by 1979 Haddu u-Mha had become president of the customary law tribunal at Zawiya Ahansal – which had been resuscitated in a very low-key way well after the rescinding of the 1930 Berber Dahir at independence in 1956. By 1986 he was the *qa'di n-l-qa'ida*, the tribunal's *qa'di* of customary law, in its localised and low-profile revival; and he was evidently doing nicely. His contacts with Bashir bin Tahami – who was still in prison – were long over.

What can we learn from these small-scale tribal uprisings during the immediate post-colonial period in Morocco, especially from the vantage point of 35 years of hindsight? Gellner, who stressed, correctly, that the language of all of these tribesmen (i.e. Berber) is not the official language of the state in which they live, then went on to mention three features about them which he found surprising at the time, especially in the light of Moroccan historical examples: (1) the fact that the uprisings collapsed fairly easily; (2) the fact that their leaders, when captured, were treated with leniency; and (3) the fact that they literally did not make sense, in that tribesmen who proclaimed themselves supporters of X staged a rebellion while X himself was in office as Prime Minister (Gellner 1973 p.361 n.1).

We would hold, on the other hand, that no matter what the intrinsic interest of these points may be, they all tend to obscure the facts. We will dispose of the last one first. Point (3) could only possibly have been made to apply to the 1960 uprising in Bni Mallal and the Central Atlas, not to either of the others; and we have already demonstrated that in our own informant's view, which we see no reason not to accept, the revolt was carried out in the name of the older Istiqlal Party while its new breakaway wing, the UNFP, was in power, and not in the name of the latter. So this issue, though doubtless interesting as a point for speculation, can now be rejected out of hand.

As for Point (1), it should not be forgotten that all three uprisings occurred in the immediate years after independence, at a time when all effective armament had been removed from tribal hands by the protecting powers, France and Spain, anywhere from 20 to 30 years earlier, after their 'pacification' of the country in the name of the sultan. Virtually all the armament in the country was therefore, very soon after independence, in the hands of the new Royal Moroccan Army and the auxiliary forces, the *mkhazniya*, the gendarmerie and the police. So given the virtual monopoly on firepower in Morocco by its armed forces, the imminent collapse of these uprisings does not seem so surprising after all.

With respect to Point (2) – the supposedly lenient treatment of the leaders of these revolts, in the sense that they were awarded long prison sentences but not the death penalty – it should be remembered not only that 'Addi u-Bihi's appeal was turned down and that he died in jail before his death sentence could be carried out, but that Muhammad nj-Hajj Sillam was condemned to death *in absentia*, as indeed he did. It is quite true that one major Rifian complaint was with respect to the under-administration and general neglect of their region (ibid. p.363). However, the fact that King Hasan II did not see fit to revoke these death sentences just because it was his late father, King Muhammad V, and not he, who had decided to hand them out does not necessarily indicate any special tendency toward leniency, as the later publicly staged and televised execution by an army firing squad of no less than ten rebellious army generals, almost all of them Berbers and who had been stripped of their decorations after the *coup manqué* at Skhirat in 1971, also bore out – with a vengeance.

What may well be something relatively new, however, and something that Gellner failed to comment upon, has been the tendency for both 'Alawid kings, father and son, to proclaim amnesty and clemency for those political prisoners whose behaviour has been good on the occasion of canonical Muslim feasts such as the 'Ayd al-Kabir in the final month of the Muslim lunar year. To our knowledge, such clemency, hedged though it may be, has no historical precedent.

BIBLIOGRAPHY

Ben Barka, Mehdi, *Opcion Revolucionaria para Marruecos y Escritos Politicos, 1960–1965* (Barcelona: Ediciones de Cultura Popular, SA 1967; originally published in Paris: François Maspero 1966).

Blair, Leon B., *Western Window on the Arab World* (Austin TX and London: University of Texas Press 1970).

Eickelman, Dale F., *Moroccan Islam: Tradition and Society in a Pilgrimage Center.* Modern Middle East Studies No.1 (Austin TX and London: University of Texas Press 1976).

Gellner, Ernest, 'Patterns of Rural Rebellion in Morocco During the Early Years of Independence' (1962), in Ernest Gellner and, Charles Micaud (eds.), *Arabs and Berbers: From Tribe to Nation in North Africa* (London: Duckworth 1973) pp.361–74.

Hart, David M., 'The Tribe in Modern Morocco: Two Case Studies', in Gellner and Micaud (above) pp.25–58.

——, *The Aith Waryaaghar of the Moroccan Rif: An Ethnography and History.* Viking Fund Publications in Anthropology, No.55 (Tucson: University of Arizona Press 1976).

M'Barek, Zaki, *Résistance et Armée de Libération: Portée Politique et Liquidation, 1953–1958* (Tangier: ETEI 1987).
Ouardighi, Abderrahman, *La Grande Crise Franco-Marocaine, 1952–1956* (Rabat: Imprimerie de l'Etoile 1975).
Waterbury, John, *The Commander of the Faithful: The Moroccan Political Elite – A Study in Segmented Politics* (London: Weidenfeld and Nicolson 1970).
Zartman, I. William, *Morocco: Problems of New Power* (New York: Atherton Press 1964).

NOTE

1. Michael Peyron has noted that during the attack on the *Affaires Indigènes* outpost at Immuzar n-Imarmushen (Immouzer-des-Marmoucha) in the eastern Middle Atlas in the winter of 1955–56, the Imarmushen attempted a push northwards to bring their neighbours of the Ait Warayin into the fray, because the then custodian of the Taffert mountain-hut, on the north-western slopes of the Jbil Bu Iblan, was involved in an amusing episode in connection with this. In a truly remarkable attempt to hedge his bets, he deliberately set fire to the hut at the time it was under threat from Imarmushen raiders (and siding with them, so to speak), but as soon as they withdrew he actually fought the flames and proceeded to put out the blaze, so as not to be seen by the French authorities at Aharmumu (Ahermoumou) as having aided the 'rebels' . This notwithstanding, Peyron reports that this man has been applying, unsuccessfully, to acquire *ancient résistant* status ever since Independence, and even though he has no hope of ever doing so, his son, the present custodian, continues to badger Peyron whenever the latter goes there by insisting that he put in a good word for his father 'with the Ministry in Rabat' (Michael Peyron, personal communication, 23 May 1995).

Part II

Northern Morocco

The Rif and the Rifians:
Problems of Definition

The Arabic term *rif* has the meanings both of 'cultivable land' and of 'seacoast' and is used to denote specific areas both in Egypt and in Morocco. In the Egyptian case it refers to the narrow strip of cultivable or arable land along the Nile and in the Moroccan one to the northern coastal range of mountains bordering the Mediterranean such that in one context one meaning is stressed and, in the other, the other comes to the fore. The poverty and infertility of the land in the Moroccan case and its over-cultivation – to say nothing of its overpopulation (cf. Hart 1976) – are very real factors, but not ones which are built into the name itself.

Physical geographers tend to refer to the whole mountain chain of northern Morocco, which extends from Tangier and Ceuta in the west to Melilla in the east and which is a continuation of the Spanish Cordillera Penibetica and of approximately the same late geological age, as 'the Rif'. Whereas this is certainly the case physically, it is not so linguistically or culturally. The geographical designation results, for example, in the Sinhaja Srir region between Ktama and Targist, the highest part of the chain being labelled 'Central Rif' (cf. Maurer 1968*a*; 1968*b*) – which ethnically and linguistically it is not. The ethnic and linguistic centre of the region is further east: it is bounded on the north by al-Husayma and the Mediterranean, on the west by Snada and Bni Bu Frah, on the south by Aknul, and on the east by Midar and Bu Dinar, and comprises the tribal groups of the Ibuqquyen (or Buqquya), the Aith Waryaghar (or Bni Waryaghal), the Aith 'Ammarth (or Bni 'Ammart), the Igzinnayen (or Gzinnaya), the Axt Tuzin (or Bni Tuzin) and the Thimsaman (or Timsaman). Further east, the eastern Rifian tribes include the Aith Sa'id (or Bni Sa'id), the Aith Wurishik (or Bni Wulishk), the Thafarsith (or Tafarsit), the Ibdharsen (or Mtalsa), the Aith Bu Yihyi (or Bni Bu Yihyi), the five-tribe confederacy of the Iqar'ayen (or Qal'aya), and the Ikibdhanen (or Kibdana), while the western ones are the Aith Yittuft (or Bni Ittuft) and the Aith Bu Frah (or Bni Bu Frah), both of which have Arabic-speaking sections. Indeed, the last-mentioned are almost entirely Arabophone and only have one or two Rifian-speaking communities.

As is well known, the inhabitants of the chain are more generally and inclusively divided into two broad traditional ethnolinguistic categories, the Arabic-speaking Jbala ('mountaineers') in the west and the Thamazighth/Tharifith-speaking Rifians in the east, with the dividing line and watershed at Targist. The western half of the chain, too, has far more vegetation and normally receives considerably more rain than the eastern, although east of Midar and on to Nador-Melilla the chain flattens out into open rolling country (Mikesell 1961).

Nonetheless, if a proper inventory is to be taken, the ethnolinguistic picture is in fact more complicated than this. Most of the tribal groups or *qba'il* (sing. *qbila*, and Rif. *dhiqba'ir* (sing. *dhaqbitsh*)) in the west are Jbala except for a congeries of nine small tribes of the Ghmara confederacy along the coast above and east of Shawen and from Wad Law to Jibha, all of which are Arabic-speaking, although a non-Rifian Berber speech has been recorded among sections of two of them, the Bni Bu Zra' and the Bni Mansur (Colin 1929). But Jbala Arabic is more like the urban *hadriya* Arabic of the northern cities than like the 'Bedouin' Arabic of most of the rest of rural Morocco, and one of its peculiarities is a propensity for a 'Latin' -esh suffix which terminates the names of certain communities.

Further east, centred on Ktama and Targist, are the nine small tribes correspondingly of the Sinhaja Srir (or 'Gunstock Sinhaja') confederacy, most of which still speak a different dialect of Berber which evidently resembles the Tashilhit of the Western Atlas and the Anti-Atlas as much as it does Tharifith (Vidal 1945). The names *Ghmara* and *Sinhaja* also represent relict names of medieval Berber confederacies which were moved or transferred to new localities as there are two other entirely Arabic-speaking groups also known as Sinhaja (the Sinhaja Ghaddō and the Sinhaja Musbah south and west of the Sinhaja Srir, and a southern Jbalan tribe, the Masmuda). Then there are also a few leftover tribes which, properly speaking, do not fit either category, such as the Aith (or Bni) Mazduy, the Targist, the Bni Gmil, the Mstasa and the Mtiwa in the western Rif; and the Ulad Stut and possibly the Aith Iznasen in the east. Legend, however, links them all through the great and probably mythical Ghmara-Sinhaja war in which all the tribes in the region are held to have joined one side or the other (Montagne 1930; Coon 1931).

With respect to the historical background very little is known of the prehistory of the region, but the history of the Jbala seems to be relatively well documented since early Islamic times and the propagation of Islam from the Hajrat al-Nsar. The early Islamic history of the Rif properly speaking, through the Salihid dynasty of the Nakur, whose members invoked Yemeni origins from the Banu Himyar, and which lasted from pre-Idrisid until Almoravid times with the fall of the Madinat al-Nakur (i.e. 710–108´ CE) is relatively well documented, but from then until the mid-nineteenth century Rifian history seems to be an almost total blank. The existence and position of key tribes in the area (the Aith Waryaghar, the Igzinnayen and the Thimsaman, for example) are attested for the Salihid period by al-Bakri (who wrote in the eleventh century) and one of the gates

of the Madinat al-Nakur was known as Bab Bni Waryaghal. As the whole
region consisted of sedentary agricultural tribesmen except for the small-
scale transhumance in the Eastern Rif of the Ibdharsen and the Aith Bu
Yihyi, and apart from the usual traditions that almost every existing social
group originated from somewhere else not too far away, the chances are that
the core populations of most of the tribes have been in their present
locations for close to a millennium, if not longer.

There are, of course, economic and cultural differences: the Jbalan use
of oxen yoked by their horns for ploughing as opposed to the Rifian use of
cows and the neck yoke; the Jbalan use of thatch (which has today become
converted into corrugated iron) for the roofing of their houses as opposed to
flat Rifian adobe roofs; and the additional use of peaking in roofs in the
Jbala, the Ghmara and the Sinhaja, all areas of heavier rainfall than the Rif
proper. The Jbala also have true villages with houses clustered together,
while the Rifians traditionally have dispersed homesteads each located at
least 300 metres from the next, even though both types of community are
called *dshar* (pl. *dshur*; for Jbalan diagnostics, cf. Vignet-Zunz 1991).
Rifian labour migration to French colonial Algeria began in the mid-
nineteenth century while it never existed in the Jbala at all until after
Moroccan independence in 1956. Music and dancing, it might be added, are
also very different: in the Jbala musicians play the *ghayta* (a form of
clarinet) and the *tbul* (drum), and dancing is generally performed by boys,
whereas in the Rif musicians, who belong to a socially and occupationally
inferior class called *imdhyazen* and who generally come from one tribe, the
Axt Tuzin, play the *addjun* (tambourine) and the *zammar* (a kind of bass
clarinet with two stems to which cows' horns are attached), and unmarried
girls dance to the standard refrain of *ay-aralla-buya*.

Sociopolitical differences include the fact that in the Jbala, the *shaykh* or
the *qa'id* of a tribe usually had greater dominance than in the Rif, where in
the precolonial period the real power lay in the hands of the *imgharen* (sing.
amghar), the members of the collective *aitharbi'in* or tribal council, who
were the real administrators of tribal customary law. Feud and vendetta
were much more common in the Rif than in the Jbala where *liff* alliances,
collective oaths and *haqq* fines for murder, which were payable to the
councillors for murders committed in the markets (cf. Hart 1976), were all
evidently unknown. However, banditry in the Jbala, conversely, was much
commoner than in the Rif (Hart 1987). Attitudes to women differed as well:
in the Rif they were both more respected and more secluded and in the Aith
Waryaghar there are still special women's markets from which men are
rigorously excluded (Troin 1975; Hart 1976).

Among religious differences there has always been a greater
proliferation both of saints or *shurfa'* (descendants of the Prophet) and of

tariqa-s or religious orders in the Jbala than in the Rif, where most homegrown holy lineages (except perhaps for the Dharwa n-Sidi Hand u-Musa in the Igzinnayen) had only localised reputations as *baraka* dispensers and conflict arbiters, not regional ones. The Rifians, however, were much affected by the politico-religious reforms of Muhammad bin 'Abd al-Krim al-Khattabi who, as a former *qa'di*, during the Rifian War which he led against Spain and France (1921–26), did his best to eradicate customary law and substitute the Shari'a for it, with notable success (Hart 1976).

During the protectorate period (1912–56) and after independence (from 1956 on), Spanish colonial rule tended to bring Rifians and Jbala together (despite their numerous and undeniable differences and despite the strong feeling of superiority which the former manifest toward the latter) as the poor 'North Zone' relations of the far larger and economically far more privileged French protectorate, which became the 'South Zone' at independence. The Rifians in particular have long felt themselves to be somewhat apart from the rest of Morocco, a fact which is clearly manifest today in the way they look toward the European labour market and in the way that many of them plough their earnings back not so much into their own region but into towns and cities in adjacent parts of Morocco where they have come to settle: for as their recognition of the fact of overpopulation in their homeland is acute, there are too many of them now to remain restricted to their natal area of the Rif.

The question remains, however, whether the definition of the latter should remain restricted to the area of Rifian speech and culture between Targist and Melilla as evinced by the tribal groups enumerated above. Our own view is that it should be, for the more inclusive any definition becomes the greater the number of ambiguous and 'catchall' cases with which it must contend and we feel that the major point of this exercise, the exclusion of the Jbala from this definition, has been amply demonstrated.

Herewith a final word: in the same or a similar vein, might it not be possible on a larger scale to propose a three-way geographical division of North African Berbers, of Imazighen n-Tmazgha, on a north–centre–south basis, and more or less 'across the board'? In such a context, the Rifians in northern Morocco and the Kabyles in north-central Algeria would form the northern group; the Imazighen of the Middle-Central Atlas, the Saghru and the pre-Saharan oases, and the Ishilhayen of the Western Atlas, the Sus Valley and the Anti-Atlas, all in Morocco, as well as the Shawiya of the Aures and the oasis-dwelling Mzabites in central Algeria, and other oasis Berber-speakers at various points in the northern Sahara (e.g. Figig, Tuwat, Gurara, Tidikalt, Ghadamas, Ghat, Awjila, Murzuq and Siwa) would form the central group; while the southern group would be restricted to the various groups of Tuareg as well as to those Mauritanian *zwaya* tribes which still retain Berber speech or admit to Berber ancestry. This very tentative suggestion for a classification, which is admittedly more geographical and cultural than it is linguistic, is offered for whatever it may be worth. We might add that it makes no pretence of corresponding to the now outmoded French colonial categorisation of Berber dialects as Masmuda, Sinhaja or Zanata, which was based not only on medieval classifications which did not survive as such even into immediate precolonial times, but also on an overly free interpretation of Ibn Khaldun which was also selective, slanted and downright questionable (cf. Hart 1982).

BIBLIOGRAPHY

Colin, Georges-S., 'Le Parler Berbère des Ghmara', *Hesperis* IX (1929) pp.43–58.
Coon, Carleton S., *Tribes of the Rif*. Harvard African Studies IX (Cambridge MA: Peabody Museum 1931).
Hart, David M., *The Aith Waryaghar of the Moroccan Rif: An Ethnography and History*. Viking Fund Publications in Anthropology No.55 (Tucson: University of Arizona Press 1976).
——, 'Masmuda, Sinhaja and Zanata: A Three-Ring Circus', *Revue d'Histoire Maghrebine* IX/27–8 (Tunis 1982) pp.361–5.
——, *Banditry in Islam: Case Studies from Morocco Algeria and the Pakistan North-West Frontier*. MENAS Studies in Continuity and Change (Wisbech, Cambridgeshire: MENAS Press 1987).
Maurer, Gérard, *Les Montagnes dō Rif Central: Etude Géomorphologique*. Faculté des Lettres et Sciences Humaines (Paris: Université de Paris 1968a).
——, 'Les Paysans dō Haut Rif Central', *Revue de Géographie du Maroc* 14 (1968b) pp.3–70.
Mikesell, Marvin W., *Northern Morocco: A Cultural Geography*. University of California Publications in Geography No.14 (Berkeley and Los Angeles: University of California Press 1961).
Montagne, Robert, *Les Berbères et le Makhzen dans le Sud du Maroc: Essai sur la Transformation Politique des Berbères Sédentaires (Groupe Chleuh)* (Paris: Felix Alcan 1930).
Troin, Jean-François, *Les Souks Marocains: Marches Ruraux et Organisation de l'Espace dans la Moitié Nord du Maroc* (2 vols., Aix-en-Provence: Edisud 1975).
Vidal, F.S., 'Ensayo sobre Linguistica en el Rif Occidental', *Africa* 46–7 (Madrid 1945) pp.32–7.
Vignet-Zunz, Jawhar, 'Treize Questions sur une Identité' in Jawhar Vignet-Zunz and Ahmed Zouggari (eds.), *Jbala – Histoire et Société: Etudes sur le Maroc du Nord-Ouest* (Paris: Editions du Centre National de la Recherche Scientifique (CNRS); Casablanca: Wallada 1991) pp.133–99.

Spanish Colonial Ethnography in the Rural and Tribal Northern Zone of Morocco, 1912–56: An Overview and an Appraisal

There has to date been very little recent scholarly research on the northern Spanish protectorate of Morocco, particularly by comparison with the now very considerable literature on the corresponding French Moroccan protectorate, its very much larger neighbour to the south. To the best of our knowledge, all there is, barring a résumé produced by one of its principal Spanish administrative functionaries and actors in its drama the year after it ended (Garcia Figueras 1957), is just one single important general study by Morales Lezcano (1984), plus our own much shorter assessment of the protectorate's role and function as seen through the career and the ethnographic output of one of its most gifted tribal administrators, to which the assessment in question acts as an introduction (Hart 1958; Hart and Blanco Izaga 1975 Vol. I pp.1–44). One good reason for this unfortunate state of affairs is that as of the date of writing (1995), the bulk of the Spanish Protectorate archives (currently housed in the Archivo de la Administracion in Alcala de Henares outside Madrid) has not yet even been classified and catalogued, let alone declared open to researchers for inspection. This article attempts to fill the gap only insofar as the published ethnological and ethnographic record for the rural and tribal areas of the Spanish Zone are concerned, although attention is occasionally drawn to certain historical works of significance as well as to unpublished works or reports if these are accessible. However, before examining any of this literature, which is both widely scattered and highly disparate in quality, it behoves us first to consider a number of points of a more general nature which have a direct bearing on the matter at hand.

To a considerable extent the Spanish Protectorate can be regarded as a much smaller mirror-image of the French one, of which, by virtue of the 1906 Treaty of Algeciras, it was a kind of joint junior partner; and this can be seen in its administration, with its *khalifa* in Tetuan, acting as the representative of the Moroccan Sultan in Rabat. On the other hand the Spanish Alto Comisario or High Commissioner functioned as the counterpart of the French Resident-General, and the *cuerpo de intervenciones militares*, which came to represent the structure of tribal administration throughout the zone, was modelled on the French military *bureaux arabes* dating from the previous century in Algeria. The blueprint for the *intervenciones* system was the brainchild of Capt. Candido Lobera

Girela, the influential founder-editor of the Melilla newspaper *El Telegrama del Rif*, and it had been set forth by him there just the year before the Algeciras Treaty (cf. Lobera Girela 1905 pp.31–42): for quite irrespective of the validity of its claims to them, Spain had held its two major *presidios* or *plazas de soberania*, the enclaves of Ceuta (Sibta) and Melilla (Mlilya), plus three other smaller ones, on the Moroccan Mediterranean coast, ever since the fifteenth century.

A major war with Morocco in 1859–60, the so-called 'Guerra de Africa', with its theatre of operations around Tetuan, resulting in a disastrous defeat for the Moroccans and in the ruination of their treasury, plus other later campaigns further east near Melilla in 1893 and in 1909–12, led to the implantation of the Spanish Protectorate in the last-mentioned year, as soon as its French counterpart to the south had been put in place. But from a standpoint of security this implantation was more on a *de jure* than on a *de facto* basis, because what with the early resistance to Spain mounted on an off-again, on-again basis by Raysuni in the Jbala from 1913 until 1919 and the later, much fiercer and very ongoing resistance offered by bin 'Abd al-Krim in the Rif first to Spain and then, later but simultaneously, to France as well, from 1921 to 1926, the total 'pacification' of the Spanish Zone was not achieved until July 1927, while the last single dissident in the l-Khmas tribe, near Bu Halla and above Bab Taza, was not killed in fact until June 1929.

In view of this, the perceptive critique applied by Rabia Hatim to Spanish novels about the Morocco of this and of an earlier period can almost, as we shall see, be transferred to Spanish thinking about Moroccan ethnography. This is that Morocco the Myth was a combination of visions of a hypothetical and romantic Muslim Near East and of an equally hypothetical and romantic Muslim Granada, plus the various patios of its Alhambra, while Morocco the Anti-Colonial Reality was bin 'Abd al-Krim and the heat, dust and mercilessly accurate rifle fire of Rifians at war (Hatim 1990 p.148).

From the beginning of the Spanish Protectorate in 1912 until its end in 1956, it is significant, first of all, that developments within it were much more closely linked to developments in Spain itself than developments in the French Zone were with those in France. Although there is not the space here to discuss the matter, this was the case, curiously enough, despite the often pointed lack of contact and communication between the small, exclusive and ethnocentric club of Spanish Arabists in the peninsular universities and the rather more vociferous Africanists and colonialists both in Madrid and on the other side of the straits (Lopez Garcia 1990 pp.35–69). The latter were determined to undertake the colonial adventure in Morocco both as an infinitesimal recompense for the loss of their colonies in the New

World and the Philippines in 1898 and in spite of strong popular protest at home. Secondly, the spiny northern tier of Morocco is one of the poorest areas of the country, as well as one of the most heavily populated. Thus the almost total lack of economic development by Spain of its protectoral zone, compared with the French development of the Gharb as an integral part of Marshal Lyautey's conception of *le Maroc Utile* – in which, of course, the utility in question was purely for the benefit of the French settler-colons who set themselves up there –, was countered, in a sense, by its usage as, above all, a training ground for the Spanish Army. There is little question, indeed, about the fact that it was to no little extent Spanish Moroccan troops, the majority of whom were Rifians, the sons of the same men who had fought against Spain only a decade earlier, who had then proceeded to win the Spanish Civil War of 1936–39 for Franco and the Nationalist cause.

Almost the whole of the *interventor* corps after 1939, furthermore, was made up of Spanish nationalist army officers who had commanded these same Moroccan troops or who had fought against their fathers in the Rifian War. There were only a few significant publications in Spanish on Moroccan ethnography prior to 1939, when the Civil War ended. Both before and after that year on until Moroccan independence, the books and articles that existed were authored largely by lieutenant-colonels, majors, captains and even lieutenants. Most of these men were right-wing *Africanistas* whose primary duty, as they saw it, was to serve the nation and who dabbled in local ethnology purely as a sideline to their administrative duties as *interventores* (for a synopsis and critique of Spanish *Africanismo*, cf. Laarbi 1990). It is significant that there was not a single professional social scientist among their number – except for Julio Caro Baroja, who spent a month in the Ghmara in 1955 (cf. Caro Baroja 1957), after his earlier and more intensive fieldwork in the Western Sahara, which was also brief in duration but which enabled him to write what is still unquestionably the best piece of colonial anthropology of what is today effectively part of Greater Morocco (Caro Baroja 1955, republished 1990). Ironically enough, prior to Moroccan independence, the only other properly anthropological fieldwork in the zone was done in the Rif by two Americans, Carleton Coon (1931; also 1932, 1933 and 1962 pp.311–19) who, however, concentrated on physical anthropology (1931, 1939 pp.480–89) and, later, the present author, who was one of Coon's students (cf. Hart 1954, reprinted in Hart and Blanco Izaga 1975 Vol. I pp.45–95; Hart 1976a; Hart and Blanco Izaga 1995, for further bibliography); and in the Jbala by an English disciple of Westermarck, Walter Fogg (1938, 1940 and 1942), who concentrated on the economic organisation of a single market, Suq t-Tnin Sidi l-Yamani. Another American, this one a geographer, Marvin Mikesell, also did fieldwork just prior to and at the time of independence, on the human and cultural geography of the zone (Mikesell 1958, 1961). Still later fieldwork was also done by two anthropologists, one French, Raymond Jamous (1981), and one English, David Seddon (1981), in the Eastern Rif well after independence, but the main thrust of their work is toward the precolonial and colonial periods. The same is true, although less so, of another American anthropologist, Roger Joseph (Joseph and Joseph 1987), who worked on marriage ceremonies in the Central Rif, and of a Moroccan one, Paul Pascon, who worked on the social ecology of the Bni Bu Frah (Pascon and van der Wusten 1983). The major trend, since 1970, toward labour migration in the European Economic Community has been covered by the work of certain Dutch scholars, notably Heinemeijer et al. (1977) and Paolo de Mas (1978, 1981).

But we are concerned here specifically with the Spanish contributions to the ethnography of northern Morocco, and it is therefore to the Spanish bibliography on the subject that we now turn. It must be stated at the outset that the great bulk of it is, unfortunately, characterised by an extreme degree of mediocrity: untrained, unimaginative and derivative themselves in the social sciences, Spaniards had long tended to rely on translations of works by foreigners rather than on original research by their own people. Hence there was always an awareness, even a realisation, by the Spanish military aficionados de etnologia that their French counterparts, under the able tutelage first of Lyautey himself and the members of his zawiya (cf. Monteil 1962; Bidwell 1973) and then under that of the in-house academic of the Residence-Générale, Robert Montagne (cf. Montagne 1930, 1931, 1973, 1986), were producing far better ethnography in their zone during the 1920s and early 1930s than they were in their own; but lacking the necessary anthropological and often the necessary language training required, there was little or nothing they could do about it. Spanish ethnography in the North Zone compares in fact more closely in quality with what French colonialism produced in Tunisia (Albergoni and Pouillon 1976; Pouillon 1984) than what the French came to produce in Morocco, where their major talents in this line were to develop. Indeed, in some cases, like that of the early and otherwise quite useful study by Capt. Mauricio Capdequi y Brieu on Yebala (1923) – a work which was also posthumous, as its author was killed in action near al-'Ara'ish (Larache) the year before his book appeared – there is evidence of outright cribbing without acknowledgement; and in this particular instance the cribbing in question was done from an earlier monograph by Edouard Michaux-Bellaire (1911), who had been the founder-instigator of the French Mission Scientifique au Maroc headquartered in Tangier and dating back to the beginning of the century. Nonetheless, Capdequi's work remains a useful summary of Michaux-Bellaire's material and we shall shortly consider it in somewhat more detail.

We must also stress that we will make no attempt here to cover all the available literature, given the fact that much of it is highly dispersed in a number of different journals, such as the monthly *Africa* (approximately 1941–56), the *Archivos del Instituto de Estudios Africanos* series (circa. 1948–65?), from the Consejo Superior de Investigaciones Cientificas, and the *Cuadernos de Estudios Africanos* series (circa. 1946–60?) from the Instituto de Estudios Politicos, all out of Madrid; the *Seleccion de Conferencias Pronunciadas en la Academia de Interventores* series (1946–53) and the *Diario de Africa* newspaper files (the latter are excellent for assiduous coverage of events in the neighbouring French Zone, 1945–56), both out of Tetuan; and the bi-monthly *Mauritania* (circa. 1945–60?), out of the Franciscan mission in Tangier. The files of all of these publications, either complete or nearly so, can be found open for inspection in the Garcia Figueras Collection in the Seccion Africa y Mundo Arabe at the Biblioteca Nacional in Madrid, which also contains many other scattered materials, both published and unpublished, in its *Folletos* and *Miscelanea* series. The Spanish military archives at the Servicio Historico Militar, also in Madrid, are likewise open for inspection and research.

However, the bulk of the unpublished archives from the Spanish Moroccan Protectorate itself (including the often very valuable *Monografia de Kabila* series, circa. 1952–55, undertaken as a prize-winning competition among the various *interventores* in the zone at the behest of Tomas Garcia Figueras, the then Delegado de Asuntos Indigenas or Delegate of Native Affairs in Tetuan – with the best monographs probably being those of Capt. José Rodriguez Erola, *El Caidato del Alto Guis (Beni Urriaguel): Estudio Economico-Social* (1953) and of José Ojeda del Rincon, *La Kabila de Beni Tuzin: Estudio Economic-Social* (1954) are housed, along with similar materials from the ex-colonies of Ifni and the ex-Spanish Sahara, in the Archivos de la Administracion at Alcala de Henares, outside Madrid; and these, to the best of our knowledge, are all still closed. The last time we checked on the matter, in 1985, most of the materials concerned were still strewn around in packing crates and had not even been catalogued.

This said, we may now move on to a cursory examination of some of the better works in the Spanish ethnographic repertory from the North Zone of Morocco. Our concentration is on books; articles are dealt with only if they are of exceptional interest, but a fairly representative bibliography is included. As the zone itself was broadly divided into two major areas, one in the west, of Arabic speech, the Jbala (comprising the former *territorios* and present provinces of the Jbala, the Lukkus and the Ghmara – or Tetuan, al-'Ara'ish/Larache and Shawen, respectively), and the other, in the east, of Berber speech, the Rif (comprising the former *territorios* and present provinces of the Rif and the Kart – or al-Husayma and Nador, respectively), we shall indicate in each instance whether the work in question is of regional or overall zonal import. Works are also considered both regionally and chronologically, in order of publication; and note also that if there is more emphasis placed upon the Rif than upon the Jbala in this article, it is simply because we ourselves know the former region far better, as well as the literature dealing with it, as we did our initial and longest stint of fieldwork there among the Aith Waryaghar (Bni Waryaghal) during two separate but lengthy stages, the first toward the end of the colonial period, in 1953–55, and the second after independence, in 1959–65 (cf. especially Hart 1976a).

Although we have been unable to consult it personally, possibly the earliest piece of descriptive ethnography in Spanish on the Jbala may be by a long-time Spanish resident of Tangier, Ricardo Ruiz Orsatti, 'La Kabila de Uadras' (Wadras) (1913, which is cited for its evidently numerous references to banditry in the area in question, very frequent at the time and indeed a sociocultural diagnostic of the period, in Bernaldo de Quiros and Ardila 1978 p.226; and cf. also Hart 1987 pp.6–26). A considerably fuller and more rounded ethnographic account of the north-western Jbala appeared ten years later, with the publication in 1923, as noted, of Capt. Capdequi y Brieu's posthumous *Yebala*. Although much of this work was, as noted, not original with its author and appears simply to have been lifted by him, without acknowledgement, from an earlier and much more detailed account by Michaux-Bellaire (1911), it has, nonetheless, the great virtue of being an excellent résumé of the ethnography of tribal groups such as the Bni Gurfat, Bni 'Arus, Sumata, Bni Yisif, Ahl Srif, Bni Yidir, l-Ghzawa and l-Khmas, and precisely the kind of work which could lead to further investigation in greater detail. To this reader, the giveaway factor indicating that Capdequi cribbed his book from Michaux-Bellaire is in his unacknowledged use of the latter's notion that the Jbala constituted an intermediate zone or area between the *bilad al-makhzan* and the *bilad al-siba*, neither completely one nor the other but sharing elements of both. This was especially deemed to be the case insofar as religious taxation ordained by Islam, in the form of *zakah* and *'ashur* payments, were not deposited in the *bit al-mal*, the sultanic treasury, but were given to the local *shurfa'* and *zawiya*-s, both of whom and which were and are exceedingly numerous in the region. Quite apart from the fact that the crudeness of the *makhzan-siba* dichotomy resulted in a classificatory device bolstered by colonialism to support a theory of divide-and-rule and that since Moroccan independence it has been subjected to stringent revisionism if not completely scrapped (for in attenuated ways and in certain cases it can still be useful), the actual existence on the ground in precolonial north-western Morocco of such an intermediate zone – which Michaux-Bellaire labelled *bilad at-taraf* – is in

116   TRIBE AND SOCIETY IN RURAL MOROCCO

itself problematical, a point which a recent and otherwise very good critique of Michaux-Bellaire's voluminous output (Houroro 1988) fails to consider. But Michaux-Bellaire, no matter how interesting or debatable his work may be, was not Spanish but French, and hence he has no real place in the present discussion. The import of this is to point out here that what Capdequi did was to present in a useful capsule form Michaux-Bellaire's ethnography of the Jbalan tribes, touching on virtually every facet of their lives (economics, agriculture and its related associations, village organisation, the *jma'a*, the division of the tribe into *tlat*, *rbu'* or *khmas*, or thirds, fourths or fifths, *qa'id*-s and *shaykh*-s and the relationship of the tribe to the wider world, the role of *shurfa'*, that of *zawiya*-s and religious orders, Qur'anic instruction, etc.) save perhaps kinship, which had not yet become a subject of special study either in the European anthropology of the period or in its manifestations under colonial rule. The point is that Capdequi on the *Yebala* can still be read with some profit if the reader bears firmly in mind the fact that like much, if not most, colonial sociology is limited itself to ethnographic description of the region under consideration during the immediate precolonial period, and was in no way concerned with any socioeconomic or sociopolitical change brought about by contact with the colonial power. Indeed, the same caveat may be levelled at almost all the rest of the literature under consideration here. But of course the colonisers had to learn something first about the existing social system.

A somewhat later work on the Jbala which is worthy of mention is Cmdte. Uriarte, *Cofradias Religiosas en Yebala y Diversas Taifas de Xorfas, Zauias y Santuarios* (1930). This study, as its title indicates, concentrates on the *shurfa'*, shrines and *zawiya*-s of a region which has a great many of all three, with the shrine of Mawlay 'Abd al-Salam bin Mashish in the Bni 'Arus recognised as the most important of the first two categories (with seven pilgrimages to his shrine in seven successive years equalling, in the popular mind, one to Mecca) and the Awlad al-Baqqal, whose main *zawiya* is in the l-Ghzawa, as the major local representative of the third. In this same connection, a much later work, dating almost to the end of the protectorate, is Ramon Touceda Fontenla, *Los Heddaua de Beni Aros y Su Extraño Rito* (1955), about an itinerant order which was headquartered in the Bni 'Arus as well, not far from the shrine of Mawlay 'Abd al-Salam. It flourished up until the end of colonialism, but it was forcibly disbanded and liquidated at independence in 1956 by the Moroccan Army of Liberation, ostensibly, at least, because of the unappealing image projected by its members, who never bathed, dressed in rags, smoked *kif*, practised sodomy and were invariably surrounded by bands of hungry cats. However, it is unfortunate that Touceda's study did not get the attention it deserved because another, much longer book on just the same subject was published in French and in the same year by René Brunel, *Le Monachisme Errant dans l'Islam: Sidi Heddi et les Heddawa* (1955), for Heddawa adepts wandered far to the south in the French Zone, where they also had one or two daughter *zawiya*-s.

But probably the most important Spanish work on the ethnography of the Jbala was, despite its much more inclusive title, Valentin Beneitez Cantero, *Sociologia Marroqui* (1952). Cmdte. Beneitez was also the author of numerous articles, almost all on the Jbala, both in *Africa* and in the *Archivos del Instituto de Estudios Africanos*, but this book, which should have been entitled *Etnologia de Yebala*, was his major work. In it he pulled most of his material together, as is suggested by a listing of its table of contents: territory, population, languages and dialects, psychology (subheaded by 'Moroccan idiosyncrasies' and 'superstitions'), religion, law, education and instruction (for which cf. also Valderrama Martinez 1955), government, economy, corporations (by which is meant the urban craft guilds of Tetuan, much smaller than those of Fez, for instance, but almost as representative), arts, social life and rites, Jews and Evolution of Morocco (under Spanish tutelage, of course). The book was based upon a two-course manual of the same name, *Sociologia Marroqui*, brought out by the Instituto Hispano-Marroqui de Enseñanza Media of the Delegacion de Educacion y Cultura in Tetuan in 1949. It is totally descriptive and is designed as a handbook more than anything else, a compilation of factual materials unrelieved and uninfluenced by any particular frame of theory, and in it the account given of life in the Jbala is made to be read as the norm for the zone. It is to Beneitez' credit, however, that wherever and whenever the ethnography of other regions further east, the Ghmara, the Sinhaja Srir and, in particular, the Rif, shows significant divergences from that of the Jbala, these are generally indicated as such in the text. There is a bibliography which, except for Père Ange Koller, OFM, *Essai sur l'Esprit des Berbères Marocains*, 1949 (which had such an impact on the Spanish Zone that Padre Esteban Ibañez, also OFM, translated it into Spanish as *Los Bereberes Marroquies: Estudio Etnologico*, 1952), consists entirely of Spanish entries.

Yet although it is purely factual and reads rather woodenly, Beneitez' book manages at the same time to contain a great deal of background information that any incipient fieldworker in the region would still do well to assimilate. It contains, in addition, remarkably few factual errors that we could spot, even though, in our view, greater detail on a good many matters discussed in it would have been welcome, for in some respects the book seems little more than an outline (which is not surprising, given that its author's original intention was to provide a manual for the *cuerpo de intervenciones*). To revert again to Capdequi, Michaux-Bellaire and the *makhzan-siba* dichotomy, for example, Beneitez mentions this briefly on p.51 but then seems to assume that the reader knows all about it, for he dismisses it after defining only the former and not the latter category, about which he gives the earlier and highly erroneous impression on p.34 that it was built up over a vast surface area of the country as a whole, not just that of the northern Spanish protectorate, through a kind of generalised and ubiquitous *liff*-type network of factional alliance systems between tribes, much as if rural Morocco at large had been made up exclusively of Berber-speaking regions like the Rif and the Western High Atlas. This may not have been intentional, of course, but since Beneitez' book is both reliable and accurate on most matters of detail, it should therefore be said that he sometimes shows signs of missing the significance of the bigger picture. As noted, his work is definitely in the *Etnologia de Yebala* rather than in the overall *Sociologia Marroqui* mould, and as such and as a manual for the *intervenciones militares*, it should not be read prejoratively (even though it is now dated), its insights are few and its theoretical advances over Capdequi's work a quarter century earlier are virtually nil. For the Ghmara, the coastal neighbours of the Jbala to the east, there is the article by Caro Baroja (1957) already mentioned on history and tradition, a study by Carlos Pereda Roig (1939) on collective storehouses in the Bni Zjil, and an analysis of a *qanun* or customary law document by Manuel Llord O'Lawlor (1957).

Also worthy of mention is the valuable work of Muhammad ibn 'Azzuz Hakim on folklore, folktales, proverbs, popular poetry, maxims, etc., of the Jbala and the Ghmara regions (ibn 'Azzuz Hakim 1953, 1954*a*, 1954*b* 1955*a*, 1955*b*, 1958, 1959; and Gil and ibn 'Azzuz 1977) as well as on Moroccan history (ibn 'Azzuz 1949), while adequate overall accounts of the geography and history of the zone are covered by Cabello Alcaraz (1950–51, 1953). It may also be noted, if only in passing, that the history of the north-western Jbala during the whole first quarter of the present century is intimately bound up with the biography of one man, the *sharif* Mawlay Ahmad ar-Raysuni of the Bni 'Arus (circa. 1871–1925), who started life as a bandit and always remained one at heart, though he rose to warlord status and played an on-again, off-again game with Spain until his capture by his younger rival the Rifian leader bin 'Abd al-Krim, in 1924 and his death in one of the latter's jails early the following year (for details, cf. Hart 1976*a* pp.390–94; 1987 pp.19–26). In this connection it is worth citing not only Rosita Forbes' splendid biography *The Sultan of the Mountains* (1924) but also Tomas Garcia Figueras, *Del Marruecos Feudal: Episodios de la Vida del Cherif Raisuni* (1930), as well as a shorter study by the latter author of Raysuni's onetime lieutenant Hmidu l-Khriru, who went over to bin 'Abd al-Krim in 1924 and became instrumental in his former chief's capture the same year (Garcia Figueras 1953), and in a collective work by the Intervenciones Militares de la Region de Yebala Central, *Memoria Relativa* *a las Kabilas Que Integran Esta Regional* (1934), which is concerned with the tribes of the Anjra, Fahs of the Spanish Zone, Bni Msawwar, Jbil Habib, Bni Yidir, Bni Hassan, Bni Layit, Bni 'Arus, Bni Yisif, Bni Zakkar and Sumata, and which provides additional ethnographic and historical information on all of them.

We may now move on to the Rif, and here the Spanish name which stands out most clearly as a landmark for the ethnography of the region is unquestionably that of Col. Emilio Blanco Izaga (1892–1949). As we have already discussed Blanco's work, both published and unpublished, in considerable depth and detail in three previous publications of our own (Hart 1958; Hart and Blanco Izaga 1975 Vol. I pp.1–44, 1995 pp.25–62), the second and third of which are our own edited and annotated translation and a later Spanish rendition of all that he wrote (or of all that we could find in his papers) pertaining to 'traditional' precolonial Rifian sociopolitical structure, there is little point in giving it more than a cursory survey here. Although there is, to be sure, a certain amount of ethnographic work on the Rif by other Spanish investigators (as e.g. Sanchez Perez (1943) on the special Aith Waryaghar institution of women's markets; Martos de Castro (1946) on social structure; and Paniagua y Santos (1948, 1950) on certain features of customary law), and although some of this is certainly worthwhile (such as Rodriguez Padilla (1930) on religious orders, *shurfa'* and *zawiya*-s; Vidal (1945) on linguistics, which contains a detailed breakdown of the complex mixture of Arabic and Berber linguistic affiliations among the tribes of the Sinhaja Srir; an equally detailed study by Rodriguez Erola (1952) on the Shurfa' Khamalsha or Ikhamlishen of the same region; Ojeda del Rincon (1952) on the eastern Rifian trashumant tribes of the Ibdharsen or l-Mtalsa and the Aith/Bni Bu Yihyi; Sanchez Perez (1951) on cooperation in agricultural tasks; Benedicto Perez (1949) on Rifian labour migration in Algeria; and, finally, four articles in English, one by Vidal (1950) on religious orders in Moroccan politics, two by ourselves (Hart 1954; 1957) on an ethnographic survey of the Aith Waryaghar and on their annual pilgrimage to Sidi Bu Khiyar, and a third co-authored by us with Rodriguez Erola on Rifian Morals (Hart and Rodriguez Erola 1956), most of it pales into insignificance when compared to the quality of the output of Emilio Blanco.

Blanco's major published work on the Rif consists of three separate items: a treatise on the Rifian house, its furnishings and surroundings, and on Rifian settlements generally (*La Vivienda Rifeña*, 1930), which is beautifully illustrated with his own line drawings; a translation of and commentary upon a series of Rifian *qanun*-s or customary law documents (*El Rif*, 1939), which was to have formed the second volume of a two-volume study on Rifian customary law and of which only a part of the first volume had been completed at the time of his death and which is translated and annotated *in extenso* in our own compendium of his work (Hart and Blanco Izaga 1975); and a three-instalment study of Rifian dances and dance forms ('Las Danzas Rifeñas', 1946*a*), also illustrated with remarkable line drawings, for Blanco was a consummate artist as well as an extraordinarily perceptive ethnographer. This last work indeed goes beyond mere dance forms to become to some extent its author's interpretation of the whole Rifian ethos – an interpretation which, we might add, is nonetheless more esthetic than anthropological. The studies on the Rifian *qanun*-s and on the dance are both first-class, but it is the former in particular which, in our view, puts Blanco on the map as an ethnographer and which we now consider in somewhat more detail. Our observations, however, are limited only to the published 1939 study of the *qanun*-s and to Blanco's commentary on them, and do not include the whole previously unpublished corpus of his other work on the same and related subjects that we ourselves brought out in 1975 (Hart and Blanco Izaga 1975; 1995).

   Los Canones Rifeños Comentados has 15 chapters, of which the first is a general introduction, while three others are essays which, although they do not refer to any particular or specific *qanun*-s as documents, deal with fishing in the Bay of al-Husayma, with the division of irrigation water in the plain of the same name bordering this bay on the south and thus constituting the northern lowland neck of the tribal territory of the Aith Waryaghar, and with hunting and the division of spoils from the chase, spoils that normally involve only partridges and rabbits. The remaining 11 chapters consist of photocopies of original *qanun*-s in Arabic, the translations thereof (which Blanco notes in his preface to have been done not by him personally but by an official office interpreter, Juan Gomez Jaen), and Blanco's commentaries. Note for the record that although the customary law of Muslim communities, in contradistinction to the Shari'a, is generally conceived as being oral, or at least unwritten, there have, even among Moroccan Berber-speaking groups, been numerous individual exceptions to this rule; and it is with these exceptions (which constitute exceptions only because of their codification, so to speak) that Blanco's study is concerned. In terms of content, they are not exceptional at all: most *qanun*-s consist of lists of 'do nots', lists of varying lengths, of offences and of the punishments, usually given in terms of fines to be levied on the person of the offender by the tribal assembly or moot, which they incur. The *qanun*-s in Blanco's study fall fully into this category.

   Although two short earlier *qanun* documents concerning irrigation water are dated 1130 AH/1737 CE and 1250 AH/1835 CE respectively, and although one of the *qanun*-s pertaining to a local community (Thamasind, in the centre of the Aith Waryaghar tribal territory) is dated 1285/1868, most of the remainder are dated later, during the first two decades of the present century. They thus fall squarely into the time frame of 1898–1921 (bracketed in the first instance by Bushta l-Baghdadi's punitive expedition against the pirates of the Ibuqquyen or Buqquya/Baqqiwa and in the second by the beginning of the Rifian War) which Rifians refer to, possibly in retrospect, as the *Ripublik*. This period immediately predates that of Muhammad bin 'Abd al-Krim al-Khattabi and his 'Rifian Republican State' (which had no connection with the preceding dispensation of the *Ripublik*, despite the superficial similarity in nomenclature: cf. Hart 1976*b*), created as a wartime measure early in 1923 during the Rifian War of 1921–26 against first Spain and then France.

It was a period of upheaval and violence in Morocco generally, and one in which, in the Rif in particular, although colonialism had not yet been solidly implanted, its presence was nonetheless strongly felt and greatly detested. A violent resistance to it, which had already broken out on two previous occasions further east, in 1893 and in 1909–12, around Melilla and Nador, where Spanish occupation was more effective, was just around the corner in the mountainous back-country behind the Bay and Plain of al-Husayma – which did not itself come into being as a town until after the effective establishment of colonialism, when it became known as Villa Sanjurjo. As most or a large part of the back-country in question forms the tribal territory of the Aith Waryaghar, from whose ranks the Rifian resistance leader bin 'Abd al-Krim was soon to emerge, it is therefore highly appropriate that all but two of the *qanun*-s discussed by Blanco also emanated from and focus upon different sections of this very same tribe. They too all date from this immediate precolonial period of government by the *aitharbi'in* assemblies, of a network of factional *liff* alliances both within tribes and extending somewhat beyond individual tribal borders, of ferociously heavy feuding and vendetta, and of equally heavy fines (*haqq*) for murder or any other infractions if committed in the tribal *suq*-s or markets. This harsh atmosphere, which shows major institutional differences from that prevailing in the Jbala, is powerfully conveyed throughout Blanco's book, as is the intense and inner-directed life of the Rifian local community, as manifested in the Aith Waryaghar *qanun*-s of the *jma'ath* (pl. of *jma'th*, from Ar. *jama'a*, 'assembly') of Imhawren (undated), Thamasind (1285/1868) and Thazurakhth (1336/1918).

A few examples will suffice. In the *qanun* of the Aith 'Abdallah section, dated 1335/1917, it is stipulated that anyone who commits a murder in the market will be shot on the spot if he is caught; but if he has already fled as a fugitive seeking refuge in a neighbouring section or tribe (the usual course of action for homicides), he will be fined 2,000 duros hasani and his house will be burned down to its foundations by the council members. The same fine is to apply if he commits his murder on any path leading to or from the market either on market day (Tuesday, in this case), the one day of peace or truce during the week, or on either of the days immediately preceding or immediately following it (here, Monday and Wednesday); and if more than one person is involved in the murder, each one will be fined 2,000 duros. Woundings under the same circumstances are fined half this amount, only 1,000 duros. The *qanun* of the Aith 'Adhiya section, dated 1332/1914, is only slightly less severe: according to the recorded agreement made among the members of the eight local communities belonging to this section, an agreement further sanctified by the ritual slaughter of two bulls at the shrine of Sidi r-Hajj 'Amar in ar-Rabda, anyone who should commit a murder away from the market or not in front of witnesses must suffer both the burning of his own house and those of his agnatic lineage-mates, as well as the extraction of a 1,000 duro fine by the *aitharbi'in*, a fine which is doubled to 2,000 duros if the murder is committed in the market or in front of witnesses. The earlier *qanun* of the Aith Khattab, bin 'Abd al-Krim's own section and the origin of his *nisba* of al-Khattabi, which is dated 1325/1907, keeps the fine for murder in the market down to only 500 duros, so that between this date and that of the Aith 'Adhiya *qanun*, drawn up just before World War I began, the Rif may have experienced something of a currency inflation, an economic fact which represents one of the few contingencies not covered in Blanco's otherwise excellent commentary.

But Blanco's talents as an ethnographer probably reach their highpoint in his long chapter on the division of irrigation water from the Ghis and Nkur Rivers in the Plain of al-Husayma (Blanco Izaga 1939 pp.101–36; Hart and Blanco Izaga 1975 Vol. II pp.350–79, 1995 pp.379–421). This is a masterpiece of ethnographic analysis, particularly with respect to the intermittent and intercalated rights of one intrusive lineage, irrigating from a particular ditch emanating from the Ghis River, to the water which three other lineages, all from a different section, traditionally receive from the ditch in question: for the patterns by which the three resident lineage users make room for the intrusive group during periods of water scarcity are unfolded, step by intricate step, by Blanco with a very sure hand (Blanco Izaga 1939 pp.113–18; Hart and Blanco Izaga 1975 Vol. II pp.363–7, 1995 pp.399–409). This is as good in its way as his later description and discussion, in his study on the dance, both of the dances traditionally performed by unmarried girls, all of them veiled, among the Aith Waryaghar during the wedding season in late summer after the harvest has been brought in, and of the war dance of the *ibarudiyen*, traditionally performed on foot by two men from the same tribe, while brandishing and firing off their flintlock guns. This war dance was outlawed by bin 'Abd al-Krim as a wartime measure in order to save ammunition, and it was never resumed thereafter, for all firearms had to be turned over to the Spanish authorities once the Central Rif was effectively occupied (Blanco Izaga 1946a pp.547–51; cf. also Hart 1958 pp.228–37). In short, Col. Emilio Blanco Izaga was easily the best and most talented ethnographer produced by the Spanish colonial administration in northern Morocco.

As with the Jbala, however, we should still mention some of the more important Spanish sources on the history of the Rif. For the early Islamic period, Sanchez Perez (1952) should be consulted, as should the historically oriented tribal monographic studies by Ghirelli on the Axt/Bni Tuzin (1923), on the Ibuqquyen or Buqquya (1955) and on the Aith/Bni Yittuft (1956), as well as Vidal on the last-mentioned group (1947). For the late nineteenth and early twentieth centuries, two major sources are both contained in biographies of the Moroccan Rogi or Pretender Bu Hmara ('the man on the she-donkey') by, first, (Cmdte.) Luis Jimenez Benhamu (1949), in a long article, and secondly, and in book form, by (Col.) Eduardo Maldonado Vazquez, *El Rogui* (1952), whose two additional collections of essays published under a pseudonym, Et-Tabyi ('the artilleryman'), *Miscelanea Marroqui* (1953) and *Retazos de Historia Marroqui* (1955), are also worthy of consultation. Both of the Bu Hmara biographies are valuable, that by Maldonado in particular, because even though it is badly organised and written in a crabbed style, as well as not being organised into chapters and lacking an index, the book contains important information not to be found, to our knowledge, in any other published source. Bu Hmara's career began and ended in the first decade of the twentieth century, and it has recently been most succinctly summed up in two articles by Dunn (1980, 1981).

Although only a Jibli peasant or tribesman from Zarhun, Bu Hmara claimed as of 1902 to be, nonetheless, the eldest son of Sultan Mawlay al-Hasan I (1873–94), and as such he was able to gain a large following in the area around Taza in order to combat Mawlay 'Abd al-'Aziz, then on the throne in Fez. But before the latter was ousted by his own brother, Mawlay 'Abd al-Hafiz, in 1908, Bu Hmara, who through his connivance and anti-sultanic manoeuvres had gained financial and even some military support from both the future protectorate powers of France and Spain, had moved up to the Eastern Rif. There, in September of the same year and on the banks of the Nkur River, he was given a thorough trouncing by the Aith Waryaghar, who were for once on the side of the *makhzan* and who evidently recognised Bu Hmara for the fraud that he was. He wound up being captured back in the Jbala, his area of origin, by Mawlay 'Abd al-Hafiz the following year and then put in a cage to be fed to the latter's lions. In any event, what is of interest here is his vicissitudes in the Rif, which are gone into in detail both by Jimenez Benhamu and by Maldonado, and which are summarised as well in a major work of our own, one which devotes a whole chapter to the events that took place in the Rif during the *Ripublik* period (Hart 1976*a* pp.355–68).

For contemporary or near contemporary Spanish insights on bin 'Abd al-Krim and the Rifian War, the best and most inclusive overall account is easily that of (Gen.) Manuel Goded, *Marruecos: Las Etapas de la Pacificacion* (1932), but supplementary information can be found on bin 'Abd al-Krim and his treatment and the subsequent ransom of the numerous Spanish prisoners captured during the initial Rifian victories of 1921, in an early work by Andres Sanchez Perez (circa. 1931), then a captain, on the decisive action taken against bin 'Abd al-Krim toward the end of the war, and in a four-volume account, informative but not always reliable, by Hernandez Mir (1926–27) on 'From Disaster to Victory', as seen, of course, from the Spanish point of view, of which Tomas Garcia Figueras, in *Marruecos: La Accion de España en el Norte de Africa* (1955), among a legion of others, also provides an adequate summary. Sanchez Perez, who finally became a general, was also to provide two further articles on bin 'Abd al-Krim, each one at later stages in his career (Sanchez Perez 1950, 1973); and both of them contain valuable insights and information. However, we must note also, for the record,, that most of the scholarly output dealing with bin 'Abd al-Krim and the Rifian War only began to appear well after Moroccan independence, and that little if any of it was in Spanish: we need cite, in order of publication, only Woolman (1968), whose analysis of the Spanish military record is very good indeed, Bu 'Ayyashi's two volumes in Arabic (out of three projected, 1974) on the Rifian War of Liberation, by a former Aith Waryaghar *qadi*-turned-*qa'id* after independence, a 1973 colloquium in Paris on *Abd el-Krim et la République du Rif* (Hart 1976*b*), our own work on the Rifian leader within the sociopolitical context of his own Aith Waryaghar tribe (Hart 1976*a* pp.369–403), Germain Ayache's study of the origins of the Rifian War (1981), which culminates in the Rifian victory at Anwal in 1921, as well as his article on Rifian society and the Moroccan central government, 1850–1920 (Ayache 1983 pp.199–227), and finally Richard Pennell on *A Country With A Government And A Flag* (1986), which for a number of reasons not worthy of enumeration here we ourselves regard as the best single study of the Rifian War to date.

We close this account of colonial ethnography in the Spanish Protectorate of Northern Morocco, one which has had of necessity to take certain historical questions into consideration as well, with a commentary on one of the most ambitious and, in our view, least successful works which that protectorate produced: the three-volume study of Tomas Garcia Figueras and Rafael de Roda Jimenez on *Economia Social de Marruecos*

(1950–55). The quality of these three volumes runs in descending order: the first one seems to us to be the best, and the third the worst. Hence some explanation is in order. Garcia Figueras, who wrote voluminously and whose enormous and very valuable personal collection now forms the basis, as already noted, of the Seccion Africa y Mundo Arabe in the Biblioteca Nacional in Madrid, was at the time the Delegate of Native Affairs (*Delegado de Asuntos Indigenas*) in Tetuan, with a long background as an *interventor* in the Jbala, while de Roda Jimenez, as far as we can determine, had pretensions to being a sociologist. Volume I (1950) of their joint effort is in fact what Beneitez' *Sociologia Marroqui* (1952) should have been: an overall ethnographic coverage of the whole North Zone as it was at the time of publication, a few years after World War II. The coverage of both the Jbala and the Rif is good as well as even, and the work is copiously illustrated with well chosen photographs. There are detailed sections on natural and geographical factors, human factors, spiritual factors, social factors, political factors, property, work, production (not in any Marxist sense, but rural, industrial and commercial), historical factors and conditions of existence (subsuming standards of living); and each section has its own bibliography. It contains most of the detail of Beneitez' book, but is a more finished production analytically and makes for more interesting reading, probably because it is not designed as a manual. This is not to say that it is totally devoid of errors; but it still stands up on its own and is still worth consulting as a historical document.

Unfortunately the same cannot be said of Volumes II (1952) and III (1955) of the same work, both of which are devoted largely to notions of economic and political development which were still at best only in the planning stage when independence came to catch the authors short in 1956. They are pretentious in scope and execution, relying heavily on statistical tables which may well have been doctored as well as on largely extraneous exemplary material taken for the most part, of course, from peninsular Spain. They would have appeared pretentious even if they had appeared under the auspices of a protecting power such as France, which had put far more, both qualitatively and quantitatively, into the economic development of its much larger southern zone of Morocco than Spain had into the country's spiny northern ridge. In retrospect, given the minimal development of the Spanish Zone as a whole (for it had at best only 500 kilometres of paved roads throughout the whole of its territory at independence), these last two volumes are quite useless; and they detract from the undeniable value of the first one. It is saddening to have to render the verdict that under the Franco regime the development of Spanish ethnography and of anthropology and the social sciences in general in the North Zone of Morocco was quite on a par with its economic development, which is to say, with only a few exceptions, minimal if not virtually nil. It is with regret, too, that we have to note that those members of the Spanish military who practised this kind of amateur ethnography were blissfully unaware that a mere *aficionado* can seldom aspire to professionalism, especially when and if a whole range of what passes for monographic studies cannot get beyond the *usos, costumbres y supersticiones de la zona* stage. But then this was part and parcel of the paternalistic attitude that was such a hallmark of colonialism in general.

BIBLIOGRAPHY

Abd el-Krim et la République du Rif. Actes du Colloque International d'Etudes Historiques et Sociologiques, 18–20 Janvier 1973 (Paris: François Maspero 1976).

Albergoni, Giovanni, and François Pouillon, 'Le Fait Berbère et sa Lecture Coloniale', in Henri Moniot (ed.), *Le Mal de Voir.* Cahiers Jussieu 2, Collection 10/18 (Paris: Union Générale d'Edition, Université de Paris VII 1976) pp.349–96.

Ayache, Germain, *Les Origines de la Guerre du Rif* (Paris: Publications de la Sorbonne; Rabat: Société Marocaine d'Editeurs Reunis (SMER) 1981).

——, 'Société Rifaine et Pouvoir Central Marocain (1850–1920)', in idem, *Etudes d'Histoire Marocaine* (Rabat: SMER 1983) pp.199–227.

Benedicto Perez, Fernando, 'Trabajadores Rifenos en Argelia', *Conferencias Desarrolladas en la Academia de Interventores 1948* (Tetuan: Delegacion de Asuntos Indigenas 1949) pp.5–17.

Beneitez Cantero, (Col.) Valentin, *Sociologia Marroqui* (Ceuta: Imprenta Imperio 1952).

Bernaldo de Quiros, Constancio, and Luis Ardila, *El Bandolerismo Andaluz* (Madrid: Ediciones Turner 1978).

Bidwell, Robin, *Morocco Under Colonial Rule: French Administration of Tribal Areas, 1912–1956* (London: Frank Cass 1973).

Blanco Izaga, (Col.) Emilio, *La Vivienda Rifeña* (Ceuta: Imprenta Imperio 1930).

——, *El Rif (2a. Parte: La Ley Rifeña) – II – Los Canones Rifeños Comentados* (Ceuta: Imprenta Imperio 1939).

——, 'Las Danzas Rifeñas', *Africa* V/55, (Madrid 1946a) pp.315–16; V/56–7 (1946a) pp.414–19; V/59–60 (1946a) pp.547–51.

——, 'Politica Africana', *Cuadernos de Estudios Africanos* (Madrid: Instituto de Estudios Politicos I 1946b) pp.43–56.

Brunel, René, *Le Monachisme Errant dans l'Islam: Sidi Heddi et les Heddawa.* Publications de l'Institut des Hautes Etudes Marocaines XLVIII (Paris: Larose 1955).

al-Bu 'Ayyashi, Hajj Ahmad, *Harb ar-Rif at-Tahririyawa Marahil an-Nidal* (2 vols., Rabat: Privately Printed 1395/1975).

Cabello Alcaraz, (Cmdte.) José, *Apuntes de Geografia de Marruecos* (Tetuan: Editora Marroqui 1950–51).

——, *Historia de Marruecos* (Tetuan: Editorial Casado 1953).

Capdequi y Brieu, (Capt.) Mauricio, *Yebala: Apuntes sobre la Zona Occidental del Protectorado Marroqui Español* (Madrid: Editorial San Fernando 1923).

Caro Baroja, Julio, *Estudios Saharianos* (Madrid: CSIC/IDEA 1955; 2nd edn., Gijon: Jucar 1990).

——, 'Una Encuesta en Gomara: Historia y Tradicion', in idem, *Estudios Mogrebies* (Madrid: CSIC/IDEA 1957) pp.123–51.

Coon, Carleton S., *Tribes of the Rif.* Harvard African Studies IX (Cambridge MA: Peabody Museum 1931).

——, *Flesh of the Wild Ox: A Riffian Chronicle of High Valleys and Long Rifles* (New York: William Morrow 1932).

——, *The Riffian* (Boston: Little, Brown 1933).

——, *The Races of Europe* (New York: Macmillan 1939).

——, *Caravan: The Story of the Middle East* (2nd revsd. edn., New York: Holt, Rinehart and Winston 1962).

de Mas, Paolo, *Marges Marocaines: Limites de la Coopération au Developpement dans une Région Périphérique – le Cas du Rif* (The Hague: NUFFIC/IMWOO/Projet REMPLOD 1978).

——, Pascon, Paul, and Herman van der Wusten, *A Balance of Curses and Blessings: Government Policy and Development in Beni Bou Frah* (Sociaal-Geographisch Instituut, Universiteit van Amsterdam, Paper No.1, 1981).

Dunn, Ross E., 'Bu Himara's European Connexions: The Commercial Relations of a Moroccan Warlord', *Journal of African History* XXI (1980) pp.235–53.

——, 'The Bu Himara Rebellion in Northeast Morocco: Phase I', *Middle Eastern Studies* XVII/1 (1981) pp.31–48.

Fogg, Walter, 'A Tribal Market in the Spanish Zone of Morocco', *Africa* XI/4 (London 1938) pp.428–45.

——, 'Villages, Tribal Markets and Towns: Some Considerations Regarding Urban Development in the Spanish and International Zones of Morocco', *Sociological Review* XXXII (1940) pp.85–107.

——, 'The Organization of a Moroccan Tribal Market', *American Anthropologist*, n.s., 44/1 (1942) pp.47–61.

Forbes, Rosita, *The Sultan of the Mountains: The Life Story of Raisuli* (New York: Henry Holt 1924).

Garcia Figueras, Tomas, *Del Marruecos Feudal: Episodios de la Vida del Cherif Raisuni* (Madrid, Barcelona and Buenos Aires: Compania Ibero-Americana de Publicaciones 1930).

——, 'Un Cabecilla de Yebala: Ahmed ben Mohammed el Hozmari (a) El Jeriro', in idem, *Miscelanea de Estudios Varios sobre Marruecos*, Vol. III (Tetuan: Editora Marroqui 1953) pp.73–118.

——, *Marruecos: La Accion de España en el Norte de Africa* (4th edn., Tetuan: Editora Marroqui 1955).

——, *España y Su Protectorado en Marruecos (1912–1956)* (Madrid: CSIC/IDEA 1957).

——, and Rafael de Roda Jimenez, *Economia Social de Marruecos* (3 vols., Madrid: CSIC/IDEA 1950–55).

Ghirelli, Angelo, *Monografia de la Kabila de Beni Tuzin* (Madrid 1923).

——, 'Monografia de la Cabila de Bokoia', *Archivos del Instituto de Estudios Africanos* VIII/32 (1955) pp.27–83.

——, 'Apuntes sobre la Cabila de Beni Iteft', *Archivos del Instituto de Estudios Africanos* IX (1956) pp.7–56.

Gil Grimau, Rodolfo, and Muhammad ibn 'Azzuz Hakim, *Que Por la Rosa Corrio Mi Sangre* (Madrid: Instituto Hispano-Arabe de Cultura 1977).

Gil Ruiz, Severiano, *Prisioneros en el Rif* (Melilla: Marfe 1990).

Goded, (Gen.) Manuel, *Marruecos: Las Etapas de la Pacificacion* (Madrid, Barcelona and Buenos Aires: Compañia Ibero-Americana de Publicaciones 1932).

Hart, David M., 'An Ethnographic Survey of the Rifian Tribe of Aith Waryaghar', *Tamuda, Revista de Investigaciones Marroquies* II/1 (Tetuan 1954) pp.51–86; republished in Hart and Blanco Izaga (below) Vol. I, pp.45–95.

——, 'An *'Imarah* in the Central Rif: The Annual Pilgrimage to Sidi Bu Khiyar', *Tamuda* V/2 (1957) pp.239–45.

——, 'Emilio Blanco Izaga and the Berbers of the Central Rif', *Tamuda* VI/2 (1958) pp.171–237.

——, *The Aith Waryaghar of the Central Rif: An Ethnography and History*. Viking Fund Publications in Anthropology No.55 (Tucson: University of Arizona Press 1976a).

——, 'De *Ripublik* à République: Les Institutions Sociopolitiques Rifaines et les Réformes d'Abd el-Krim', in *Abd el-Krim et la Republique du Rif*, Actes du Colloque International d'Etudes Historiques et Sociologiques, 18–20 Janvier 1973 (Paris: François Maspero 1976b) pp.33–45.

——, *Banditry in Islam: Case Studies from Morocco, Algeria and the Pakistan North-West*

Frontier. MENAS Studies in Continuity and Change (Wisbech, Cambridgeshire: MENAS Press 1987).
—— (ed.), and Blanco Izaga, *Emilio Blanco Izaga: Colonel in the Rif* (transl.). Ethnography Series, HRAfLEX Books MX3-001 (2 vols., New Haven: Human Relations Area Files 1975).
—— (ed.), and Blanco Izaga, *Emilio Blanco Izaga: Coronel en el Rif*, Biblioteca de Melilla No.8 (Melilla: Ayuntamiento de Melilla, Fundacion Municipal Sociocultural, y UNED-Centro Asociado de Melilla 1995).
——, and José R. Erola, 'Rifian Morals', in Vergilius Ferm (ed.), *Encyclopedia of Morals* (New York: Philosophical Library 1956) pp.481–90.
Hatim, Rabia, 'Marruecos, Mito y Realidad: El Oriente y el Rif', in Victor Morales Lezcano (ed.), *Africanismo y Orientalismo Español.* In *Awraq: Estudios sobre el Mundo Arabe e Islamico Contemporaneo*, Anejo al Volumen XI (Madrid: Instituto de Cooperacion con el Mundo Arabe 1990) pp.131–48.
Heinemeijer, W.F., van Amersfoort, J.M.M., Ettema, W., de Mas, P., and van der Wusten, H.H., *Partir Pour Rester: Incidences d'Emigration Ouvrière à la Campagne Marocaine.* Institut Socio-Géographique de l'Université d'Amsterdam, Publication No.2 (Amsterdam: IMWOO/NUFFIC/Projets REMPLOD 1977).
Hernandez Mir, F., *Del Desastre a la Victoria (1921–1926)* (4 vols., Madrid: Fernando Fe 1926–27).
Houroro, Faouzi M., *Sociologie Politique Coloniale au Maroc: Cas de Michaux-Bellaire* (Casablanca: Afrique Orient 1988).
ibn 'Azzuz Hakim, Muhammad, *Epitome de Historia de Marruecos* (Madrid: Instituto de Estudios Politicos 1949).
——, *Glosario de Mil Quinientas Voces Españoles Usadas entre los Marroquies en el Arabe Vulgar (Ensayo)* (Madrid: Consejo Superior de Investigaciones Cientificas (CSIC)/Instituto de Estudios Africanos (IDEA) 1953).
——, *Refranero Marroqui*, tomo I (Madrid: CSIC/IDEA 1954*a*).
——, 'Refranero Agricola de Gumara', *Cuadernos de Estudios Africanos* 28 (1954*b*) pp.65–8.
——, *Cuentos Populares Marroquies*, tomo I: *Cuentos de Animales* (Madrid: CSIC/IDEA 1955*a*).
——, *Pensamientos y Maximas de Sidi Abdurrahman el Maxdub* (Madrid: CSIC/IDEA 1955*b*).
——, *Diccionario de Supersticiones y Mitos Marroquies* (Madrid: CVSIC/IDEA 1 1958).
——, *Folklore Infantil de Gumara el Haila* (Madrid: CSIC/IDEA 1959).
——, 'Leyendas y Tradiciones de Gumara', *Archivos del Instituto de Estudios Africanos* XIV/53 (1960) pp.41–84.
Intervenciones Militares de la Region de Yebala Central, *Memoria Relativa a las Kabilas Que Integran Esta Regional* (Tetuan: Casa Gomariz 1934).
Jamous, Raymond, *Honneur et Baraka: Les Structures Sociales Traditionnelles dans le Rif* (Cambridge: Cambridge University Press; Paris: Editions de la Maison des Sciences de l'Homme 1981).
Jimenez Benhamu, (Col.) Luis, 'Bu Hamara', *Conferencias Desarrolladas en la Academia de Interventores durante el Curso de 1948* (Tetuan: Delegacion de Asuntos Indigenas 1949) pp.157–215.
Joseph, Roger, and Terri Brint Joseph, *The Rose and the Thorn: Semiotic Structures in Morocco* (Tucson: University of Arizona Press 1987).
Koller, Padre Angel, OFM, *Los Bereberes Marroquies: Estudio Etnologico* (transl. by Padre Esteban Ibañez, OFM (Tetuan: Instituto General Franco/Editora Marroqui 1952).
Laarbi, Ali Mohamed, 'Contribucion para la Comprehension del Africanismo Español', *Aldaba* VIII/15 (Melilla 1990) pp.83–8.
Lobera Girela, (Capt.) Candido, *Memoria sobre la Organizacion y Funcionamiento de las Oficinas de Asuntos Arabes en Argelia: Proyecto de Bases para la Creacion de Organismos Analogos en las Plazas en el Norte de Africa* (Melilla: Tipografia 'El Telegrama del Rif' 1905).
Lopez Garcia, Bernabe, 'Arabismo y Orientalismo en Espana: Radiografia y Diagnostico de un Gremio Escaso y Apartizado', in MORALES LEZCANO, Victor, Ed., *Africanismo y*

Orientalismo Español, in Awraq: Estudios sobre el Mundo Arabe e Islamico Contemporaneo, Anejo al Volumen XI, Marid: Instituto de Cooperacion con el Mundo Arabe, 1990: 35–69.

Llord O'Lawlor, Manuel, 'Un Canon Bereber Tripartito', *Tamuda* V/2 (1957) pp.305–9.

Maldonado Vazquez, (Col.) Eduardo, *El Rogui* (Ceuta: Imprenta Imperio circa. 1952).

—— (pseud. Et-Tabyi), *Miscelanea Marroqui* (Tetuan: Editora Marroqui 1953).

—— (pseud. Et-Tabyi), *Retazos de Historia Marroqui* (Tetuan: Instituto General Franco/Editora Marroqui 1955).

——, 'Constantes Norteafricanos', *Archivos del Instituto de Estudios Africanos* XVI/61 (1962) pp.47–62.

Martos de Castro, José, 'Lo Bereber en Marruecos y Sus Relaciones con lo Ibero', in Alta Comisaria de España en Marruecos, *Labor de España en Africa* (Barcelona 1946) pp.309–33.

Michaux-Bellaire, Edouard, *Quelques Tribus de Montagne de la Region du Habt*, in *Archives Marocaines* XVII (Paris: Honoré Champion 1911).

Mikesell, Marvin W., 'The Role of Tribal Markets in Morocco: Examples from the "Northern Zone"', *Geographical Review* 48 (1958) pp.494–511.

——, *Northern Morocco: A Cultural Geography*. University of California Publications in Geography Vol. 14 (Berkeley and Los Angeles: University of California Press 1961).

Montagne, Robert, *Les Berbères et le Makhzen dans le Sud du Maroc: Essai sur la Transformation Politique des Berbères Sédentaires (Groupe Chleuh)* (Paris: Felix Alcan 1930).

——, *La Vie Sociale et Politique des Berbères* (Paris: Editions du Comité de l'Afrique Française 1931).

——, *The Berbers: Their Social and Political Organization* (translated with introduction by David Seddon, London: Frank Cass 1973).

——, *Regards sur le Maroc: Actualité de Robert Montagne*, Cinquantenaire du CHEAM (1936–86) (Paris: Centre des Hautes Etudes sur l'Afrique et l'Asie Moderne, 1986).

Monteil, Vincent, *Maroc*. Collection 'Petite Planete' (Paris: Editions du Seuil 1962).

Morales Lezcano, Victor, *Espana y el Norte de Africa: El Protectorado de Marruecos (1912–1956)* (Madrid: Universidad Nacional de Educacion a Distancia 1984).

—— (ed.), *Africanismo y orientalismo Espanol*, in *Awraq: Estudios sobre el Mundo Arabe e Islamico Contemporaneo*. Anejo al Volumen XI (Madrid: Instituto de Cooperacion con el Mundo Arabe 1990).

Ojeda del Rincon, José, 'Las Tribus Nomadas de Beni Buiahi y Metalza', *Seleccion de Conferencias y Trabajos Realizados durante el Curso de Interventores 1951–1952* (Tetuan: Delegacion de Asuntos Indigenas 1952) pp.85–112.

——, *La Kabila de Beni Tuzin: Estudio Economico-Social*, ms. (1954).

Paniagua y Santos, José Maria, 'Notas sobre el Derecho Consuetudinario de la Propiedad en el Rif', *Archivos del Instituto de Estudios Africanos* IV (1948) pp.7–44.

——, *La Prescripcion y el Retracto en el Derecho Consuetudinario del Rif* (Madrid: CSIC/IDEA 1950).

Pascon, Paul, and Herman van der Wusten, *Les Beni Bou Frah: Essai d'Ecologie Sociale d'une Vallée Rifaine (Maroc)* (Rabat: Institut Universitaire de la Recherche Scientifique (IURS0), and Institut Agronomique et Veterinaire Hassan II (INAV); Amsterdam: Faculté de Géographie Sociale de l'Université d'Amsterdam 1983).

Pennell, C.R., *A Country with a Government and a Flag: The Rif War in Morocco, 1921–1926* (Wisbech, Cambridgeshire: MENAS Press 1986).

Pereda Roig, Carlos, *Los Horreos Colectivos de Beni Sech-yel* (Ceuta: Imprenta Imperio 1939).

Pouillon, François, 'Du Savoir Malgré Tout: La Connaissance Coloniale de l'Extreme-Sud Tunisien', in Jean-Claude Vatin (ed.), *Connaissances du Maghreb: Sciences Sociales et Colonisation* (Paris: Editions du Centre National de la Recherche Scientifique (CNRS) 1984) pp.79–93.

Rodriguez Aguilera, Cesareo, *Manual de Derecho de Marruecos* (Barcelona: Bosch 1952).

Rodriguez Erola, (Capt.) José, 'Los Chorfa Ajamelichen', *Seleccion de Conferencias y Trabajos Realizados durante el Curso de Interventores 1951–1952* (Tetuan: Delegacion de Asuntios

Indigenas 1952) pp.49–84.

——, *El Caidato del Alto Guis (Beni Urriaguel): Estudio Economico-Social*, ms. (1953).

Rodriguez Padilla, Isaias, *Cofradias Religiosas en el Rif y Diversas Taifas de Xorfas, Zauias y Santuarios* (Ceuta: Imprenta Imperio 1930).

Ruiz Orsatti, Ricardo, 'La Kabila de Uadras', *Boletin Oficial de la Zona de Influencia Española en Marruecos*, 10–25 May 1913.

Sanchez Perez, (Capt.) Andres, *La Accion Decisiva Contra Abd el-Krim* (Toledo: Sebastian Rodriguez circa. 1931).

——, (Cmdte.), 'Zocos de Mujeres en Beni Urriaguel', *Africa* (Madrid, May 1943) pp.22–3.

——, (Lt.-Col.), 'Abd-el-Krim'. *Seleccion de Conferencias y Trabajos Realizados por la Academia de Interventores durante el Curso 1949–1950* (Tetuan: Delegacion de Asuntos Indigenas 1950) pp.59–76.

——, (Lt.-Col.), 'Aprovechamientos Comunales y Formas de Cooperacion en el Rif', *Seleccion de Conferencias Pronunciadas en la Academia de Interventores durante el Curso 1950–1951* (Tetuan: Delegacion de Asuntos Indigenas 1951) pp.95–104.

——, (Col.), 'Datos Historicos sobre Ciudades Rifeñas', *Seleccion de Conferencias y Trabajos Realizados durante el Curso de Interventores 1951–1952* (Tetuan: Delegacion de Asuntos Indigenas 1952) pp.29–47.

——, (Gen.), 'Abdelkrim', *Revista de Historia Militar* XVII/34 (Madrid 1973) pp.123–57.

Seddon, David, *Moroccan Peasants: A Century of Change in the Eastern Rif, 1870–1970* (Folkestone, Kent: Dawson 1981).

Touceda Fontenla, Ramon, *Los Heddaua de Beni Aros y Su Extraño Rito* (Tetuan: Instituto General Franco/Editora Marroqui 1955).

Uriarte, (Cmdte.), *Cofradias Religiosas en Yebala y Diversas Taifas de Xorfas, Zauias y Santuarios* (Ceuta: Imprenta Imperio 1930).

Valderrama Martinez, Fernando, *Manual del Maestro Español en la Escuela Marroqui* (Tetuan: Editora Marroqui 1955).

Vidal, F.S., 'Ensayo sobre Linguistica en el Rif Occidental', *Africa* 46–7 (Madrid, Oct.–Nov. 1945) pp.32–7.

——, 'Breve Historia de la Kabila de Beni Itteft', *Africa* 61–2 (Madrid 1947) pp.49–54; 66–7 (1947) pp.32–9.

——, 'Religious Brotherhoods in Moroccan Politics', *Middle East Journal* IV/4 (1950) pp.427–46.

Woolman, David S., *Rebels in the Rif: Abd el-Krim and the Rif Rebellion* (Stanford: Stanford University Press 1968).

Origin Myths, Autochthonous and 'Stranger' Elements in Lineage and Community Formation, and the Question of Onomastic Recurrences in the Moroccan Rif

Despite the accent which Bedouin Arabs, for example, have always placed upon genealogy and patrilineal descent, the great majority of tribal groups in Morocco (and probably in most of the rest of north-west Africa), whether Arabic- or Berber-speaking, are composite and thus heterogeneous in origin, as Pascon, for example, has noted (Pascon 1971, 1978). By this is meant that in terms of their own traditions or myths (and between these two concepts, for present purposes, no distinction seems necessary), either the tribes themselves as wholes or simply some of their component sections or segments see themselves as having come from somewhere else. Note at the outset that one striking exception to this rule, one that we have examined elsewhere in considerable detail, is that of the Ait 'Atta, Berber-speakers in the south-centre of the country; but despite their vigorous insistence on descent from their ancestor Dadda ('Grandfather') 'Atta, their eponymous ancestor in the patriline who lived in the late sixteenth century, the Ait 'Atta are unable to demonstrate such descent on a step-by-step genealogical basis. Hence, despite its vigour, it must remain only an asseveration. But few if any other Moroccan tribes, or at least tribes made up solely of lay members, can make such a claim, for long and recitable genealogies, committed to memory, are both the prerogative and the stock-in-trade of holy lineages, those consisting of *shurfa'* (sing. *sharif*) or descendants of the Prophet, whose abundance in the country far exceeds (or has in the past far exceeded) the demand. Such asseverations, and the reasons for them, will be discussed in this article where relevant. Such is not at all the case for the much shorter genealogies of lay tribesmen, which even among the Ait 'Atta do not go above four ascending generations from the speaker, and always in the patriline (Hart 1981, 1984).

Although in the Rif, the northern mountain chain bordering Morocco's Mediterranean coast, the lineage depth of lay tribesmen runs from four to seven ascending generations, it must be said that, unlike among the Ait 'Atta, holy lineages or even whole tribal sections into which they may have grown also became integral members, or member units, of the lay tribes into which they were incorporated: for every Rifian tribe has a large number of 'stranger' elements of which these holy lineages form an often quite significant part. Indeed, in three out of the six cases discussed here, the stranger elements show themselves to have higher percentages than the local or autochthonous ones, whereas among the Ait 'Atta and other southern transhumant Berber tribes, holy lineages tend to be interstitial in a territorial sense in that they are located at the borders between lay tribes and do not form integrated parts of the latter. In addition, the southern transhumant tribes tend to have clearer, or at least less confused, origin myths, probably because most of them are considerably more recent in historical time.

As Coon pointed out, and correctly, in our view, over 60 years ago, such lack of clarity in itself indicates antiquity (Coon 1931 p.19). As we shall show, he was sometimes wrong in detail, but his grasp of the overall Rifian picture in this respect was sound. Each tribe was composite, with a greater or lesser number of elements of 'stranger' accretion, but each also had a well-defined local and autochthonous core. Note also that these tribes are unquestionably among the oldest in the country: the names of at least three of them, Thimsaman (Timsaman), Aith Waryaghar (Bni Waryaghal) and Igzinnayen (Gzinnaya), are associated with the Salihid kingdom of the Nakur (710–1084 CE), held to be of Yemeni origin, which preceded even the Idrisids of Fez. Thus this association is with the earliest beginnings of Islam in Morocco. The Thimsaman were allegedly the earliest tribe in the Nakur region, but as the south-eastern gate of this little kingdom's capital, the Madinat al-Nakur, was known as the *Bab Bani Waryaghal*, we also have here an unmistakable identification with the Aith Waryaghar. As the construction of the city, which was destroyed by the Almoravids somewhat over three centuries later, was evidently completed about 760, it may be inferred that the gate in question, and hence the tribal name it bears, dated to about the same time. These two names, as well as those of the Igzinnayen and the Marnisa (the latter no longer a Rifian-speaking tribe today), are all to be found in al-Bakri's eleventh century *Description of North Africa* in association with the Salihid dynasty, whose rulers probably regarded them as 'the barbarians at the gates' (cf. Hart 1976 pp.343–7).

The early and medieval Arab historians, however, are not of great assistance when it comes to identifying the Rifian tribes, and indeed there is a major contradiction in the *Kitab al-'Ibar* of ibn Khaldun – translated by de Slane as *Histoire des Berbères et des Dynasties Musulmanes de l'Afrique Septentrionale* (ibn Khaldoun 1925–56) – over the identification and origins of both the Aith Waryaghar and the Igzinnayen (or Bani Waryaghal and Gzinnaya). In one context they are listed as descendants of Mklata ibn Ittuwaft ibn Nafzaw of the Butr line of Berber tribes (ibid. Vol. I p.227) and in another they – or at least the Aith Waryaghar, the Ibuqquyen and the Thafarsith – are listed as Sinhaja 'of the third race' and hence as stemming from the line of Branis as opposed to that of Butr (ibid. Vol. II p.123).

Moreau, for example, lists the full genealogy given by ibn Khaldun for the descendants of Nafzawa as providing the core groups of the Nafzawa of southern Tunisia – amongst whom the Rifians of the Aith Waryaghar and the Igzinnayen are, perhaps unwittingly, included (Moreau 1947 p.76; Hart 1976 p.237 n.1).

In a later context ibn Khaldun also mentions the Aith Waryaghar (Bani Waryaghal) as Sinhaja inhabiting the region of Bijaya in eastern Algeria (ibn Khaldoun 1925–56 Vol. II p.56) – which at least is somewhat closer to the Moroccan Rif than is southern Tunisia. It is only when he mentions them along with the Ibuqquyen, as noted above, that he gets the locations of the Madinat al-Nakur and its port al-Muzimma correctly. But the Ibuqquyen are here shown as inhabiting the environs of Taza, whereas in fact and today they border the Aith Waryaghar on the north-west, while the Axt Tuzin (or Bni Tuzin) are held to be Zanatan and hence more recent, descended from the Bani Tujin of the central Maghrib (Western Algeria), who contributed to the formation of the Marinid dynasty (656–869 H/1258–1465 CE). Hence we can see that the arguments of Gautier and his successors about Berber origins are largely predicated upon the alleged and almost certainly mythical opposition between the Butr and the Branis groups as postulated by al-Bakri and, following him, by ibn Khaldun. This bears as little relevance to explaining the distribution of Berber dialect groups today as does the 'three-ring circus' of Masmuda, Sinhaja and Zanata to which it was claimed to have given rise. The latter was also a pseudo-explanation for a problem which cannot be solved adequately in genealogical terms and which will probably remain conjectural in any case (Hart 1982). The whole exercise, in fact, seems like an attempt to simplify or even to cover up the very real and very tangled complexities of Rifian origins as seen by Rifians themselves.

Such a verdict may also be extended to the mythical war between the Sinhaja and the Ghumara in northern Morocco. Both these groups, significantly, have present-day namesakes, which are nonetheless much reduced in size and are located west of the Rif. As Coon, Montagne and others have noted, all the tribes of northern Morocco are held to have joined in this fight, on one side or the other (Coon 1931 pp.17–18; Montagne 1930, map facing p.208). According to Coon's Sinhaja and Ghmara informants, the whole world, indeed, took part, and in the small Sinhajan tribe of Taghzut he himself was asked which side the Americans were on (Coon 1931 p.17). He concludes that it was the presence of both the Aith Waryaghar and the Igzinnayen on the Sinhajan side that allegedly won the war for them (ibid. p.18). Strikingly, however, there was no reference to this mythical war on the part of his Rifian informants, while our own informants from just the same area a quarter century later were totally unaware of it. A case of negative evidence, one might say.

Finally, it is worth mentioning that there are two further traditions of a more generalised nature. The first of these, faint but still present in the Central Rif, relates to the alleged onetime occupation of the region by the Swasa, or Susis, of south-western Morocco, who then departed from it, as Coon noted in greater detail both for the Ghmara and the Sinhaja Srir to the west of the Rif properly speaking. His informants also mentioned the desert region of Sagiyat al-Hamra in the Western Sahara as well as the Sus as having been a point of origin of these people. This particular tradition is also discussed in still further detail by Pascon and van der Wusten for the Bni Bu Frah of the Western Rif (Coon 1931 pp.16–17; Pascon and van der Wusten 1983 pp.55–60). The second and considerably more widespread tradition relates to the later occupation of the area by the 'Portuguese', about whom our own Rifian informants said that their ancestors chased them out of the region with sickles, given the historical fact that they did not yet have guns at the time. Such folk memories of a mythical Portuguese occupation, relating to the initial invasions of the country in the fifteenth and sixteenth centuries by a foreign and Christian enemy, appear frequently in Berber-speaking regions of Morocco such as the Rif and the Central Atlas (Hart 1976 p.343; Gellner 1969 p.175 n.1), in areas precisely where the real Portuguese, whose enclaves were confined entirely to the Moroccan Atlantic coast, never in fact set foot, while those of a previous Susi (and Muslim) occupation seem confined to the north. This is almost certainly because the real Portuguese occupation of the coast produced far more concern and ferment in the Moroccan hinterland.

This said, we may now begin our own exercise by citing the percentages of autochthonous, local and home-grown lineage groups as opposed to those of 'stranger' lineage groups from anywhere outside, even though 'outside' may only mean, in certain contexts, from a neighbouring or nearby Rifian tribe. Our original calculations were that for the Ibuqquyen, this figure is 42 per cent; for the Aith 'Ammarth, the lowest of the lot, it is only 31 per cent (and in any case their name means 'people of the filling-up'); for the Igzinnayen, only 32 per cent; for the Axt Tuzin, 55 per cent; for the Aith Waryaghar, 58 per cent; and for the Thimsaman, 78 per cent (Hart 1976 pp.235–6). This gives an average of 49 per cent of autochthonous lineages for the region as a whole. More recently, however, we have been able to emend the Igzinnayen figure upwards to 47 per cent, thus giving an overall regional average of 52 per cent (Hart, in preparation). We now discuss each case individually, commenting on those of the Aith 'Ammarth, Igzinnayen and Aith Waryaghar in more detail than the others simply because we were able to obtain more in-depth information on them while in the field. Individual origin traditions within each tribe (Rif. dhaqbitsh (pl. dhiqba'ir), from Ar. qabila) will be considered below in terms of its constituent sections (*rba'* (pl. *r-urbu'*), or *khums* (pl. *khmas*)) and of the local communities (*dshar* (pl. *r-udhshur*)) and/or lineage groups (*dharfiqth* (pl. *dharfiqin*)) within these, particularly in instances where the ones may differ from the others.

Ibuqquyen (Ar. Buqquya or Baqqiwa)

For the Ibuqquyen, the *ex post facto* folk etymology of the tribal name as derived from Moroccan Arabic *baqi wahid* ('still one left') may be completely discounted. An alleged linkage of the name Ibuqquyen with that of another Rifian lineage, the Ibittuyen, to be found both among the Aith Sa'id (or Bni Sa'id) of the eastern Rif and among the Aith Waryaghar, seems scarcely less dubious, because of the obvious difference in their consonantal roots, and this despite the fact that ibn Khaldun would have us believe that the former were a branch of the latter (1925–56 Vol. III p.123).

The Ibuqquyen have three sections, Izimmuren (lit. 'wild olive trees'), Azghar and Thaghidhith, all of which are place names. The oldest lineage groups in the tribe are held to be the Aith 'Aru Hmid (Ait 'Ali u-Ahmad), the Aith r-Qadi and the Ibannudhen of the Izimmuren section and the I'araben, the Aith Tizi Maya, and the I'athmanen of that of Azghar, with the ancestors of the last two said to have come from the Sus. Curiously enough, these oldest lineages remained neutral and aloof in all intra-tribal conflicts which were to follow. One lineage in the Aith Tizi Maya, the Iharwash, is held to have had 'Portuguese' ancestry. But a principal founder-genitor of the Izimmuren section came in later, from the Yinn Sa'id Ikhrif (or Ulad Sa'id Ikhlif) section of the Aith 'Ammarth (a tradition which is given in precisely the reverse direction in the latter tribe), and established himself in the community of Tafinsa, where he had three sons, Hammu, Rahmun and Ziyyan. The second son, Rahmun, was the ancestor of the Irahmunen lineage of Tafinsa, but the other two sons moved further afield: Hammu to Isummar to father the Aith Hammu, and Ziyyan to Tawrirth u-Fuith to engender the Aith Ziyyan. The Aith u-Fulayin are descended from a stepson of the original founder from the Aith 'Ammarth. Apart from these, one stranger lineage in Igar 'Ayyash of the Izimmuren section is that of the Idsuliyen, whose ancestor came from the Dsul tribe in the south-eastern Jbala, while two more in Tawssarth (lit. 'old woman') in the same section are those of the I'abbuthen from the lineage of the same name in the Thimsaman and the Ishshuyen from the Bni Gmil tribe in the western Rif. The whole of the Thaghidhith section is made up of descendants of the Imrabdhen n-Ibubakriyen of I'adduz, who were its first settlers.

Aith 'Ammarth (Ar. Bni 'Ammart)

The land now inhabited by the Aith 'Ammarth was held to have been originally empty. Two saints, Sidi 'Abdallah and Sidi 'Ari n-Dawud (Sidi 'Ali bin Dawud), came there and wanted to settle with their families, but each one wanted the other out of the way. Sidi 'Abdallah brought in sheep to eat the grass, so Sidi 'Ari n-Dawud brought in jackals to hunt the sheep. Hence Sidi 'Abdallah angrily brought in slougis to hunt the jackals. But when they finally decided to abandon the territory, other people from all over the Rif began to filter in and settle. Thus the Aith 'Ammarth got their name, 'people of the filling-up'. Sidi 'Abdallah is buried beside the Monday Market (Suq ath-Thnayn) of the Aith 'Ammarth and Sidi 'Ari n-Dawud is buried in the neighbouring Arabic-speaking and Jbalan territory of the Marnisa.

The Aith 'Ammarth are made up of four sections, the Yinn Sa'id Ikhrif (or Ulad Sa'id Ikhlif), Aith r-Hsayn (or Ulad l-Hsayn), Ija'unen (or Ja'una) and Aith 'Abbu (or Ulad 'Abbu), and one account of the 'filling-up' process runs as follows: in the Yinn Sa'id Ikhrif section – descended, it appears, from two entirely unrelated individuals, Sa'id and Ikhrif, the second of whom left no descendants but the first of whom did, in the community of Buhuth – most of Buhuth is held to have come from Tawssarth in the Ibuqquyen (in the reverse of the Ibuqquyen tradition of Aith 'Ammarth origin, above), Iznagen (unidentified) is said to have come from the Iqar'ayen in the eastern Rif, the communities of Aith Mikhfadh, Sammar and Khazziyath are all from the Branis in the south-eastern Jbala, that of Ijwawen (from possibly the same root as Zwawa and/or Igawawen, the generic term for the Kabyles of the Algerian Jurjura?) is held to have come from the Bni Zarwal in the southern Jbala, while the people of Aghir Hmid (who are mistakenly identified by Coon as 'eastern Arabophone Sinhaja': cf. 1931 p.19) may have come from the Ulad Stut, intrusive Arabs in the eastern Rif.

In the Aith r-Hsayn section, the Isiqqimen lineage is said to have come from the Aith Dris lineage of the Aith 'Abdallah (or Bni 'Abdallah) section of the Aith Waryaghar by way of the Ija'unen section, while the bulk of the communities of Tainast, Agnis and Aith Finathen are descended from two brothers, Yusif u-Sa'id and Hammu u-Sa'id, who came from the Sagiyat al-Hamra in the western Sahara to found the lineages of the Aith Yusif u-Sa'id and Aith Hammu u-Sa'id, which bear their names.

In the Aith Dris subsection of the Ija'unen section, the communities of Ujdiya, r-Quddjth (Ar. Qulla) and parts of those of Arma Ibawen (lit. 'beanfield') and Taghzuth are all from the Aith Dris subsection of the Aith 'Abdallah section of the Aith Waryaghar, while part of the community of

Ufis is from Tufist in the Aith Yittuft and that of Yanith from the Branis; the rest of it, along with the rest of that of Arma Ibawen, is from the Ulad Dris near Fez. In the Aith Ma'sum subsection of the Ija'unen section, part of the community of I'ashban is held to have come from that of Tamjund in the Asht 'Asim section of the Igzinnayen and the people of Sidi Bushta are both from the Sagiyat al-Hamra and from the Bni Zarwal, while those of the rest of I'ashban, Taghzuth, Tamshtt (lit. 'comb') and Aith Ma'dh are held to have come from the Branis.

Finally, in the Aith 'Abbu section, the people of the community of Aith Hmid, as well as parts of those of Thazruth, Aghir Bandu and Ibuyibbughen, are also held to have come from the Branis; one lineage in the community of Aith Msitha, the I'allaliyen, is from the Igzinnayen, while an unnamed ancestress of another, the Ikibdhanen, is held to have come from the tribe of that name in the eastern Rif. In another community, Thazruth, in the same section, two further lineages show complementary filiation from the Aith Waryaghar: Dharwa n-Twaryaghatsh ('sons of the Aith Waryaghar woman'), whose mother came from the Aith Tihar lineage in the community of Tfsast of the Timarzga section, and Aith Tamkhrufth, whose mother came from the community of Aith Bu Khrif (Bni Bu Khlef) in the Aith Bu 'Ayyash section – although Coon is correct in saying that a large part of the community of Aghir Bandu, also in the Aith 'Abbu section, is descended from a purely local individual named Bandu, although the latter's descendants would probably not like to think of him as having been a heathen. Other than this, most of the remaining traditions he gives for the Aith 'Ammarth appear to be mistaken in detail (Coon 1931 p.19).

Finally, there are four lineages of *shurfa'* in the Aith 'Ammarth: those of the Zawith Ughir Hmid from the Marnisa; the Shurfa' Iharramen from Mawlay 'Abd al-Salam bin Mashish in the Bni 'Arus of the north-western Jbala; a branch of the Shurfa' Ikhamlishen from the Zarqat tribe in the Sinhaja Srir; and a branch of the Shurfa' Ibaqqaliyen from the l-Ghzawa tribe in the Jbala.

Igzinnayen (Ar. Gzinnaya)

The etymology of the tribal name Igzinnayen is held to be derived from *izinnayen* ('libertines, fornicators'). The Igzinnayen, like certain other Berber groups in south-eastern Morocco, are also considered locally to be Dharwa n-Jallut ('sons of Goliath'), and are hence jokingly referred to by their northern neighbours of the Aith Waryaghar as *r-'adhawth n-Sidna Dawud* ('the enemy of our lord David'). They have six sections: the Asht 'Asim (or Bni 'Asim), the Asht 'Aru 'Aisa (i.e. Ait 'Ali w-'Aisa or Ulad 'Ali bin 'Aisa), the Asht Yunis (or Bni Yunis), the Asht Mhand (or Bni

Mhammad), the Imzdurar (lit. 'mountaineers') and the I'utawiyen or Asht r-Udha (or Ulad l-Uta, lit. 'plainsmen').

In the Asht 'Asim section, all the lineages of the community of Ikhuwanen (lit. 'thieves'), barring those of Hibir and of Iznagen/Iznayen (of which name more is said later), are held to be brothers. It may not be out of place to note, moreover, that among the Aith Turirth of the Aith Waryaghar it is said that the ancestor of the Ikhuwanen was killed in their territory, in Bulma. His wife escaped and went back to Ikhuwanen, where she remarried a man of the Ibinyusifen lineage, the founding one of the community; and hence people referring jokingly to the Ikhuwanen say that they had no grandfather and that the Ibinyusifen ancestor was a thief who stole their grandmother, and therefore the name. Two later lineages, the Yinn Si Mhand and the Yinn Mhand w-'Amar (the latter of which was to produce the Hajj Biqqish, an unsuccessful rival of bin 'Abd al-Krim in the Rifian War against Spain and France, 1921–26), are held to be descended from Sidi 'Abdallah al-Khulali al-Wazzani who came most probably from Tamda in the Aith Siddat tribe of the Sinhaja Srir (and not, again, from the 'eastern Arabophone Sinhaja', as Coon has it: cf. 1931 p.19). In the community of Iharrushen, as Coon has correctly noted, the lineages of the Asht 'Abd r-Mumin and the Asht Tadmuth as well as those of the communities of Iqarru'an and Asht Fars are all descended from brothers who came into the Igzinnayen from the east, through the Aith Bu Yihyi (ibid.). Again in Iharrushen, the lineages of Thariwin claim to have come from the Aith 'Aru Musa (i.e. Ait 'Ali u-Musa) subsection of the Aith 'Abdallah section of the Aith Waryaghar (ibid.), while precisely the reverse claim is made by the latter. Still in Iharrushen, the lineages of Thirmist and r-Mquddam n-Sidi Musa claim to have come from the community of Aith Msitha in the Aith 'Abbu section of the Aith 'Ammarth, while the I'aisathen of Tharusht, on Coon's evidence, again (ibid. p.19), say they came from the community of Aghir Hmid in the Yinn Sa'id Ikhrif section of the same tribe. In the community of Tamjund, only the Imrabdhen lineage, from the community of Aith 'Aziz in the Imrabdhen section of the Aith Waryaghar, represents a stranger accretion; all others, both there and in the community of Buridh, are local and autochthonous.

The section of the Asht 'Aru Aisa is entirely made up of Idrisid *shurfa'*, of the line of the Dharwa n-Sidi Hand u-Musa, descended from Sidi Musa bin Mashish, the brother of the great saint Mawlay 'Abd al-Salam bin Mashish (d. 1227–28 CE) and buried beside him in the Bni 'Arus tribe of the Jbala.

The Asht Yunis section is also largely made up of stranger lineages: the Asht Uzru, in the community of Azru (lit. 'rock', but referring here to the mountain of Azru Aqshar, 'bald rock', at 2,010 metres the highest in the

Central Rif), are regarded as Andalusiyin, or descendants of Muslims who had to leave southern Spain after 1492; the Asht Tghirasth (lit. 'people of the she-panther') are considered to be descendants of Sidi Ya'qub al-Badisi, buried in Badis on the Bni Bu Frah coast in the western Rif; the Ihadriyen are from the Jbarna, in the Igzinnayen lowlands; the Asht r-'Arqub/'Aqub are descended either from Sidi 'Azzuz or Sidi r-'Arqub/r-'Aqub, buried in Taza; the Ikhabbaben are from the Bni Khalid section of the Branis; and the Asht Hazim are from the Ulad Bu Hazim section of the Aith Iznasen near Oujda.

The whole Asht Mhand section is held to have come from the Jbil Sidi Sa'id in the Ibdharsen (Ar. l-Mtalsa) in the eastern Rif.

There are evidently fewer stranger lineages in the Imzdurar section. The Asht Marar (Malal) are descended from Sidi 'Athman from 'Ayn Zuhra in the Ibdharsen (l-Mtalsa); the Inhanahan are local except for two lineages in the communities of Thighambuyin and Iharshriyen which are descended, respectively, from a Sidi Hmid, buried in Thighambuyin, and from a descendant of Mawlay Idris, the founder of Fez; while Thara Tazzugwakhth (Ar. 'Ayn Hamra, lit. 'red spring') is entirely local and autochthonous.

In the I'utawiyen section, the Ishawiyen are held to be descended from Abu 'Amama, the *basha* of the Igzinnayen during the Marinid period and a member of the Rashidiyin lineage of the Imrabdhen n-Iya'gubiyen; the Dharwa Haddu derive from the Dharwa 'Abdallah w-'Assu section of the Aith Bu Yihyi in the eastern Rif; the Swiyah or Suyah Rashidiyin are Idrisid *shurfa'*, as are the Imrabdhen n-Wawizaghth; while the Jbarna are partly from the Imzdurar section (Hart and Blanco Izaga 1975 Vol. I p.141) and partly composed of recent arrivals from the Branis (Coon 1931 p.19). The rest are local and autochthonous.

Axt Tuzin (Ar. Bni Tuzin)

The Axt Tuzin have five sections: the Igharbiyen (lit. 'Westerners' or 'Moroccan Arabs'), the Axt Bir'aiz (or Bni Bil'aiz), the Axt 'Akki (or Bni 'Akki), the Axt Ta'ban (or Bni Ta'ban) and the Axt Tsafth (lit. 'people of the holly oak'). Except for one autochthonous lineage, the Axt Maqrin, the Igharbiyen section is considered to have come from Fez. The Axt Bir'aiz section is entirely local and autochthonous except for one lineage of Idrisid *shurfa'*, the Axt Sidi Bu Jiddayn. In the Axt 'Akki section, all lineages are autochthonous and local; and it may not be entirely accidental that this section is the one held to have produced the various low status occupational groups for which the Axt Tuzin as a whole are well known, such as the *imziren* (blacksmiths) and the *imdhyazen* (musicians) who double as mule and donkey breeders. The Axt Ta'ban section is also entirely local and autochthonous, and it evidently gave rise to the Aith Ta'ban section in the Thimsaman tribe as well. The ancestors of the Axt Tsafth section, however, are held to have come from Tlemcen in western Algeria and may possibly correlate with the 'Zanatan' Bani Tujin of ibn Khaldun.

The following lineages of Idrisid *shurfa'* in the Axt Tuzin should also be noted: the Dharwa nj-Hajj 'Ari, whose *zawiya* is in the Axt Tsafth section; the Dharwa n-Si 'Ari t-Tuzani, whose ancestor is buried in Taza and which produced Sidi Muhammad Bu Jiddayn, himself buried in the Axt Bir'aiz section; and the Dharwa n-Sidi Yihya, who are to be found both in the Igharbiyen section and in that of the Axt Tsafth and who are from the Bni Ukil near Oujda.

Thimsaman (Ar. Timsaman)

The Thimsaman have five sections: the Aith Marghanin (or Bni Marghanin), the Aith Ta'ban (or Bni Ta'ban), the Rba' r-Fuqani, the Aith Bu Idir (or Bni Bu Idir) and the Truguth. Of these, all the constituent lineages of the Aith Marghanin section are local and autochthonous. Conversely, all those of the Aith Ta'ban section are descended from the Axt Ta'ban section of the Axt Tuzin, as noted above. In the Rba' r-Fuqani section, all lineages, again, are local and autochthonous save the Idrisid *shurfa'* of the Aith Sidi Bu Ya'qub, the Aith 'Azza, who are held to have come from the Aith Iznasen, and the Ushshannen (lit. 'jackals', with reference to a wily and crafty ancestor) of Amzawru, who are partly from the Aith Iznasen, again, and partly from the Axt Tuzin. In the Aith Bu Idir section, only the *shurfa'* of the Aith Zawith n-Tighza are of the Wazzaniyin branch of the Idrisids; while all other lineages are local and autochthonous. The same is true of the Truguth section: only the Imrabdhen n-Bu Zwiqa are *shurfa'* of the Baqqaliyin branch of the Idrisids, and all other lineages are local and autochthonous.

Aith Waryaghar (Ar. Bni Waryaghal)

Most of our informants had no idea of the exact meaning of the tribal name *Waryaghar*, but all were agreed that it refers to three specific points (or possibly only one, if all three are fused in local recollection) in the mountain massif of the Jbil Hmam (Mor. Ar., lit. 'mountain of doves') in the southern bulge of the tribal territory, held by all to be the tribal cradle or point of origin. Its highest peak, the Adhrar n-Sidi Bu Khiyar (lit. 'mountain of Sidi Bu Khiyar'), where the tribe's patron saint Sidi Bu Khiyar is buried, is some 1948 metres, and is located near the community of Bu Ma'dan in the territory of the Timarzga section. The three points in question are

Dhawragh/Thawragh, between the communities of Isrihan in the Aith Yusif w-'Ari (Ait Yusuf w-'Ali) section and r-Maqsuridh in that of the Timarzga; Iwraghen, near the community of Aith Yusif in the Timarzga; and Adhrar u-Waryaghar in the section of the Aith 'Arus. It may be worth noting that *awragh* is the generalised Berber term for 'yellow', which is possibly tied in with the popular and long-held, although totally erroneous, local belief that the Jbil Hmam was a source of gold and silver – and hence the name Bu Ma'dan, 'place of mines' (Hart 1976 p.239).

Two further traditions indicate that the Jbil Hmam was inhabited prior to its first Aith Waryaghar occupants. The first specifies once again that these original inhabitants were Susis, who left much buried treasure there (and the association of Susis or Swasa with buried treasures is an integral piece of Moroccan folklore generally) and who were chased out by a fearful seven-day fog, recalling a similar myth also noted above. The second specifies that the Susis were chased out by people called Imarzgiwen (lit. 'bitter, hard people'), who were ancestral, in part at least, to the Timarzga section also alluded to above. After this, a man named 'Ari ('Ali) from the Ibdharsen (Ar. l-Mtalsa) in the eastern Rif came to live with the Imarzgiwen, where he married a young widow. This woman had already had a son, named 'Ayyashi, by her first husband, thus accounting for the Aith Waryaghar section name of the Aith Bu 'Ayyash (Bni Bu 'Ayyash); and now, by 'Ari, she subsequently had three more sons, Yusif, 'Ari and 'Abdallah, hence accounting for three more Aith Waryaghar section names, those of the Aith Yusif w-'Ari (Ait Yusuf w-'Ali), Aith 'Ari (Ait 'Ali) and Aith 'Abdallah (Bni 'Abdallah).

We have noted elsewhere (ibid. p.240) that although this tradition makes no mention of an ancestor for the Aith Hadhifa section or for their 'brothers' of the Aith 'Arus, it does establish the fact that the Aith Yusif w-'Ari and the Aith 'Ari (w-'Ari, implied) are 'brother' sections. It also includes the Aith 'Abdallah with them and stresses that they are closer kin to each other than they are to the Aith Bu 'Ayyash. The latter, in turn, according to another tradition, are 'brothers' of the Aith Hadhifa and the Aith 'Arus in the Jbil Hmam, while the Aith Turirth (lit. 'people of the hill') and Timarzga sections are held to be 'brothers' and allies of the Aith Yusif w-'Ari and the Aith 'Ari, respectively. Both of these last two sections are located further north, in the plain of al-Husayma, where they border each other and were traditionally hostile to each other, a hostility dating from a quarrel between the two brothers Yusif w-'Ari and 'Ari w-'Ari said to have arisen after one of them cut the head of the other while shaving it. The sections of the Aith Yusif w-'Ari, Aith 'Ari, Aith 'Abdallah, Aith Turirth and Timarzga all came to be known collectively as the Aith Khattab – hence the name of the Rifian resistance leader Muhammad bin 'Abd al-Krim al-Khattabi, who came from the lowland community of Ajdir in the Aith Yusif w-'Ari, the name of which is itself derived from another point in the Jbil Hmam known as Thajdirth, in Isrihan in the highland Aith Yusif w-'Ari. The sections of the Aith Bu 'Ayyash, Aith Hadhifa and Aith 'Arus correspondingly came to be lumped collectively under the name Aith Bu 'Ayyash (ibid. pp.240–41). The intrusive section of Idrisid *shurfa'* known as the Imrabdhen presumably only came in after their ancestor Sidi Ibrahim al-A'raj ('the Lame'), the first of his line in Aith Waryaghar territory, died and was buried in Fez, presumably at some point between 1284–85 and 1322 CE (ibid. p.257 n.40).

Several further traditions also underscore the Jbil Hmam as the original home of the Aith Waryaghar, as well as emphasising the fact of lineage accretion and of the beginnings of occupation of the lower lands to the north. One of these has it that six individuals, all ancestral to communities or lineages currently located in the lowlands, moved into Aith Waryaghar territory from the south, probably from the Igzinnayen, and then bought land further north. These men were 'Abd r-Mumin, the ancestor of the Dharwa 'Abd r-Mumin lineage of the Aith Ughir Izan subsection of the Aith Yusif w-'Ari, located in the community of Aith Hishim; Ashshuyi or Ishshu, the ancestor of the Ishshuyen lineage in the community of Ikattshumen (or Ikultumen), in the Isrihan subsection of the Aith Yusif w-'Ari; Amzuri or Amzur, who gave his name to the present community of Imzuren, which is mixed in terms of sectional affiliation but which has elements from at least three sections, the Aith Yusif w-'Ari, the Aith 'Ari and the Imrabdhen; Amhawr, the ancestor of the Imhawren subsection of the Aith 'Ari; Aqamrawi, who gave his name to the present community of Aith Qamra, in which Imrabdhen elements predominate but which also contains Aith Yusif w-'Ari and Aith 'Ari lineages; and Am'aru, the ancestor of the Im'arwen lineage of the Aith Ughir Izan subsection of the Aith Yusif w-'Ari, but located discontinuously both in Isrihan, the other subsection of the Aith Yusif w-'Ari, and in Tafrasth of the Aith 'Ari.

All of these men are said both to have inherited land in the mountains and to have bought additional land in the vicinity of the plain of al-Husayma. The people of Ikattshumen alluded to above settled the original community of this name in the northern foothills of the Jbil Hmam; this community became known as Upper Ikattshumen when some of them moved north to become reduplicated in Lower Ikattshumen. The same happened with Thajdirth in the Jbil Hmam (where the oldest known Aith Yusif w-'Ari lineage is that of the I'arrasen) and Ajdir, though the latter, bordering the Bay of al-Husayma, soon became bigger than the former. It also happened with the Aith Mhand u-Yihya, also of the Aith Yusif w-'Ari, who also have terriorially discontinuous highland and lowland communities. This is additionally true of both the Aith Bu Minqad and

Iswiqen communities of the Aith 'Ari section, of the Izakiren and Ighmiren communities of that of the Aith Bu 'Ayyash, while a segment of the Aith Ufaran lineage of the Aith Turirth section, which is still located integrally in the Jbil Hmam, scissioned off to settle further north in Tazurakhth in the Aith Bu 'Ayyash. Finally, the Aith 'Abdallah and Aith Hadhifa sections also both lived formerly only in the Jbil Hmam, and when the former moved north-west, they purchased all of their land west of the Ghis River from the Aith Yittuft (or Bni Yittuft). One reason for all this movement, even though it never went beyond a radius of 60–70 square kilometres, was of course natural increase, but another and possibly more compelling one was that of individuals who were exiled as a result of bloodfeuds at home, for, as we have shown elsewhere, the rates of both the bloodfeud and the vendetta were higher among the Aith Waryaghar than anywhere else in precolonial Morocco (ibid. pp.313–38; 1989; in preparation).

There are, however, additional origin myths which attribute the ancestorship of the different Aith Waryaghar sections to various companions of the Prophet, and these can almost certainly be dismissed out of hand. They include the claim of the Aith Khattab to descent from the second of the 'rightly guided' caliphs of Islam after the Prophet's death, 'Umar ibn al-Khattab (634–44 CE), that of the Aith 'Abdallah to descent from Sidi 'Abdallah ibn Ja'far, that of the Aith Hadhifa to descent from Sidi Hudhayfa al-Yamani and that of the Aith Bu 'Ayyash to descent from an almost certainly apocryphal Sidi Ku'aish. The same is also almost certainly true for the Amrabit Bu M'awiya, whose name recalls that of Mu'awiya ibn Abi Sufyan (661–80 CE), the first caliph of the Umayyad dynasty in Damascus, and who is often credited with the ancestry of the sections of both the Aith Turirth and the Timarzga (Hart 1976 pp.238–41). These represent attempts, frequent in Berber history, to manufacture an illustrious Arab ancestry out of whole cloth. Nonetheless, the members of the Imrabdhen section, quite unlike those of any of the lay sections of the tribe, are able to document, and fully, their own descent as Idrisid *shurfa'* from the Prophet's daughter on a step-by-step genealogical basis (ibid. pp.256–60,481–97). However, the Aith 'Arus, regarded by their neighbours in the Jbil Hmam as the hardest headed and most feud- and vendetta-addicted of all the Aith Waryaghar sections, are jokingly regarded as *ayyawen n-trumith* ('grandchildren of the Christian woman'), a nickname which infuriates them. Although they may claim a very distant kinship with the Bni 'Arus of the north-western Jbala, they are never allowed to go there on pain of death, for one tradition has it that their ancestor is also held to have murdered the leading saint of the region and one of the leading saints of Morocco generally, Mawlay 'Abd al-Salam bin Mashish, who is buried in the Bni 'Arus (ibid. p.238 n.10).

For the Aith Waryaghar, we can provide statistics for local and autochthonous lineages as opposed to accreted stranger lineages for each section and subsection: (1) for the Aith Yusif w-'Ari section, the Aith Ighir Izan subsection is 69 per cent local, that of the Isrihan is only 34 per cent local, while that of the Aith Turirth is 65 per cent local, giving an overall sectional average of 56 per cent; (2) for the Aith 'Ari section, the Tigarth subsection is 73 per cent local, the Imhawren subsection is 50 per cent local, the Aith r-'Abbas subsection is also 50 per cent local and the Timarzga subsection is 100 per cent local, giving an overall sectional average of 68 per cent; (3) for the Aith 'Abdallah section, the Aith 'Aru Musa subsection is 60 per cent local and that of the Aith Tmajurth is 71 per cent local, giving a sectional average of 66 per cent; (4) for the Aith Bu 'Ayyash section, the 'true' Aith Bu 'Ayyash subsection (comprising the communities of Izakiren at nil per cent local, Aith Tfarwin at 96 per cent local, Isufiyen and Aith Ta'a at 60 per cent local, and Aith Bu Khrif at only 22 per cent local) shows an average of 45 per cent local lineages, while that of the Aith 'Adhiya (comprising the communities of Aith Bu Qiyadhen at 89 per cent local, ar-Rabdha at 78 per cent local, Ighmiren at 35 per cent local, Imnudh at only 11 per cent local and Tazurakhth at 31 per cent local) shows an average of 41 per cent local lineages, thus giving an overall sectional average of 43 per cent for localised lineages; (5) for the Aith Hadhifa section, the Aith Bu Jdat subsection shows no less than 100 per cent localised lineages, while that of Iraqraqen (lit. 'frogs') shows one of 98 per cent, giving an overall sectional average of 99 per cent; (6) the Aith 'Arus section shows localised lineages as constituting 98 per cent of their own total and the small I'akkiyen section again shows 100 per cent for the same, thus providing an average of 99 per cent; and (7) the Imrabdhen section, consisting entirely of intrusive Idrisid *shurfa'*, shows, not surprisingly, nil per cent of localised lineages. These figures place the tribal average as a whole at 58–59 per cent, and thus the 'stranger' accretions at 41–42 per cent, as already noted (ibid. pp.236–7, Table 10.1).

We now consider the origin traditions of individual lineages, section by section, in order to distinguish further the autochthonous lineages from the accreted stranger ones. In the Aith Ughir Izan section of the Aith Yusif w-'Ari, the Aith Ujdir ('people of Ajdir', of whom the oldest lineage is that of the Aith 'Aru 'Aisa), the Isifsafen/Izifzafen and the Aith Buham all originated in Tawragh and in Isrihan w-Udhrar in the Jbil Hmam, as did the originating lineages of both the Aith Mhand u-Yihya and the Ikattshumen. A variant tradition, however, has it that the Aith Mhand u-Yihya went to the Jbil Hmam from their earliest home among the Ulad 'Azzam (in the Bni Qurra of the Sinhajat l-Uta or Arabophone Sinhaja) along the Wargha River. In Aghridh, in the northern Jbil Hmam foothills, one lineage, the Isikkaken, is from the Thimsaman, a second, the Iznagen, is from the Axt Tuzin (as is the lineage of the same name in the Aith Turirth, about which we shall have more to say later), and a third, the Aith Sa'id, is from the tribe of that name in the eastern Rif, from whence the Im'arwen in Tafrasth of the Aith 'Ari section may also have come. In the Isrihan section, and in the community of Lower Isrihan, the Aith r-Ahsin lineage is from the Aith 'Ammarth, while the Imjjawiyen lineage is from the Amjjaw section in, once again, the eastern Rifian tribe of the Aith Sa'id, while in Upper Isrihan, where the founder lineage is that of the Aith Yikhrif w-'Amar, only the Ighmaden lineage is external, descended from *imziren* (blacksmiths) from the Axt Tuzin. In Upper Ikattshumen, the Aith Mahsin lineage is also from the Axt Tuzin, while that of the Ishshuyen is held to be made up of Aith Ya'ra (Ar. Bani Ya'la), descendants of the Bani Marin.

In the Aith Turirth section, the founding lineages are the Aith Yikhrif u-'Amar of the Aith Ughzar (lit. 'people of the river', referring to the Nakur; whether this particular lineage group of Aith Yikhrif w-'Amar is the same as that of the Upper Isrihan, mentioned in connection with the Aith Yusif w-'Ari section, is not certain, but seems likely); the Aith Mhand u-Sa'id in Ignan; the Yinn Hand w-'Abdallah in Bulma; and the Aith 'Amar in Thizimmurin. In Aith 'Aru Musa, again, further autochthonous lineages include the 'true' Aith 'Aru Musa and the Dharwa n-'Ari Muhand Uqshar (whose grandfather must have suffered from favus, and hence his nickname *aqshar*), while the Aith Yikhrif u-Hand in l-Wad, the Aith Uswir in Aswil, the Aith Ufaran in Tufatsh and the Ihammuthen in Aith 'Aru Musa are also autochthonous (ibid. pp.270–74). But there are a number of stranger lineages as well: the Aith Hand u-Misa'ud, from the Aith 'Ammarth; the Aith r-'Arqub, in the community of Habbu, from Asht r-'Arqub in the Asht Yunis section of the Igzinnayen; the Iznagen and the Ihawtshen, both in the community of Thigzirin, from the Axt Tuzin by way of the Igzinnayen in the first instance and from the Axt 'Akki section of the Axt Tuzin directly in the second; and finally the Imjjat, in l-'Ass, a direct case of scission on the part of an individual escaping the consequences of a mid-nineteenth century killing in Hibir in the Asht 'Asim section of the Igzinnayen (for details, cf. ibid. pp.329–38). Further additional information on the multiple onomastic recurrences of the lineage names both of the Imjjat and of the Iznagen are detailed in the final sections of this article.

In the Tigarth subsection of the Aith 'Ari section, the lineages of the Aith Musa u-Hmid, Iyihyathen and Aith r-'Arbi are all from the Aith Sidar (Bni Sidal) tribe of the Iqar'ayen (Qal'aya) confederacy in the eastern Rif, while that of the Imjjudhen is evidently derived, again, from the Imjjat lineage of Hibir in the Asht 'Asim section of the Igzinnayen. The other Aith 'Ari subsections, as well as the section of the Timarzga, are composed almost entirely of local and autochthonous lineage groups.

In the Aith 'Aru Musa subsection of the Aith 'Abdallah, the community of Thariwin (lit. 'springs') is, mirror-image-wise, held to have come from Thariwin in Iharrushen of the Asht 'Asim section of the Igzinnayen (where, as noted above, just the opposite tradition prevails); and this classificatory 'brotherhood' between the two Thariwin-s was invoked late in 1955 when those from Iharrushen sent their wives and children to stay with those in the Aith 'Abdallah during the campaign of the Moroccan Army of Liberation against the French in the Igzinnayen. Other stranger lineages in the Thariwin vicinity include, in the community of Awthib, the Aith 'Amar from the Bni Ulid in the Wargha region, and the Aith r-Ahsin from the Axt Tuzin; in that of Thamugzind, the Aith Si 'Abdssram z-Zarhuni from I'adduz in the Ibuqquyen, and the Yinn Hammush w-'Aisa from Maya in the Ibuqquyen; in Thafarishth, the Dharwa Umrabit Haddu from the Imrabdhen n-Kammun, of the Imrabdhen section of the Aith Waryaghar, the Dharwa 'Abdallah Abdars from the Ibdharsen (l- Mtalsa) and the Aith "Amarush n-Murud, *imziren* from the Axt Tuzin; in Aith Sa'id, the Aith 'Ari nj-Ahsin, also *imziren* from the Axt Tuzin, the Aith Hmid l-Ghurfi from the Bni Wanjal in the Wargha region, and the Ibarda'iwen (lit. 'pack-saddlers') from the Amjjaw or Imjjawiyen section of the Aith Sa'id in the eastern Rif; in Iqanniyen (lit. 'rabbits'), the Aith Si Hmid Iqanniyen from the Imrabdhen n-Zawith n-Sidi Yusif of the Imrabdhen section of the Aith Waryaghar, the Aith Sha'ib u-l-Muluk from the Imrabdhen n-I'athmanen (again of the Imrabdhen section), and the Aith Tahtah from the Axt Tuzin. The Aith Zkri are 'brothers' of the Izikrithen lineage in the Asht 'Asim section of the Igzinnayen.

There are fewer stranger lineages in the other Aith 'Abdallah subsection, that of the Aith Tmajurth: in Aith Musa, the Aith Ya'qub are from the Aith 'Ammarth, and in Bu Khalifa there are two lineages from the Bni Khalid and Bni Rzin tribes of the Ghmara.

In the Aith 'Adhiya subsection of the Aith Bu 'Ayyash, in the community of Ighmiren, the lineages of the Aith Fars and the Aith Tizi are both Aith Ya'ra, supposedly descended from the Bani Marin; that of the Ishtiben is from the Ghmaran tribe of Bni Silman; and that of the Imziren, the oldest in the community, is held to be from the Sinhaja. In the community of ar-Rabdha, only the Ihamdiwen lineage is from the Imrabdhen n-Aith 'Aziz of the Imrabdhen section of the Aith Waryaghar; all the rest are local. In the community of Igar w-Anu (lit. 'the field of the well'), the people of Aghzar Imziren ('river of blacksmiths') are from the Aith Sidar tribe of the Iqar'ayen, and all other lineages there save one are from the Aith Bu Ifrur tribe in the same confederacy. The exception is the lineage of the Dharwa nj-Hajj bin Dirha, from the Yinn Bu Qabut lineage in the community of Bu Sa'ida in the section of the Aith 'Arus. In the community of Imnudh, the Aith Umnudh, or Dharwa n-Talib 'Amar, are Ibaqqaliyen *shurfa'* descended from Sidi r-Hajj Yusif, who is buried in Imnudh. In the same community, the Aith Kharbush lineage of the Aith Ishshu are from the Ibdharsen (or l-Mtalsa) in the eastern Rif; the Isi'arithen (also of the Aith Ishshu) are descendants of the Aith Ya'ra or Bani Marin; the Aith Fir'awn are *shurfa'* from Asht r-'Arqub in the Asht Yunis section of the Igzinnayen; and the Ighmiren n-w-Udhrar ('Mountain Ighmiren'), although evidently the originating lineage of the community of Ighmiren, give their point of origin as the Bni Silman in the Ghmara. In the community of Thazurakhth, the Aith Tizi Marda lineage is from the Aith Sa'id in the eastern Rif, the Aith Tihar from the Timarzga section of the Aith Waryaghar, and the Aith Ufaran, as noted, from that of the Aith Turirth. In the same community, the Aith 'Aisa w-Anu lineage is from Aith 'Amar u-Sa'id in the Aith Hadhifa section, as is that of the Aith Injin (Hart and Blanco Izaga 1975 Vol. I pp.134–5).

In the 'true' Aith Bu 'Ayyash subsection of the Aith Bu 'Ayyash, in the community of Izakiren, the Aith 'Alla lineage is from the Aith Bu Ifrur of the Iqar'ayen; the Aith Tigrin lineage from the Axt Tuzin; the Ihaddjiyen lineage from the Aith Tmayith section of the Aith Sa'id (Eastern Rif); that of the Aith Bu Srama (Bu Slama) either from the Aith Bu Ifrur or the Ibdharsen; and the Itukuken ('cuckoos') from the Aith Bu Ifrur. All the lineages in the community of Aith Tfarwin (lit. 'people of the plough handles'), on the other hand, are completely local and autochthonous. In the community of Iriyanen, the Izakiren u-Sasnu are from the Ibdharsen. In the community of Isufiyen, the Ihaqqunen, Imdihiriyen and I'adwiyen lineages are also all from the Ibdharsen. In the community of Aith Bu Khrif, the Aith Wuzghar lineage (that of the late and legendary Qa'id r-Hajj Haddu n-Muh Amzzyan, d. 1955) and that of the Ait Bu Stta, normally affiliated with the Aith 'Adhiya subsection (cf. Hart 1976 p.254), are held to be Aith Ya'ra or descendants of the Bani Marin, the Aith Yunis are descended from the Asht Yunis section of the Igzinnayen, the I'addiyen are from the Axt Tuzin, and the Imrabdhen n-Aith Tumritsh and the Imrabdhen n-Aith Tizza are from the Ibdharsen. In this community, only the Dharwa Umrabit Haddu lineage is from the Imrabdhen n-Aith 'Aziz of the Imrabdhen section of the Aith Waryaghar (Hart and Blanco Izaga 1975 Vol. I pp.133–4).

In the Aith Hadhifa section, only the Ibunaharen and Thirkuzin lineages in the community of Aith 'Amar u-Sa'id are from the communities of the same name in the Aith Tmajurth subsection of the Aith 'Abdallah. All other lineages are local and autochthonous.

In the Aith 'Arus section, the only stranger lineage is that of the Iznagen, in the community of Maru (lit. 'shade'), from the same Iznagen lineage in the Aith Turirth. All other lineages are, once again, local and autochthonous. Members of the I'akkiyen section assert that they too are autochthonous to their section; but members of other neighbouring sections suggest that as many of them are butchers, another low-class occupational speciality. The Axt 'Akki section of the Axt Tuzin must have been their true point of origin, as is suggested by their name.

The present section of this article consists largely of a description of a document in Arabic which for various reasons we were personally unable to see or consult. The description of the document in question was afforded us verbally by our onetime top fieldwork assistant in the Rif, in whose possession it remains, in 1981, well after the publication of my Aith Waryaghar study (Hart 1976). We give his observations as we took them down.

In August 1981 this man and his only surviving patrilateral uncle received identical *shajara*-s or genealogical documents from the Wizarat al-Sharifat al-Malikiya in Rabat or Royal Ministry of Sharif-hood. This document evidently attests to the fact that his own lineage, the Imjjat, located both in l-'Ass of the Aith Turirth section of the Aith Waryaghar (his own branch) and in Hibir of the Asht 'Asim section of the Igzinnayen, is made up of Idrisid *shurfa*'.

The document itself – which its recipients were evidently surprised and delighted to receive – was described as a scroll of some 1.6 metres in length. It bears the royal seal of King Hasan II and is signed by numerous central and provincial authorities in the ministry in question. The four branches or *ijujga* (sing. *jajgu*) of the Imjjat lineage in Hibir in the Igzinnayen each have copies also and in the copy received by our ex-assistant the genealogies were evidently updated to include his own name and that of his uncle as well.

The document holds that the point of origin of the Imjjat was Sidi bil-'Abbas in western Algeria; and it was from this point that their odyssey began. They were ejected by the local rulers because they fought incessantly and made a nuisance of themselves. From Sidi bil-'Abbas they evidently headed south-west to the Sagiyat al-Hamra in the Western Sahara (a legendary point of origin for saints or *shurfa*' in its own right), again, it was specified, fighting all the way. Once again they were expelled and this time they headed north to Glaymim (Goulimine). Here too it was the same story, and now they headed north-east to Marrakesh, where it happened yet a fourth time.

At this juncture four agnates, the survivors of the last battle, headed north. Two of them, Hajj Musa bin Mashish and his more illustrious brother Mawlay 'Abd al-Salam bin Mashish, went to the Bni 'Arus in the north-western Jbala, where they died and were buried, while the other two,

Ahmad bin al-Hajj Musa bin Mashish and Yusuf bin Mashish, went to the Igzinnayen in the Rif and died there. The first of these last two, Ahmad bin Musa, is the ancestor of the large lineage of the Dharwa n-Sidi Hand u-Musa (Hand u-Musa being the Rifian rendition of Ahmad bin Musa), which embraces the whole section or clan of the Asht 'Aru 'Aisa. In this section 'Aru 'Aisa or 'Ali bin 'Aisa himself, who is buried in the local community of Dwayyar, emerged as a point of fission several generations further down the genealogy. The second of the last two men mentioned, Yusuf bin Mashish, turns out to have been the ancestor of the Imjjat lineage and is buried in the community of Ihadriyen in the section of the Asht Yunis. Yusuf's son 'Abd al-Halim was evidently the point of fission of the Imjjat lineage in the Igzinnayen, while the latter's grandson, Muhand n-'Ari n-'Abd r-Harim (or Muhammad bin 'Ali bin 'Abd al-Halim), acted as their point of scission, once again to the north, into the Aith Turirth of the Aith Waryaghar.

There are also many Imjjat near both Meknes and Taza who are not accounted for by this tradition, although the Western Sahara and Anti-Atlas groups bearing the name are indeed taken into consideration by it. (Our ex-assistant equated verbally the Meknes Imjjat with the religious order of the 'Aisawa, the followers of Sidi Mhammad bin 'Aisa, in an obvious error.) But the gist of the legend is that they were expelled from every place they went to because they did nothing but fight, and that four surviving brothers (or rather, three surviving brothers and the son of one of them) finally ended up in the Rif.

Some commentary on the content of this *shajara* as described is now in order. It appears, first of all, to present a nice 'just-so story'. Although it may not actually 'prove' the Idrisid *shurfa'*-hood of the Imjjat, it nonetheless sheds considerable light on certain other issues, including that of the segmentary process, at least in terms of equality of segments of the same order of segmentation, in that five copies of it were sent to the five outstanding Imjjat lineage groups in the Central Rif, four of them in the Igzinnayen and one in the Aith Waryaghar. It also sheds some light on the time-honoured practice of genealogical rearrangement, telescoping and foreshortening, in which the past is generally rearranged to suit the present: for between Mawlay 'Abd al-Salam bin Mashish and the Fqir Azzugwagh (Muhand n-'Ari n-'Abd r-Harim), the ancestor of the Imjjat in l-'Ass of the Aith Turirth, there is a time gap of over six centuries! This discrepancy is particularly glaring when we consider that in terms of the information as presented here, there is implicitly a difference of only four to six generations between them, which not even the most fabled cases of Muslim Middle Eastern or North African longevity could possibly account for. Gellner has already commented on this fact in one context, that of the Ihansalen of the

Central Atlas (Gellner 1969 pp.261–78) and we ourselves have done so in another, that of the Imrabdhen of the Aith Waryaghar (Hart 1976 pp.256–60, 481–97).

But the odyssey also shows up, and in the richest possible manner, a third factor, that of 'movement and energy' as suggested for Morocco by Geertz (1977 p.161). Geertz's specific context is that of the last expedition of the Sultan Mawlay al-Hasan I to the Tafilalt in 1893–94, but it can be made to apply equally to earlier periods, as exemplified in the above legend recounting the fighting and unruly Imjjat behaviour from Sidi bil-'Abbas to the Sagiyat al-Hamra to Glaymim to Marrakesh, and then on northward to the Bni 'Arus of the Jbala (where Hajj Musa bin Mashish and Mawlay 'Abd al-Salam bin Mashish are buried) and on to the Igzinnayen and the Aith Waryaghar of the Rif. Finally, a fourth and very Rifian feature of the odyssey is that of 'fighting among themselves', *minghan jirasen*, as well as with the local people in each locality where the Imjjat stopped.

This whole exercise may merely represent an obvious attempt to establish a claim for agnatic kinship, the degree of which remains unspecified and undemonstrated, between and among various groups in widely different parts of Morocco. These groups bear the same *nisba* or attribute in the name *Imjjat*, itself probably a Berber (Tamazight) plural form of *amjjud/amjjut* ('favoid individual' or 'scabhead'), a term which in Rifian, as noted, would be rendered as *aqshar*. In such an attempt the three Idrisid *shurfa'* brothers as well as the son of one of them may have been thrown in to provide respectability. The basis for this is further underlined by the inclusion of the Sagiyat al-Hamra, well known as a breeding ground for *shurfa'*: for this particular *shajara* is more *ta'rikh* ('history') than it is *shajara* in a purely genealogical sense. Significant too is that although two of the brothers and the son of one of them are only locally known, Mawlay 'Abd al-Salam bin Mashish is nationally known throughout Morocco. Even more significant is the fact that although both Mawlay 'Abd al-Salam and Hajj (or Sidi) Musa, as well as the latter's son Sidi Ahmad bin Musa (or Sidi Hand u-Musa), all occupy prominent points of definition and/or fission on the genealogy of the Dharwa n-Sidi Hand u-Musa, or the Asht 'Aru 'Aisa in the Rifian tribe of the Igzinnayen, as we recorded it elsewhere (cf. Hart, in preparation), Yusuf bin Mashish, the alleged ancestor of the Imjjat (who may also have been Yusuf u-Yihya?) does not figure in it anywhere.

It seems possible, therefore, that the attempt in this particular *shajara* to establish the *bona fide* Idrisid *shurfa'*-hood of the Imjjat lineage may be a complete fabrication through interstitial planting, an attempt to graft a new line or element onto a pre-existing genealogy. If so, by no means would it be the first time that such a technique has been utilised. There is also the present-day political factor to be considered: as the Idrisid *shurfa'*, individually or collectively, represent no threat to the 'Alawid monarchy, it may well be that in handing out *shajara*-s of this kind King Hasan II has merely bestowed harmless favours on the recipients by recognising them as fellow *shurfa'*, albeit of a different and at present less exalted line. Certainly the reaction of our ex-assistant on receiving it was one of complete surprise. His pleasure over it only came later and we refrained pointedly from passing any critical judgements on it at the time.

By way of conclusion, it now seems worthwhile to bring in some additional and wider evidence from other parts of Morocco. Mezzine, for example, indicates that the lineages of the Zawiya Dila' in the Middle Atlas were also known as Imjjat, and that most of them remained in the Upper Mulwiya region after the Dila'i-s had emigrated to Ait Ishaq in the Tadla, possibly in the sixteenth century (Mezzine 1987 pp.51–2). It is, or should now be, obvious that Imjjat is a Morocco-wide lineage name, found in one form or another in all parts of the country where Berber is still spoken, and in at least one instance where Arabic is spoken as well: the Zawiya Darqawiya, the mother-lodge of the Darqawa order, at Amjjut in the Bni Zarwal of the southern Jbala. Unfortunately Mezzine does not provide the tribal affiliations or identification of the Upper Mulwiya Imjjat, nor the date or motive for the Dila'i move to the Tadla. Writing about the same general region, however, Chiapuris notes suggestively that the Imjjat/Mjjat tribe was originally a member group of the Ait Idrasen confederacy of the Middle Atlas, and that they settled in the Upper Mulwiya plain in the fifteenth century, between Midelt and Tunfit, while the Zawiya Dila'iya (Ait Iddila in Tamazight) was founded about 1566 in the region between the plain in question and Khanifra in the western Middle Atlas, taking its name from the site where it was built (Chiapuris 1979 p.17).

Drague has noted, too, that the founder of the original zawiya of Dila', razed by the 'Alawids in 1668, was a Sinhaji Berber named Abu Bakr bin Muhammad bin Hammi bin Sa'id bin Ahmad bin 'Amr al-Ujjari al-Zammuri, of the Mjjat tribe, which he also informs us were mountaineers at the time, with a zone of transhumance from the source of the Wad al-'Abid to that of the Umm al-Rabi' (Drague circa. 1951 p.127). In addition, LeCoz makes it clear, through a historical map of *gish* tribal movements, that the Mjjat entered Morocco from the south as a *gish* or paramilitary tribe in the service of the reigning dynasty in both the Marrakesh and, later, the Meknes cases, by coming north with the Ahl Sus in the sixteenth century (LeCoz 1965 p.2). But it might be noted, even so, that their Rifian namesakes, in both the Igzinnayen and in the Aith Turirth section of the Aith Waryaghar, were anything but *gish* in their behaviour, if our *shajara* is to be believed.

We discovered subsequently two further pockets of Imjjat/Mjjat both among the Ait Attab in the Azilal province and at Suq l-Had Mjjat in the Imi

n-Tanut administrative circle of the Marrakesh province (Royaume du
Maroc 1962 pp.155, 466–7). Yet a third pocket of Imjjat, in the Rif itself, is
that registered by Biarnay as Imjjat in the Aith Tmayith/Tmasht section of
the Aith Sa'id (Biarnay 1910 p.112). However, the name does not appear
either in the 1955 *Nombres de los Musulmanes Habitantes en la Zona de
Protectorado de España en Marruecos* (Alta Comisaria de España en
Marruecos 1955) nor in the 1960 *Population Rurale du Maroc* (Royaume
du Maroc 1962) for the Dar Kibdani commune in the Nador province.

The Imjjat/Mjjat near Meknes are readily identifiable from the *Carte des
Tribus du Maroc*, 1958/1962, while the Marrakesh-area group of that name
obviously refers to one located between Shishawa and Imi n-Tanut in the
Western Atlas. This too is derived from the *Carte des Tribus*, as is the
Imjjat/Mjjat confederacy in the southern Anti-Atlas, located between the Id
aw-l-Tit and the Ait n-Nuss.

Thus, through repeated lineage scission for whatever reason, there are at
least *nine* identifiable lineage or tribal groups bearing the name Imjjat/Mjjat
in the Maghrib: two demonstrably related ones in the Central Rif (in Hibir
of the Asht 'Asim of the Igzinnayen and its offshoot in l-'Ass of the Aith
Turirth of the Aith Waryaghar), a third in the Eastern Rif (in the Aith Sa'id)
and its offshoot in Battiwa in the Algerian Oranie, thereby making four; a
fifth just outside Meknes; a sixth in the Ait Attab of Azilal; a seventh in the
Western Atlas; an eighth in the Anti-Atlas: and a ninth in the Sagiyat al-
Hamra. Under the circumstances, this listing should by no means be looked
upon as exhaustive, but rather as open-ended, as there must almost certainly
be other namesake lineage groups elsewhere in the region at large.

A similar commentary might be made on the name of another Aith
Turirth lineage which would seem to stand further investigation, that of
Iznagen or Znaga and its implications, as well as its connections with
Mauritania and the Western Sahara. First, however, another connection
alleged to exist – and one accepted by ibn Khaldun – between Zanaga and
Sinhaja seems to us questionable at best, at least on the basis of the roots of
the two names. These are not the same at all, in our view, but quite different,
z-n-g as opposed to *s-n-h-j*. Znaga is also the name of a large low-lying *qsar*
in the oasis of Figig, while much closer to home, and in the Central Rif
itself, there is the Iznayen lineage of the Igharbiyen section of the Axt
Tuzin: for *Iznayen* and *Iznagen* are merely different pronunciations of the
same name, just as are *aith*, *axt* and *asht* ('people (of)'). By the same token,
a mountain on the southern borders of both the Aith Waryaghar to the west
and the Axt Tuzin to the east is known to the former as *Adhrar Aznag* and
to the latter as *Adhrar Aznay*, and the name Iznagen evidently survives in
both the Igzinnayen and the Aith 'Ammarth as well, as already indicated.
There is also the Igharm n-Iznagen among the Ait Hadiddu of Tilmi, on the

southern slope of the Central Atlas, in the Bu Maln circle of the Warzazat (Ouarzazate) province, as well as Znaga in Bu 'Arus of the Mzrawa, southwest of Tawnat in the Fez province (Royaume du Maroc 1962 pp.321, 592).

The connection between Sinhaja and Zanaga, which we regard as highly questionable, is also assumed in an otherwise very interesting essay by Sadki to be a straight one-for-one correlation of three great historical names: Masmuda/Imsmudn or Imasmuden, Zanata/Iznaten or Izanaten and Sinhaja/Iznayn or Iznagn (Sadki 1987 p.128). This seems particularly odd considering that Sadki's arguments are based on linguistic rather than on genealogical evidence. It takes us right back to the 'three-ring circus' theory so beloved of an earlier generation of Francophobe scholars (Hart 1982) – although Sadki in fact makes it four rings by adding the name of Igizzulen or Iguzuln/Guzzula or Gzula (sometimes or even usually written as Jazula) to the list.

A final and general comment may now be made. Berque, in his well-known article on the nature of the North African 'tribe' (his inverted commas), has rightly observed that the repeated occurrence – or recurrence – of such names over the North African landscape is far too frequent to be simply coincidental. In this connection, he cites five mentions of the names Zanata and Masmuda in Morocco alone (Berque 1974 p.25), while later in the same article he cites al-Bakri's *Description* as turning up the names Masmuda in six places, that of Zanata in 14, that of Sinhaja in 25 and that of Huwwara in 15 (ibid. p.30). This has the ring of truth, and it is certainly due to much more than mere coincidence that such 'onomastic emblems' are scattered so liberally all over the 'bled', the countryside.

But Berque makes no attempt to push the matter any further, nor to examine any individual cases. Furthermore, he does not pinpoint any single one of these to an exact locality. To return to our own case here under examination, and as already noted, the name *Imjjat* suggests – in Tamazight if not in Tharifith – the descendants of a scabheaded or favoid individual, while Coon tells us that among the Igzinnayen, at least, scabheads were often reputed to be men of great courage (Coon 1932 p.93). Furthermore, there is in this case the clearly demonstrable connection between the Fqir Azzugwagh, the founder of the Imjjat lineage in l-'Ass of the Aith Turirth section of the Aith Waryaghar, who had fled his own home in Hibir in the Asht 'Asim section of the Igzinnayen in a hurry in order to escape the consequences of a homicide he had committed there (indeed, it seems he killed a local *sharif*). Biarnay, in the work cited above, implies, but does not say outright, that exactly the same kind of link existed between the Imjjat of the Aith Sa'id who went to Battiwa (formerly Vieil-Arzeu and/or Saint-Leu) in western Algeria and those who stayed at home in the eastern Rif (Biarnay 1910–11). However, as we have pursued the fortunes of the Imjjat lineage both in the Aith Turirth of the Aith Waryaghar and in the neighbouring Igzinnayen elsewhere, including an account in depth of the fearful vendetta that broke out within their ranks at about the beginning of the present century (cf. Hart 1976 pp.329–38), there is no need to do so here.

At any rate, the above chronicle may account for the distribution of the name Imjjat in the Rif, but it does so less successfully for its recurrence elsewhere in Morocco, as evinced by the five remaining cases in Meknes, in the Ait Attab, in the Western (or Marrakesh) Atlas, in the Anti-Atlas and in the Sagiyat al-Hamra. In these instances it is highly probable that any recollections of whatever may have brought about such link-ups originally have faded completely from informants' memories. Hence one finds informants saying things to the effect that 'there are seven lineage groups named Aith Dris in as many different Rifian tribes' (as we recall from early field experience in the Rif in 1953). Statements like this may be of some intrinsic interest in themselves, but as they assume connections which are empirically undemonstrable, they are structurally valueless. If such connections should prove to be spurious (and informants invariably claim that such is not the case), they should be demonstrated to be so, in some kind of anti- or counter-genealogical exercise. But Berque has made no effort to establish any kind of connection, whether positive or negative. In this present exercise we have gone to further lengths to check out such onomastic recurrences, and even if our own results are not much more positive, we believe nonetheless that we have demonstrated some of the very real complexities of situations of this kind, as they exist, or existed, on the ground.

BIBLIOGRAPHY

Alta Comisaria de España en Marruecos, *Nombres de los Musulmanes Habitantes en la Zona de Protectorado de España en Marruecos: Territorios, Kabilas, Fracciones y Poblados de la Misma* (Tetuan: Editora Marroqui 1955).
Berque, Jacques, 'Qu'est-ce que c'est une "Tribu" Nord-Africaine?', in idem, *Maghreb: Histoire et Sociétés* (Algiers: Société Nationale d'Edition et de Diffusion (SNED); Gembloux: Duculot 1974) pp.22–34.
Biarnay, S., 'Etude sur les Bet't'ioua du Vieil Arzeu', *Revue Africaine* 277/2 (1910) pp.97–181; 278/3 (1910) pp.301–82; 279/4 (1910) pp.405–39; 280/1 (1911) pp.100–136; 281/2 (1911) pp.171–215; 282/3 (1911) pp.327–42.
Chiapuris, John, *The Ait Ayash of the High Moulouya Plain: Rural Social Organization in Morocco*. Anthropological Papers, Museum of Anthropology, University of Michigan, No.69 (Ann Arbor: University of Michigan Press 1979).
Coon, Carleton S., *Tribes of the Rif*. Harvard African Studies IX (Cambridge MA: Peabody Museum 1931).
——, *Flesh of the Wild Ox: A Riffian Chronicle of High Valleys and Long Rifles* (New York: William Morrow 1932).
Drague, Georges (pseud. of Georges Spillmann), *Esquisse d'Histoire Religieuse du Maroc: Confréries et Zaouias*. Cahiers de l'Afrique et l'Asie II (Paris: Peyronnet circa. 1951).

Geertz, Clifford, 'Centers, Kings and Charisma: Reflections on the Symbolics of Power', in Joseph Ben-David and Terry Nichols Clark (eds.), *Culture and its Creators* (Chicago: University of Chicago Press 1977) pp.150–71.

Gellner, Ernest, *Saints of the Atlas* (London: Weidenfeld and Nicolson 1969).

Hart, David M., *The Aith Waryaghar of the Moroccan Rif: An Ethnography and History*. Viking Fund Publications in Anthropology No.55 (Tucson: University of Arizona Press 1976).

——, *Dadda 'Atta and his Forty Grandsons: The Socio-Political Organisation of the Ait 'Atta of South-Central Morocco* (Wisbech, Cambridgeshire: MENAS Press 1981).

——, 'Masmuda, Sinhaja and Zanata: A Three-Ring Circus', *Revue d'Histoire Maghrebine* IX/27–8 (1982) pp.361–6.

——, *The Ait 'Atta of Southern Morocco: Daily Life and Recent History* (Wisbech, Cambridgeshire: MENAS Press 1984).

——, 'Rejoinder to Henry Munson, Jr., "On the Irrelevance of the Segmentary Lineage Model in the Moroccan Rif"', *American Anthropologist* 91/3 (1989) pp.765–9.

——, *Traditional Society and the Feud in the Moroccan Rif*, in preparation.

—— (ed.), and Blanco Izaga, *Emilio Blanco Izaga: Colonel in the Rif* (transl.). Ethnography Series, HRAfLEX Books MX3-001 (2 vols., New Haven: Human Relations Area Files 1975).

ibn Khaldun, *Histoire des Berbères et des Dynasties Musulmanes de l'Afrique Septentrionale*, (transl. by Baron de Slane, edited by Paul Casanova; 4 vols., Paris: Paul Geuthner 1925–56).

LeCoz, Jean, 'Les Tribus Guichs au Maroc: Essai de Géographie Agraire', *Revue de Géographie du Maroc* 7 (1965) pp.1–52.

Maroc 1.500.000e, *Carte des Tribus* (Rabat 1958, 1962).

Mezzine, Larbi, *Le Tafilalt: Contribution à l'Histoire du Maroc au XVIIe et XVIIIe Siècles*. Publications de la Faculté des Lettres et des Sciences Humaines, Série Thèses 13 (Rabat: Université Mohammed V 1987).

Montagne, Robert, *Les Berbères et le Makhzen dans le Sud du Maroc: Essai sur la Transformation Politique des Berbères Sédentaires (Groupe Chleuh)* (Paris: Felix Alcan 1930).

Moreau, Pierre, *Des Lacs de Sel aux Chaos de Sable: Le Pays des Nefzaoua*. Publications de l'Institut des Belles Lettres Arabes 11 (Tunis: Bascone & Muscat 1947).

Pascon, Paul, 'La Formation de la Société Marocaine', *Bulletin Economique et Social du Maroc (BESM)* XXXIII,/20–21 (1971) pp.1–27.

——, 'Segmentation et Stratification dans la Société Rurale Marocaine', *Actes de Durham: Recherches Récentes sur le Maroc Moderne* (13–15 July 1977; Rabat: Publication du Bulletin Economique et Social du Maroc 1978) pp.105–20.

Pascon, Paul, and Herman van der Wusten, *Les Beni Bou Frah: Essai d'Ecologie Sociale d'une Vallée Rifaine (Maroc)* (Rabat: Institut Universitaire de la Recherche Scientifique (IURS) and Institut Agronomique et Veterinaire Hassan II (INAV); Amsterdam: Faculté de Géographie Sociale de l'Université d'Amsterdam 1983).

Royaume du Maroc, Ministère de l'Economie Nationale, Division de la Coordination Economique et du Plan, *Population Rurale du Maroc: Recensement Démographique (Juin 1960)* (Rabat: Service Central des Statistiques 1962).

Sadki, Ali, 'L'Interpretation Généalogique de l'Histoire Nord-Africaine Pourrait-Elle Etre Dépassée?', *Hesperis-Tamuda* XXV (Rabat 1987) pp.127–46.

Precolonial Rifian Communities Outside the Moroccan Rif: Battiwa and Tangier

The twin factors of energy and motion as being important ones in Moroccan history have been commented upon at the macro-level by Geertz (1977) as well as by ourselves, in a context both larger than and quite different from that to be examined here (Hart 1993). But they can be made to apply equally well at the micro-level, for Moroccans, and North Africans generally, have never been strangers to movement, even in the form of travel, as the massive and ever-increasing labour migration of Maghribine workers to the countries of the EU and Western Europe has come today to bear eloquent witness. In this article our inquiry is restricted entirely to the micro-level, that of Rifian and hence originally Berber-speaking individuals or groups who established colonies outside their homeland of the Rif mountain region of north-eastern Morocco in the precolonial period, insofar as known, with the subsequent relations of these communities with the homeland in question. We will use our own work on the ethnography of one of the most representative Rifian tribal groups, the Aith Waryaghar (or Bni Waryaghal: cf. Hart 1976) and of the six other tribes that border them (cf. Hart, in preparation), as a sociocultural yardstick, even though in this article our orientation is largely sociohistorical, in the sense that as it focuses predominantly on the immediate precolonial period, considerably more use is made of earlier source materials than of near contemporary ones.

Thus the material to be presented here from Battiwa and Arziw in the Algerian Oranie on the one hand (Biarnay 1910–11; Janier 1945) and on Tangier and its environs, known as the *fahs*, on the other (Salmon 1904, Michaux-Bellaire 1921) should not serve as a mere replication of our earlier article on the Rifian community in Tangier (Hart 1957), with respect to which, in any case, some of our views have changed considerably in the interim. This is so even though no attempt will be made here to discuss post-independence developments (i.e. after 1956 for Morocco and after 1962 for Algeria). In any case, from a purely personal standpoint it seems most appropriate that we are now, in 1993, able to terminate our long ongoing Moroccan researches in Tangier, precisely where we began them over 40 years ago, in 1952. As a start, a certain distinction should be made between labour migrants, among which, as understood here, expectant rural/tribal workers move either to the cities of their own country or to those of other countries in order to look for work, but whose aim is or was always to return home eventually, and rural/tribal fugitives who fly from home simply either because of the pressure of poverty or who were, more likely, and in the past, forced into exile for other specific reasons relating to tribal politics, such as the feud or the vendetta.

In the Berber-speaking areas of the Maghrib generally, the first category has over the last century come to subsume the great majority of migrants. Most of these were Rifians to the French Algerian Oranie, working first on the farms of French settler-colons, from about 1850 to 1962 (when the Algerian frontier was closed with independence), and then moving to Western Europe and the EU from the latter date onward; or Algerian Kabyles, in a totally different labour wave, to France from about 1880 onward; or Moroccan Swasa or Ishilhayen Berbers from the Anti-Atlas to the cities of the northern Moroccan plain and littoral to pursue the trades both of wholesale and retail grocery, from mid-protectorate times, as of about 1936 onward (Montagne *et al.* 1948; Adam 1973; Waterbury 1972, 1973); or even the *izarzayen* porters' guild in Fez from the Middle Atlas village of the same name in the Ait Warayin tribe (Le Tourneau 1949 pp.194–7). Note that in Kabylia, in the Rif and in the Anti-Atlas, the Malthusian law has long prevailed: the land in all three cases is palpably too poor (especially in the Rif) to support its excess population, for which migration and the feud have always been two major avenues for trying to get out of the 'vicious circle'.

The second category is in fact only a smaller but more specific segment of the first, that of the establishment of precolonial Berber communities outside their original homelands. It is significant that, particularly in the Rif, and insofar as known, such communities were almost always established by tribesmen (or their descendants) who had had to flee from home whether because of having committed murder there, because of exile by the tribal council for the same reason or because of getting the worst of it in a feud (for details, cf. Hart 1976 pp.313–38, and Hart, in preparation).

For it was certainly within the narrower context that most of the precolonial Rifian colonies outside the Rif appear to have been formed. Our count of these should by no means be considered exhaustive, as we may well have missed a few. But in western Algeria we have, according to Coon (1931 p.105), both a community of the Aith Waryaghar, which was not confirmed by our own informants, as well as a whole quarter in the city of Oran (Ar. *Wahran*, possibly from Rif. *uhar* (pl. *uharan*, 'foxes'?)) known as Gal'aya, and commemorating the name of that confederacy in the Eastern Rif, in addition to that of a third community, Battiwa (or Aith Sa'id) in Arziw (Arzeu), which is examined more closely below.

In Morocco, there are several further Rifian communities outside the homeland. The first is one which was established by the Axt Tuzin (or Bni Tuzin) tribe in one or two villages outlying Mawlay Idris Zarhun (ibid. p.105), where the founder of Morocco's first Muslim dynasty, the Idrisids, is buried, even though Ben Talha in his study of Mawlay Idris fails to mention or to identify this particular community (Ben Talha 1965). The second is what has become a minor concentration of the Igzinnayen (or Gzinnaya) tribe on the Lamta agricultural region just west of the city of Fez. As Coon demonstrated, this particular Rifian community grew into being as the result of exiles from feuds at home, later increased by their descendants who did not return there (1932 pp.108–31; 1962 p.316). He also went on to mention several further communities, in his fieldwork dating from the late 1920s, that we were unable to corroborate in our own later fieldwork dating from the 1950s (1931 p.105). Finally, and importantly, however, there is the major Rifian community, which he also mentions (ibid.) in and on the outskirts of Tangier, which we also ran into quite independently (Hart 1957; 1976 pp.350–53). But both the Tangier community and its *raison d'être* were quite different from and more complex than the others, as we shall see shortly. Battiwa is closer to the norm, as is evident from the work of Biarnay (1910–11) and Janier (1945), and hence we consider it first.

There seems to be no question but that the origins of the Battiwa of Arziw and of what was in colonial times Saint-Leu are from the tribe of the Aith (Bni) Sa'id in the eastern Moroccan Rif, as Biarnay makes clear (1910 p.101). This important point of identification, however, is glossed over completely by Janier, who instead gives us a lengthy and not entirely relevant excerpt from ibn Khaldun (as translated by de Slane) to show that, like the Algerian Kabyles, they were sedentary Sinhaja who inhabited the Rif until the fourteenth century when they were defeated while in the service of the Marinids at Maz'una, after which some of them went back to the Rif and the rest moved on to Mustaghanim, where they stayed until 1784. In that year they moved to a site close to the Roman ruins of Portus Magnus close to the coast, a site which after 1848, and hence in the colonial period, became the European village of Saint-Leu, at a time when French Catholic saints' names were being handed out by the colonial administration to the settlers of new villages (Janier 1945 pp.238–45).

The etymology of the lineage or tribal name *Battiwa* however (an Arabic version of the Rifian original *Ibittuyen/Ibattiwen*) is, like so many other Berber anthroponyms and toponyms, not known. But in 1943 its Muslim and Rifian-descended population numbered 1400, and its European population 600 (ibid. pp.247–51). Nonetheless, the village square, in Janier's time, which corresponded to the site of the old Roman forum, was also bisected by the line of division between the two hostile *saff*-s or leagues of the village, the Bni Tmayit (Rif. Aith Tmashth) and the Zigzawa (Rif. Izigzawen), which corresponded exactly, if on a smaller scale, with an earlier or at least contemporary pair of hostile factions within the considerably larger parent tribe of the Aith Sa'id, at home in the Rif, among whom these same factions, somewhat expanded, were known as *liff*-s (ibid. p.242).

Precisely why the new community was referred to as *Battiwa* is uncertain, but the name may well derive from the Berber root *bdhu* ('to divide, to share'), despite Biarnay's misgivings on this point (Biarnay 1910 p.114). It is, however, to be found in its Rifian cognate form Ibattiwen or Ibittuyen as a lineage or a local community name in a number of different Rifian tribes, including the Aith Sa'id. Nonetheless, as Biarnay informs us, the area of the Wad Kart/Aghzar n-Kart, in or near Aith Sa'id territory, was the point of origin of this particular group of Battiwa, and he makes it clear that after a battle between two sections of the home tribe of the Aith Sa'id, the survivors of the vanquished section had to leave the country and seek exile in the east, in the Oranie. Our own view is that we are dealing here less with two sections of the Aith Sa'id than with two *saff*-s or *liff*-s, or mutually hostile leagues of alliance, which had members throughout all the original sections of the tribe and which therefore often cross-cut its quasi-segmentary and territorial organisation. As Biarnay observes, this would also explain the fact that at Vieil Arzew/Arziw l-Qdim or 'Old Arziw' (which is to say, Arziw Amslim or 'Muslim Arziw', to differentiate it from the French village of Saint-Leu) there are lineages claiming affiliation with at least half, and probably more, of the present sections of the Aith Sa'id (Biarnay 1910 p.105, as well as further corroborating evidence from unpublished papers of Col. Emilio Blanco Izaga, dated 1943, on the internal division and alliances of the same tribe).

The *saff* alliance arrangements of the Battiwa, which even preserved the old names in use (with slight rearrangement) among the Rifians of the Aith Sa'id, were still remembered as of the time of Janier's fieldwork, even though they were no longer active. But Janier also notes their much more irreconcilable hostility toward their Arab neighbours the Hamyan, who sneered at them as Berber bumpkins and who were located only two kilometres away from Saint-Leu across a ravine which, ordinarily dry, fills up with water during the winter rains. It is proof of the fact that propinquity by no means automatically engenders good relations. It seems that once two Hamyanis were walking along the ravine when a Battiwa woman passed by quite inoffensively. But they spat on the ground as she went by and began to curse the Battiwa generally. The woman, of forthright Rifian stock, quite naturally got angry and went up to the nearest one, grabbed him by the shoulders and flung him into the ravine. She then did the same to his astounded partner before he could flee. The fall did not seem to humble either of them, however, and so, as they continued to hurl insults at her from down below, she loosened a large load of stones in an avalanche which then rolled down and killed them both (Janier 1945 p.259). What a lady!

Janier now informs us that as of 1943 social pressure among the Battiwa was still very strong, for there was still no intermarriage between them and the Hamyan (ibid. p.260). Biarnay sheds further historical light on this mutual hostility by saying that in the immediate precolonial period, because the Battiwa were persecuted by the Hamyan and other neighbouring Arabs, they became auxiliaries of the Turks, when the Bey of Oran, Muhammad al-Kabir, offered them land if they helped to pacify the salt marshes of Arziw from the depredations of the Hamyan, whose activities as bandits they now began to hinder. After the French invasion of 1830, their friendliness to the invaders rendered them suspect to 'Abd al-Qadir, who dispersed them, sending some to Perregaux (today Muhammadiya) and others to Bni Shugran and l-Burj. Still others, fleeing both 'Abd al-Qadir and the French, returned to the Rif, although most of them helped the French in the defence of Mazaghran in 1839–40. After 'Abd al-Qadir surrendered to the French and was finally removed from the Algerian scene, the local colons found the Battiwa to be excellent workers, in true Rifian style, much better than the local Arabs (Biarnay 1910 pp.106–8). We have no idea to what extent they later became Algerian nationalists.

Social pressure on the Battiwa, Janier tells us, is also manifest within the 'tribe' (referred to by the universal designation, in Algerian Arabic, of *'arsh* as opposed to the Moroccan one of *qbila* or its Rifian cognate *dhaqbitsh*) in a way which has become classic in Berber regions. This is through its division into two *saff*-s or leagues which, as noted, bear different names: the Zigzawa, who live in the western part of the village, and the Bni Tmayit, who live in the eastern one. As also noted, these two *saff*-s existed previously (and continued to exist) as *liff*-s among the Aith Sa'id of the Rif. The spatial dividing line between them in Battiwa was the public square, where the tribal sheep and goats were assembled every morning and evening under the guard of a shepherd.

The division of the Battiwa into eleven sections as recorded by Biarnay (1910 pp.109–12) had ceased to exist by the time Janier came along, and in any case they were very unequal in size; the Zigzawa (Rif. Iziyzawen) had 500 members, while three others, the Hatriya (Rif. Ihatriyen), Mjjat (Rif. Imjjat) and Rahmuna (Rif. Irahmunen), had 50 members apiece, while the seven remaining ones only had ten members each. Given the overwhelming numerical superiority of the Zigzawa, they were easily able to impose their will on the remainder, which even after uniting could not even produce half the number of the latter. This situation had obviously become rectified by the early 1940s, by which time the remaining non-Zigzawa sections had been incorporated into the Bni Tmayit *saff*. As of 1943 the only two groups which still existed were the Zigzawa (Rif. *yinin waddai*, 'those below') and the Bni Tmayit (Rif. *yinin innij*, 'those above'), each with about 600 members. They were able to send this number (or presumably half this number, as women would have been excluded) to participate in the tribal council or *jma'a*. As the total population in 1943 was estimated at 1,400, there were thus some 200 souls left over. These had a tendency to build their houses at the two extremities of the village, as they feared cohabiting either with the Zigzawa or the Bni Tmayit. This remainder originated from the various Rifian tribes surrounding the Aith Sa'id, which is to say, the Aith Bu Yihyi, the Thimsaman, the Aith Wurishik and the Iqar'ayen. In the village *jma'a* they had their own representatives just as the purely Battiwa *saff*-s had: in 1943 political fractionation was much less apparent than it had been in 1908, even though the two *saff*-s were still not quite equal in size, that of the Zigzawa retaining its slight edge (Janier 1945 pp.260–61).

Janier informs us, furthermore, that as of 1943 the vitality of the *saff*-s was still manifested in the three following ways: (1) marriages were invariably contracted between men and women of the same *saff*, never between men and women of opposing *saff*-s; (2) there was always a recrudescence of *saff* rivalries on the occasion of important events in the political life of the village, and there were no municipal elections in which shots were not exchanged between men of the two *saff*-s (which may be compared and contrasted to the complete *Pax Hispanica* which reigned in the Rif after the defeat of bin 'Abd al-Krim in 1926 and the resultant confiscation of all Rifian arms by the Spanish authorities); and (3) murders between men of the two *saff*-s were evidently frequent in the past and automatically invoked the application of the *lex talionis*. In connection with this last, Janier does not even mention *diya* or bloodmoney payments, which were always regarded by Rifians to be incidental in any case to the main business of prosecution of the feud or the vendetta, as the case may have been; and he goes on to cite two short case histories (ibid. pp.262–4; cf. also Hart 1976 pp.283–338).

As for the economy of Battiwa village, Janier noted that as of 1943 almost all its inhabitants were sedentary agriculturalists, just like their cousins in the Rif. Only 68 men out of the total population of 1,400 had other occupations: these included 24 grocers, ten gardeners, five teahouse keepers, five barbers, four masons, four bakers, three butchers, three egg merchants, two tailors, two coffin-makers, two bicycle repairers, two healers, one cobbler and one potter (Janier 1945 pp.254–6). The produce of the average Battiwi farmer's land netted him a total of 30,000 francs per year in 1943, all of which was more than swallowed up by expenses: food (60 francs per day, hence 22,000 francs per year), taxes (3,000 francs per year) and restocking of tools and livestock (5,000 francs per year). The bleak result was that he was thus forced to turn to black marketing or worse, as he was quite unable to save any money (ibid. pp.258–9). Again, we have no information with respect to what extent the Battiwa villagers may have become involved in labour migration to France since Algerian independence.

Battiwa village in Janier's time boasted two local saints, Sidi Ahmad bin 'Ali and Sidi 'Amar bin Ahmad, both of whom lived in the early twentieth century, both of whom are buried in the village or near it, and both of whom had the *baraka* as manifested in an ability to work miracles. The latter, for example, remained calm and tranquil in the face of a violent storm which tore the roof off the local mosque, while on another occasion his prayers becalmed the sea when another storm arose, threatening to shipwreck a boatload of aspiring pilgrims on their way to Mecca. Four *turuq* or religious orders (sing. *tariqa*) were represented: of these the Sanusiya had the largest number of followers with their centre at Bu Girat, 30 kilometres from Mustaghanim, while the Bu 'Abdalliya had their own centre right in Battiwa itself (ibid. pp.268–71).

Under colonial rule Battiwa was what was known in French Algeria as a *commune de pleine exercice*. Its mayor was assisted by a municipal council consisting of 12 Europeans and six Battiwi-s, while the *qa'id* of the tribe was accountable to the mayor. His role was largely that of a police officer, while that of the *jma'a* which assisted him was confined to inflicting fines on locals either for wounding one another, for theft or for infractions of public order. Its own role had obviously been much greater in the precolonial past, and the memory of an *'urf* or customary law was retained in 1943 as having been different from the Shari'a, although whether it had ever been written down was not known. One significant piece of customary law which was still retained, however, was that women turned their share of the inheritance over to their brothers, exactly as they do in the Rif, but they did so only if the share in question had no great monetary value. Janier notes, correctly, that inheritance by women is considered to be dishonourable among Berbers generally, but that today the notion of interest has largely replaced that of honour (ibid. p.271). He observes that even so the retention of this archaic custom is striking.

However, it seems that even under Turkish domination customary law in Battiwa was in the process of giving way to the Shari'a. The *makhzan* or central government was even then solidly entrenched among the Battiwa and there was no question of any resistance to it. The *duwwar* of Battiwa was placed under the same jural mantle as the seven neighbouring *duwwar*-s of the nearby and hostile Arabs of the Bni Hamyan, and all of them were subject to a *qadi* resident at Arziw. In the 1940s the Shari'a adjudicated all conflicts among the Battiwa and was applied by religious personnel or holy men. Exactly like their Rifian cousins at home, the Battiwa were hot-headed and often got into fights. The victim went to the local doctor to obtain a medical certificate, bought his medicine and registered a complaint with the gendarmerie. But then the next day he generally realised that an arrangement made with the local holy man would be quicker and less costly. So both the plaintiff and the defendant went to Shaykh Bu 'Abdalli, who listened to the facts, placed the blame on the guilty party and reconciled the contestants with words of peace. After this they only had to return to the gendarmerie to have the medical certificate and the official complaint torn up. Janier concludes that it was precisely along these lines that over the last two centuries jural power in Battiwa passed from the *jma'a* to the representative of the *makhzan* and finally to the religious leader (ibid. pp.271–3).

The Rifian settlement of Tangier and its environs of the Fahs preceded that of Battiwa in the Algerian Oranie by exactly a century. It went back to February 1684 when, after the English evacuation of the town, Mawlay Isma'il, one of the earliest and strongest Moroccan sultans of the present 'Alawid dynasty (ruled 1672–1727), restocked it with an army of Rifian troops. This army, known as the *gish ar-rifi*, had been instrumental not only in driving the English out, but also, since 1678, in besieging Christian occupants and evicting them from other north-western Moroccan ports, such as the Spanish from Mahdiya three years before the Tangier evacuation, in 1681. The Rifian army blockade of Tangier had lasted six years, while the army itself, made up of men from the Thimsaman, Aith Waryaghar, Ibuqquyen and Iqar'ayen tribes, and probably from others as well, was first placed under the command of a war leader named, curiously enough, 'Amar bin Haddu al-Battiwi. The origins of this individual, however, were from the Thimsaman tribe and not from that of the Aith Sa'id, and Mawlay Isma'il had appointed him as governor of al-Qsar al-Kbir. His parallel cousin 'Ali bin 'Abdallah al-Rifi was given the pashaship of Tangier, where the besiegers built a *qasba* or fortress to house the *mujahidin* troops, the fighters for the faith. But 'Amar bin Haddu was killed at the siege of Mahdiya, after which the command of his troops passed to 'Ali bin 'Abdallah at-Timsamani, who assumed the office of pasha amid rejoicing over the Moroccan victory over the English, whose evacuation he supervised (Michaux-Bellaire 1921 pp.82–4). A résumé of the history of the Tangier *gish* is now in order; and certainly in its formative years it was emphatically not made up of escapees from feuds at home, a fact which differentiates it from the normal Rifian community away from the Rif.

'Ali bin 'Abdallah remained pasha of Tangier from 1684 until his death in 1713; and one of the first things that happened after the English departure was that the territory of the Fahs on the outskirts of the city was awarded to the victorious Rifian army which had taken it. The *mujahidin* were installed in it and were organised into a *gish* (from Classical Arabic *jaysh*, 'army'), by virtue of which they were compelled to do military service in exchange for the land they now possessed. 'Ali bin 'Abdallah and his cousin, 'Ali bin Haddu, led them to the conquest of al-'Ara'ish (Larache) in 1690, then to that of 'Azayla/Asila the following year, then to the siege of Badis and finally to that of Sibta (Ceuta), which was not lifted until 1727, the year of Mawlay Isma'il's death. In 'Ali bin 'Abdallah's time, his command included not only the Fahs environs of Tangier but also the territory around 'Azayla and the whole area between Tetuan and Badis, although Tangier remained the seat of his command (ibid. pp.85–7).

His son, Ahmad bin 'Ali, was pasha from 1713 to 1743, during a period of ups and downs. After the new sultan Mawlay 'Abdallah (1728–57) assassinated a delegation that Ahmad bin 'Ali sent to him, the pasha became anti-dynastic and backed a pretender named Mawlay al-Mustadhi whom he proclaimed as sultan in Tangier. As Ahmad bin 'Ali was also not recognised by the pasha of Tetuan, 'Amar al-Waqqash, he marched against him and took the city, killing 800 people and building a palace as a monument to the establishment of his authority. But he and Mawlay al-Mustadhi were to suffer a reversal in battle against sultanic forces in the Gharb, beside the Wad Sbu, in February 1743, where they lost 900 men. In July of the same year he was killed in another battle near al-Qsar al-Kbir and Mawlay 'Abdallah placed his head on a pike at the Bab al-Mahruq gate in Fez (ibid. pp.87–92).

He was succeeded by his brother 'Abd al-Krim bin 'Ali (1743–48), who went against the pretender al-Mustadhi; but after he was captured and blinded by the latter, he was in turn succeeded by his brother's son 'Abd as-Sadaq bin Ahmad bin 'Ali, whose pashaship from 1748 to 1766 was relatively calm. During or just after his tenure (and the pasha-providing lineage thereafter became known as the Ulad 'Abd as-Sadaq) the original *gish ar-rifi* was reconstituted and reinforced, and was made up almost exclusively of Rifians. Numbering 3,600 men, it consisted of 2,400 infantry and cavalry, 500 artillery and 700 sailors. We have noted elsewhere that the infantry and cavalry, at least, were divided into 21 *miya*-s all told, each with its own *qa'id al-miya*. Several *miya*-s (number unspecified) constituted a *raha*, under a *qa'id ar-raha*, while the artillery was under a *qa'id at-tubjiya* and the sailors under a *ra'is al-bhar*; and three *miya*-s acted as a *mkhazniya* guard for the governor (Hart 1957 p.153). Interestingly, in 1788 under the sultan Sidi Muhammad bin 'Abdallah (1757–90), an attempt was made to increase the fleet with 600 Ait 'Atta Berber tribesmen and 400 *'abid* or blacks from the Tafilalt, but as these men had never before seen salt water, the experiment was doomed to failure. In any case, by the twentieth century all the sailors had become simple fishermen and most of the soldiers, Fahsi farmers in villages on the outskirts of town. By 1902 *harka* or military force formation was down to three men levied per village, and the whole force did not exceed 200 men. Exemption from *harka* service could also be obtained by payment to the pasha of 20 duros hasani per village (Salmon 1904 p.185).

All soldiers received a salary of one *mithqal* (five francs) per month, which turned out to be insufficient, and the sultan had to give them an advance. It should be made clear that the pasha of the *gish* and the governor of the city were one and the same individual, and he distributed plots of land by delegation from the sultan. There was also a register, the *kunnash al-gish*, in which the plots and the names of their beneficiaries were inscribed. Although this organisation became increasingly lax after the death of Sidi Muhammad bin 'Abdallah, and the *gish* no longer received a salary, it continued to exist right up to, and indeed past, the establishment of the protectorate in 1912. During this whole period both the *gish* command and the city pashaship remained in the hands of the Ulad 'Abd as-Sadaq lineage from the Thimsaman (ibid. pp.93–112); there seems little point in enumerating all its incumbents here.

It might, however, be noted that during the sultanate of Mawlay al-Hasan I (1873–94), the Tangier command still consisted of considerably more territory than it did at the time of the protectorate. It comprised no less than nine tribes, in addition to the Fahs, from the neighbouring north-western Jbala: the Gharbiya, 'Amr, Mzura, Bdawa, Anjra, Wadras, Bni Msawwar, Jbil Hbib and Bni Yidir. The Anjra, however, often showed a tendency to reject the weakening authority of the pasha, a fact which Michaux-Bellaire linked to their affiliation with the Darqawa order. This separatist tendency was evidently manifested openly in 1876 with the nomination of 'Abd as-Sadaq bin Ahmad as governor. He was replaced in 1891 by his weak son Hajj Muhammad, who was then in turn replaced by a cousin, 'Abd ar-Rahman bin 'Abd as-Sadaq, because as of 1875 the pashaship was, by sultanic decree, statutorily awarded to the Ulad 'Abd as-Sadaq.

But after Hajj 'Abd as-Slam bin 'Abd as-Sadaq became pasha in 1902, his principal antagonist, from within the Fahs itself, was the famous (and very non-Rifian) Jbalan *sharif* turned bandit Mawlay Ahmad al-Raysuni, who after 1904 administered the Fahs without leaving his nearby birthplace of Zinat. He remained the *de facto* master of the Fahs and of Tangier until 1907–8, when Sultan Mawlay 'Abd al-Hafiz confirmed him in Fez as the Qa'id of the Jbala. Raysuni's star was in the ascendant: in 1904 he had also demanded and obtained the partnership from Hajj 'Abd as-Slam bin 'Abd as-Sadaq and, after his capture of the Greek–American Ion Perdicaris that same year, he then captured the English instructor of the sultan's army Qa'id Sir Harry MacLean in 1907. We have described elsewhere Raysuni's on-again, off-again relationship with the Spanish protectorate authorities (1911–24) and his eventual defeat, capture and death in the Rif in 1924–25 at the hands of the Rifian leader bin 'Abd al-Krim (Hart 1976 pp.390–93;

1987 pp.19–24). As they do not impinge upon the subject at hand, there is no need to discuss them further here.

Note, nonetheless, that as of 1907–8 the government of Tangier was reformed to include only the Fahs plus four villages of the Anjra, as the rest of Anjra territory was to be included in the new Spanish Zone of Morocco through the Franco–Spanish protectorate treaty of 1912, which had already been secretly worked out in its essentials in the Act of Algeciras in 1906. Even the southern-most slice of the original Fahs now went into the new Spanish Zone (Michaux-Bellaire 1921 p.112), and the International Zone which Tangier became from 1912 to 1956 retained the same shape as the northern Moroccan province which it became after independence. But there were no more Rifian pashas, the last one having been replaced during the international (and colonial) period by a *mindub* from a Fasi family, Si Ahmad Tazi, and, after independence, by a Moroccan provincial governor.

At independence the Moroccan Muslim population of Tangier numbered about 100,000, and of this figure we estimated originally that about 70,000, or 70 per cent, were either Rifian or of Rifian descent, mostly the latter (Hart 1957 p.154), a figure which has probably become somewhat reduced in the interim. To this we may add Michaux-Bellaire's higher estimate, from 1921, of the population of the Tangier Fahs, in which the Rifian element is even more apparent, of 85 per cent Rifian, 9 per cent Arabo–Berber from the neighbouring Jbala, and only 6 per cent Arab, properly speaking (Michaux-Bellaire 1921 p.361; Hart 1957 pp.154–5). This last estimate may err somewhat on the high side, but probably not very much. As early as 1904, in a detailed and perceptive ethnographic survey of the Fahsiya, Salmon stressed the highly composite nature of the latter as a Moroccan 'tribe', saying perspicaciously that if a working definition of a tribe or *qabila* may be that of a group of kinsmen, real or putative, descended from a common ancestor, its northern Moroccan counterpart, since the lengthy wars of the *mujahidin* to expel the Christian settlements on the Mediterranean and Atlantic coasts, has come a long way from the Arabian original: for the 'Alawid sultans, wanting to divide territory among such groups, drew boundary lines and nominated *qa'id*-s, more or less arbitrarily but at the same time officially. The tribe, Salmon notes, has thus become an administrative subdivision placed within stable limits and under the authority of a functionary of the *makhzan* or government. Some tribes still retain the genealogically based names that they bore formerly, but very few have remained intact, and certain sections, detached from their main branches, have equally become settled on the territory of other tribes. The more heterogeneous ones show a complete absence of any common ancestry and the names they are given are purely geographical terms referring to the area they occupy. Among these, for example, are the Fahs,

Hawuz, Sahil and Gharbiya, all of which are far removed from the original *qabila*-concept of Arabia (Salmon 1904 pp.149–51).

Although Fahs territory only covers about 200 square kilometres around the city limits of Tangier, from the Bay of Tangier to the Strait of Gibraltar to Cape Spartel on the west, and from there to the Wad Tahaddart on the south, with its centre in the Jbil l-Kbir, they are very much aware of their Rifian origins, or at least they certainly were in Salmon's time and even in the 1950s. (The Jbil l-Kbir, although only some 600 metres high, became known to Europeans in Tangier as the 'Old Mountain' on its north slope and as the 'New Mountain' on its south slope, while it levels off down to the Atlantic beach between Cape Spartel and the Caves of Hercules in a way that suggests, physically, a kind of *bilad al-makhzan*/*bilad al-siba* dichotomy in miniature, even though the *siba* concept was totally inapplicable in the context of Tangier.) Although they admitted the administrative term *dshar* (pl. *dshur*) or 'village' for their settlements, which with their once thatched and today corrugated iron roofed *nwala* houses close together look much like those of the neighbouring Jbalan tribes, they still referred to these settlements at the beginning of the century as *qbila* or 'tribe', simply because these village communities were a microcosm of the tribes which they or their ancestors came from in the Rif. Salmon adds, significantly, that it is clear that this tribal and ethnic fractionation was the cause of intense rivalries between villages, and especially between Rifians and Jbala, of whom the Rifians have always been scornful (Salmon 1904 p.168).

Michaux-Bellaire, who estimated the total Fahsiya population at about 14,000 in 1921 (as opposed to a figure of 22,000 given for them in the Moroccan census of 1960), gives a detailed listing of all the Fahsiya villages as well as the ethno-tribal composition of each, within the context of the entirely territorially based 'quarters' or *rbu'* (sing. *rba'*) to which they were assigned administratively, as of 1921 (Michaux-Bellaire 1921 pp.379–400; cf. also Salmon 1904 pp.190–92); but for our purposes here just a few representative examples will suffice: Dshar Bni Waryaghal, for example, was inhabited originally exclusively by members of the Aith Waryaghar tribe, while the present quarter (and onetime village) of l-Msalla was inhabited by those of the Thimsaman. Dshar Bni Tuzin was inhabited by members of the Axt Tuzin, Dshar Rifiyin (without tribal specification) by members of the Aith Yittuft and al-Farihiyin by members of the Bni Bu Frah, both these last located in the western Rif. 'Azib d-Abaqqiw was originally inhabited by the Ibuqquyen, as its name indicates, the quarters and onetime villages of Marstarkhush (said to have been a Rifianisation of a once resident Englishman named 'Mr Hodge') and Swani by the Aith 'Ammarth, and l-Gzinnaya, which after independence became a whole rural commune in its own right, by the Igzinnayen as well as by some Iqar'ayen. A few *dshur*, such as l-Hajariyin, were inhabited both by Rifians and Jbala, with, it seems, fairly frequent intermarriages between them, while others, along the lines of the percentages suggested above by Michaux-Bellaire, were Jbala. Examples of the latter were Shwiqrash, inhabited by *shufa'* of the Ulad al-Baqqal lineage of the al-Ghzawa, and Dshar bin Diban, occupied by a segment of the Anjra (Salmon 1904 pp.188–92).

In our earlier work on the subject we made a distinction between Old Rifians, which is to say, the original Rifian garrison of Tangier and their descendants, as well as the pasha-providing lineage of the Ulad 'Abd as-Sadaq, on the one hand, and New Rifians, those that have come to the city since the beginning of the present century, since the Rifian War against Spain and France of 1921–26, and particularly since the terrible drought of 1945, the 'year of hunger'; and we noted further that the Old Rifians have long been Arabised whereas the New ones still retain Berber speech and Rifian culture patterns even after having learned Arabic (Hart 1957 pp.154–5). This now seems to us overly schematic and dichotomised, for the fact of the matter is that from 1684 to the present there has been a virtually uninterrupted influx of Rifians both into Tangier and into the Fahs, as well as into Tetuan. This influx has of course been heavier at some periods than at others, but it has always remained at a fairly steady trickle in which erosion or loss of both the Rifian dialect and of tribal identity has probably been faster in the urban population of the city than in its still rural Fahsi outskirts.

Salmon noted that even as early as 1904, although most of the Fahsiya of Rifian origin still spoke *dharifith*, Arabic was already gaining heavy inroads, and recently arrived Rifians had to be able to understand it in order to maintain relations with the city. Indeed, at that time Arabic was already spoken by the majority of the southern and eastern Fahsiya, precisely where the Jbala- and Arab-descended villages are located, except for the inhabitants of l-Msalla and Swani, who had only come from the Rif in the 1870s (Salmon 1904 pp.170–71). By the 1950s, Rifian speech was generally maintained only by first-generation arrivals, whose children and grandchildren then largely ignored it to speak only Arabic, even at home. Furthermore, during the period when Tangier was under international control, many even learned Spanish, French and English (Hart 1957 pp.153–4).

Language, however, was by no means the only Rifian cultural diagnostic among the Tangier Fahsiya at the turn of the century; there were several others. Salmon tells us that in his day, quite apart from the flintlock guns that they used in powder plays on foot at weddings or religious feasts, they were, just like the Rifians at home, quite well armed with more or less modern European rifles. Each village had its target site, target practice was supervised every Friday after mosque attendance by a *shaykh ar-rma'* or chief sharpshooter, and even though he was not paid, he fined those marksmen who missed the target. Such target practice too stood the Fahsiya in good stead in the event of attempted raids or pillaging expeditions by bandits from the neighbouring Jbalan tribes of the Anjra and the Bni Msawwar (ibid. p.204). Such raids were very common at and before the turn of the century; and the Fahsiya response to them was a very Rifian one, to fight back hard. For banditry and theft were widespread among the Jbala, and indeed Salmon ends his account with a look at Raysuni, their most famous exponent (ibid. pp.260–61), while they were much less so among the Fahsiya, who had inherited the rough honesty and willingness to do hard work of the Rifians as well as the predilection of the latter toward the bloodfeud and the vendetta (and both for this and for wider cultural comparisons with the Jbala, cf. Vignet-Zunz 1992).

Salmon makes it clear that in the event of murder the Fahsiya did not admit the institution of bloodwealth or blood compensation (Salmon 1904 p.202). If and when they did so, it was only a slight amount and of secondary importance, because they preferred to prosecute the feud, in which the murderer at once became the prey of his victim's agnates. Salmon does not distinguish between feud and vendetta, nor does he tell us anything about the occurrence of the latter among the Fahsiya; but as in the Rif itself it was normally restricted to hostility between close agnates, the bloodmoney factor was almost never invoked in any case (Hart 1976 pp.313–38; Munson 1989; Hart 1989). But he does say that reciprocal murders gave rise to interminable feuds between lineage groups which sought to avenge the deaths of their members. Significantly, the pasha refrained from interfering in these feuds, the existence of which was responsible for the maintenance of a generalised hostility over most of the tribal territory at all times (Salmon 1904 p.202).

This was indeed a mirror image, on a smaller scale, of the normal situation among the parent tribes of the Fahs, at home in the Rif, in precolonial times. Even so there was, among the Fahsiya, nothing corresponding to the Rifian *qanun* documents of customary law, to the *liff* or alliance network (unlike the case in Battiwa), to the *haqq* fine for murder if committed in the market – for there was only one market, the bi-weekly one in Tangier itself, held on Sundays and Thursdays – or to the *aitharbi'in* or tribal council beyond the rudimentary level of the village assembly or *jma'a* headed by the *mqaddim d-dshar* (Hart 1976 pp.283–325). For in the Fahsiya, given its multiple and heterogeneous origins, there was no need for a tribal council, and the appointment of the *mqaddim* was ratified by the pasha.

In the Fahsiya case all of the above institutions were truncated in any case, if not short-circuited entirely, simply because the responsibility of this administrative tribal unit, as a *gish*, was directly to the pasha. Salmon notes with some perspicacity that as there was no central authority other than that of the provincial governor, *makhzan*-tribe relations in general were reduced to pasha–*dshar* relations (Salmon 1904 p.183). These relations, as noted, revolved mainly around the levying of *harka*-s by the pasha from the Fahsiya and the payment by them to him of the *hadiya*, the non-legal tax from which nobody was exempt (although the Fahsiya were indeed exempt because of their *gish* status from the Qur'anic taxes of the *zakah* and the *'ashur*) and which the pasha was required to hand over to the sultan on the occasion of the three major Muslim religious feasts (ibid. p.184). In return, the cultivated lands of the Fahsiya were decreed inalienable by virtue of having been conceded to the original *gish* by right of conquest and are no doubt therefore still today regarded as *mulk* or private property (ibid. p.228).

It is not our intention here to pursue Salmon's 'thick ethnographic description' of the Fahsiya of Tangier of nearly a century ago beyond the point, now achieved, of showing what they did or did not retain from their Rifian ancestors. Hence we leave aside some of the more complex aspects of their land tenure and socioeconomic organisation, for example, which do not derive directly from this fact. All of these are masterfully handled by Salmon, and we see no reason to dispute his findings. Indeed, the only possible point of minor difference that we can cite is with respect to what Salmon has to say about the shrine of Sidi Qasim wuld Mawlay Idris, supposedly the son of Mawlay Idris himself and the most famous saint in the Fahs, whose annual *musim* at the time of the summer solstice he fails, curiously, to mention. But Salmon does note that in his day the shrine had no cupola or *qubba*, simply because it had evidently caved in every time one was built, thus indicating, no doubt, that the saint in question preferred the open air (ibid. pp.248–9). We may add parenthetically, however, that by 1962, when we ourselves first saw and photographed the shrine, a *qubba* was firmly in place atop it.

In sum, enough has been said to show, through two examples given in some detail, that the number of those Rifian communities established in the precolonial period beyond the borders of the Moroccan Rif from whence their founders originated had and have vivid collective recollections of their Rifian origins. We would venture to say that this is still as much the case today as it was half a century ago, even though such memories may be dimming somewhat or becoming distorted with the passage of time. Let us only hope that the galloping, unbridled and cumulative pace of socioeconomic change over the last three decades does not obliterate them completely.

BIBLIOGRAPHY

Adam, André, 'Berber Migrants in Casablanca', in Ernest Gellner and Charles Micaud (eds.), *Arabs and Berbers: From Tribe to Nation in North Africa* (London: Duckworth 1973) pp.325–43.

Ben Talha, Abdelouahed, *Moulay-Idriss du Zerhoun: Quelques Aspects de la Vie Sociale et Familiale*. Notes et Documents XXIII, Faculté des Lettres et des Sciences Humaines, Université Mohammed V (Rabat: Editions Techniques Nord-Africaines 1965).

Biarnay, S., 'Etude sur les Bettioua de Vieil-Arzeu', *Revue Africaine* 277/2 (1910) pp.97–181; 278/3 (1910) pp.301–42; 279/4 (1910) pp.405–39; 280/1 (1911) pp.100–136; 281/2 (1911) pp.171–215; 282/3 (1911) pp.327–42.

Coon, Carleton S., *Tribes of the Rif*. Harvard African Studies IX (Cambridge MA: Peabody Museum 1931).

——, *Flesh of the Wild Ox: A Riffian Chronicle of High Valleys and Long Rifles* (New York: William Morrow 1932).

——, *Caravan: The Story of the Middle East* (2nd edn., New York: Holt, Rinehart and Winston 1962).

Geertz, Clifford, 'Centers, Kings and Charisma: Reflections on the Symbolics of Power', in Joseph Ben-David and Terry Nichols Clark (eds.), *Culture and Its Creators* (Chicago IL: University of Chicago Press 1977) pp.150–71.

Hart, David M., 'Notes on the Rifian Community of Tangier', *Middle East Journal* XI/2 (1957) pp.153–62.

——, *The Aith Waryaghar of the Moroccan Rif: An Ethnography and History*. Viking Fund Publications in Anthropology No.55 (Tucson: Universitty of Arizona Press 1976).

——, *Banditry in Islam: Case Studies from Morocco, Algeria and the Pakistan North-West Frontier*. MENAS Studies in Continuity and Change (Wisbech, Cambridgeshire: MENAS Press 1987).

——, 'Rejoinder to Henry Munson, Jr., "On the Irrelevance of the Segmentary Lineage Model in the Moroccan Rif"', *American Anthropologist* 91/3 (1989) pp.765–9.

——, 'Four Centuries of History on the Hoof: The North-west Passage of Berber Sheep Tranhumans Across the Moroccan Atlas, 1550–1912', *Morocco: The Journal for the Society of Morocccan Studies* No.3 (London 1993) pp.21–55.

——, *Traditional Society and the Feud in the Moroccan Rif* (Wisbech, Cambridgeshire: MENAS Press; Tetouan: Université Abdelmalek Saadi, in preparation).

Janier, Emile, 'Les Bettioua de Saint-Leu', *Revue Africaine* LXXXIX (89), 3–4 trim. (1945) pp.236–80.

Le Tourneau, Roger, *Fes Avant le Protectorat: Ertude Economique et Sociale d'une Ville de l'Occident Musulman*. Publications de l'Institut des Hautes Etudes Marocaines, Vol. XLV (Casablanca: Société Marocaine de Librairie et d'Edition 1949).

Michaux-Bellaire, Edouard (and Résidence-Générale du Protectorat Français au Maroc), *Tanger et sa Zone*, Vol. VII of series *Villes et Tribus du Maroc* (Paris: Ernest Leroux 1921).

Montagne, Robert, *et al.*, *Naissance du Poroletariat Marocain: Enquête Collective, 1948–1950*. Cahiers de l'Afrique et de l'Asie II (Paris: Peyronnet circa. 1951).

Munson, Henry, Jr., 'On the Irrelevance of the Segmentary Lineage Model in the Morocccan Rif', *American Anthropologist* 91/2 (1989) pp.386–400.

Salmon, Georges, 'Une Tribu Marocaine: les Fahcya', *Archives Marocaines* II (1904) pp.149–261.

Vignet-Zunz, Jawhar, 'Les Instruments de la Décentralisation (Administrative et Economique) dans le Rif à la Charnière des 19e et 20e Siècles', in *La Société Civile au Maroc: Approches*, in series *Signes du Présent* (Rabat: Société Marocaine d'Editions Réunies (SMER) 1992) pp.71–95.

Waterbury, John, *North for the Trade: The Life and Times of a Berber Merchant* (Berkeley, Los Angeles and London: University of California Press 1972).

——, 'Tribalism, Trade and Politics: The Transformation of the Swasa of Morocco', in Gellner and Micaud (eds.), *Arabs and Berbers* (above) pp.231–57.

Comparative Land Tenure and Division of Irrigation Water in Two Moroccan Berber Societies: The Aith Waryaghar of the Rif and the Ait 'Atta of the Saghru and South-Central Atlas

In the context of rural, and formerly tribal, Morocco, as well as, most probably, of those of many other Muslim lands in the Maghrib and the Mashriq (i.e. North Africa and the Middle East), traditional concepts both of land tenure and of the use and division of irrigation water may be regarded as being based upon three axes of classification, or, perhaps more pointedly, upon three pairs of opposed or polarised categories: (1) whether the land in question is dry-farmed or irrigated, (2) whether it is collective, and held by the *jama'a*, the community at large, or whether it consists of *mulk*, of individual, private property holdings, and (3) whether it is or remains in a state of indivision if held in common by members of the same agnatic lineage or patrilineal extended family group, or whether they have divided it as partible inheritance. All these categories fall within the available range of choice. Although no single individual could possibly have land holdings that would fit into all six of these paired opposites, those of most people would nonetheless be found to fit into more than one of them. Only marginally applicable is the concept of *habus* (known elsewhere as *waqf*) land, an essentially urban category referring to any land, and the income therefrom, which has been granted by individuals as an inalienable endowment to mosques as pious foundations for religious and charitable purposes.

We have already discussed, and in considerable detail, the land tenure systems of the two Berber-speaking Moroccan societies which form the subject-matter of this article, the Aith Waryaghar of the Rif and the Ait 'Atta of the Saghru and the South-Central Atlas, societies located at opposite ends of the country; and we have done so in the context of their overall ethnography and, in particular, in that of their sociopolitical organisation (cf. Hart 1976 pp.97–116; 1981 pp.99–133).

We have, however, up to now made no attempt to compare our findings on the subject: for generally speaking, and again we accent traditional land tenure systems, that of the Rifians of the Aith Waryaghar tends toward the individual and the particularistic, while that of the Imazighen as exemplified by the Ait 'Atta tends toward the collective. Indeed, the Aith Waryaghar may be said to present a leading Moroccan Berber argument in favour of property division, while the Ait 'Atta present an equally strong one in favour of property indivision. (Nonetheless, when the Ait 'Atta feel the need to do so, they can also show an extraordinary aptitude for division, as we shall see.) Although there are exceptions (examined later), these attitudes toward land are owing as much as anything else to the traditional economic systems of each group. The Aith Waryaghar, who numbered 77,000 in 1960, are (or were until very recently) sedentary and subsistence agriculturalists and tribal farmers, while the Ait 'Atta, who numbered an estimated 135,000 in the same year, are largely sheep transhumants, who make two well-defined moves every year: up into the mountains in spring to live in tents and pasture their flocks, and back into their permanent houses in the valleys before the autumn rains, to supplement their herding with subsistence agriculture.

But there is more to it and more behind it than this. The Aith Waryaghar, who live in an area of somewhat over 1,000 square kilometres in the gradually ascending back-country behind the Bay and Plain of al-Husayma (El Hoceima), country culminating in the Jbil Hmam massif (1,948 metres), are (or were) all, without exception, sedentary farmers on a very poor and eroded soil. Their major problems, which were those of the Rif at large, were hence those of poverty and overpopulation (and population density in the Plain of al-Husayma was well over 150 persons per square kilometre even in 1960) – until the massive exodus of migrant workers from this region to Western Europe in the 1960s and, particularly, after 1970. These hard facts have traditionally acted as stimuli to two sets of responses: labour migration, which began in concerted moves of workers to French Algeria in the mid-nineteenth century and culminated in the new direction toward Western Europe, as indicated, after Algerian independence in 1962, and the bloodfeud and/or vendetta in which the establishment and maintenance of honour by the participants was the factor of guiding importance.

The Ait 'Atta, on the other hand, do not feel such population pressure nearly as acutely, as they inhabit an enormous territory consisting of an estimated 50,000–55,000 square kilometres, running from the holly oak regions on the southern slope of the Middle Atlas range, across Mt. Azurki (3,690 metres) and the Tizi Mqqurn Pass (3,223 metres) in the Central Atlas down to the Dadss Valley and to their heartland and point of origin in the Saghru (2,712 metres at highest point). From there they extend south to the date palms of the Dra and east to those of the Tafilalt oases. It should be added that the Ait 'Atta are the dominant but by no means the only element in the population of this huge area, which also includes various Arab groups and a large number of sedentary black agriculturalists known as Haratin, a good many of whom stood formerly in a clientage relationship to the Ait

'Atta. Some Ait 'Atta groups, too, only pay the merest lip service to transhumance: the variation up and down the economic spectrum is much greater in their case than it is in that of the Aith Waryaghar, who are the only group in their own territory and who are all farmers.

The precolonial Ait 'Atta too had a very strong warrior ethos, as the precolonial Aith Waryaghar did, but it was oriented in a rather different direction, which is to say, externally, in hostility toward those neighbouring tribes which attempted to check their northward, southward and eastward expansion from the Saghru. The Ait 'Atta acquired or annexed all their present territory apart from their point of origin in the Saghru through right of conquest, a conquest which was stopped only by the arrival of the French in the early twentieth century. Major blocks against this expansion had been provided only by two other tribal coalitions – those of the Ait Siddrat and the Ait Yafalman, both of which were probably assembled for this purpose early in the seventeenth century at Moroccan dynastic and governmental instigation. Among the Aith Waryaghar, on the other hand, the enemy was very much within: not only within the tribe and/or any of its component sections, but within the local communities which made up these sections, and indeed quite often even within the agnatic lineage groups making up the communities. The Ait 'Atta conceived their own lineages as being corporate, but ideology apart, the Aith Waryaghar did not, at least in practice as opposed to theory. Hence full-blown hostility between half or even full brothers and their sons over partible inheritance was common enough to constitute quite a normal exception to a rather flexible rule (Hart 1976 pp.313–38; Munson 1989; Hart 1989).

* * * * *

In connection with the Rif, what must be established first are dates. Unlike, for example, Berque's documentary materials on the Seksawa of the Western High Atlas, some of which go back as far as the latter half of the fifteenth century (1974 p.18), our own earliest document from the Aith Waryaghar in the Rif is considerably later, at 1724 CE, in a document which notes only the sale of some pomegranate trees in r-'Attaf on the Upper Nkur River, now located in the present sectional territory of the Aith Turirth. Other names only start to appear in the second such document, dated 1736, in which a sister sells land in Thasriwin, also along the Upper Nkur, to her brother Ahmad bin Musa al-M'awti al-Waryaghli, a name which provides us with the first appearance of the tribal *nisba* al-Waryaghli (in our own materials, not necessarily those of others) preceded by that of the putative and genealogically untraceable Aith Turirth/Timarzga sectional ancestor Amrabit Bu M'awiya (cf. Hart 1976 p.507; in preparation). Nonetheless, despite this evidence with respect to two tribal sections, the Central Rifian tribal names themselves appear to be quite old: al-Bakri reports that the Aith Waryaghar, the Igzinnayen and the Thimsaman (in their Arabised equivalents of Bani Waryaghal, Gzinnaya and Timsaman) were all present and accounted for in the eleventh century, and in very much the same areas where they live today (Hart 1976 p.346).

What is significant, however, is that the bulk of our early documents from the Rif are land deeds, and bills of sale of land and trees. This indicates that as far back in Rifian history as we have detailed knowledge, land and property, generally speaking, have always been inheritable commodities that could be bought and sold. This point is of central relevance to the whole question of land tenure in the area at large – and here we refer especially to the Aith Waryaghar highland sections of the Aith Turirth and the Timarzga, located in the mountain knot of the Jbil Hmam, which is regarded as the tribal point of origin. Frequent references are made to the Aith Waryaghar lowlands as well, to the Plain of al-Husayma (El Hoceima), as we found them during the course of fieldwork in the region at large (1954–65). This is so simply because the tribal territory as a whole has a slender northern neck, its meagre outlet to the Mediterranean, from which it then sweeps up in a bulge into its massive southern mountains. Everywhere among the Aith Waryaghar – as among their neighbours, the Thimsaman, the Axt Tuzin, the Igzinnayen and the Aith 'Ammarth – local communities (*dshur* (sing. *dshar*)), traditionally, have never been in any sense a series of compact village communities, but rather extremely dispersed lots of individual homesteads with collective names. The optimum space between individual homesteads has always been at least 300 metres, usually considerably more, because this was a society which, in precolonial times until the Rifian reformer and resistance leader Muhammad bin 'Abd al-Krim outlawed them in 1922, was totally riveted to the feud and the vendetta.

In all this part of the Central Rif, in formal terms, there are (or were, traditionally, until very recently) only three kinds of real property: (1) *r-murk* (Ar. *mulk*), or privately owned land, constituting over 95 per cent of the whole; (2) *r-mishra'*, or collective land, usually used only for pasturage and held by the male members of the local community, the *jma'th*, in common; and (3) *habus* land, donated individually to mosques by pious individuals as acts of charity, with their agricultural yields being devoted to pious purposes or toward religious bequests. Among the Aith Waryaghar the first category is by far the most important, reducing the other two to purely residual status (*habus* land in particular, as it is normally to be found only in an urban context). Hence our focus here is entirely upon the Aith Waryaghar concept of private property, upon how it is divided up and irrigated (Hart 1976 p.97).

We consider first the vernacular terminology. *R-murk* refers at once to 'property' and 'ownership', both in a private sense. *Dhamurth* is the generic term for 'land', and an owner of land is *bab n-tmurth*; an owner of a house is *bab n-taddarth*; and an owner of property consisting both of houses and of arable land, whether it be irrigated (*dhamurth w-aman*) or dry-farmed (*dhamurth nj-bur*), is *bab nj-murk*. Therefore, one may speak either of *r-murk Ufqir Azzugwagh* or of *dhamurth Ufqir Azzugwagh* – the 'property' or the 'land' of the Fqir Azzugwagh ('the red-headed *fqir*, or member of a Sufi religious order and, in the event, that of the Darqawa), to take the name of the ancestor of a prominent lineage group in the Aith Turirth section, a man who had escaped there in the mid-nineteenth century from his original home in the Igzinnayen in order to avoid the consequences of a homicide. Anyone referring to his land in general calls it *dhamurth-inu* ('my land'), while reserving *r-murk-inu* ('my private property') for the land that is his personal property received through inheritance. (It may be added parenthetically that movable property consists traditionally of animals (*r-ksibth* or *r-mar*, from Mor. Ar. *l-ksiba* and *l-mal*), household furniture (*tarika*) and clothing (*'arrudh*). *R-murk* is also employed to refer to land that is currently being worked ('property'), as opposed to land that is lying fallow (*dhamurth*, 'land' in itself).)

As already implied, a major point about *r-murk* land revolves around whether it has been divided up (*dhibdha*, from *battu*, 'division') or whether it has remained in indivision (*ur ibdhi*, 'not divided'). Note here that the concept of *battu* or division is of crucial importance in Aith Waryaghar social structure, and examples are myriad: *battu dhamurth* (division of land), *battu w-aman* (division of (irrigation) water), *battu nj-haqq* (division of heavy fines formerly imposed upon murderers by the tribal council if they committed their murders in or on the way to or from the local market), *battu n-tqbitsh* (division of a tribe), *battu n-ar-rba'* (division of a tribal section), and *battu n-tarfiqth* (division of a lineage, whether through the normal processes of proliferation and fission, or through vendetta). A very common verbal usage is *ibdha ag-aithma-s* ('he has divided (land) with his agnates'), while far less common is *ur-ibdha-shi ag-aithma-s* ('he has not divided (land) with his agnates').

The issue of 'division' or 'indivision' of land almost always concerns property held in common by brothers (or by other slightly less close agnates). Contrary to a popular stereotype, the great majority of Rifians, including the Aith Waryaghar, as well as of other Berbers elsewhere in Morocco and Algeria (although the Ait 'Atta constitute a significant exception to this rule), divide their land up after the death of the lineage or extended family head, and sometimes even before he dies, if he permits it. It is generally recognised that brothers, who according to the Shari'a or Muslim Law all inherit equally, often do not get on well together. For this reason alone division is virtually automatic after the father's death. Nonetheless, in those comparatively rarer cases in which brothers do get on amicably, or in which the amount of land itself suggests a maintenance of the status quo in indivision (i.e. when there is enough land to go around comfortably among the heirs) the eldest brother becomes administrator or *na'ib* of this privately owned land on behalf of his agnates, and is thenceforth known as *amqqran n-aithma-s* ('the big one of his brothers'). Yet if they quarrel, division may occur at any time, and a special term *afiddjahuh* describes a situation in which two brothers have divided all their property right down the middle, an indication of how great the hatred is between them.

Two full brothers, members of a lineage in the community of Aith Yusif in the sectional territory of the Timarzga, did exactly this because the younger one suspected the elder of having poisoned his wife. (Because these two brothers looked enough alike to be identical twins, the writer, when he first knew them, was never quite sure which one he was addressing, and on at least two occasions this proved embarrassing, as they hated each other implacably.) They lived, in the 1950s, in a jointly owned house, inherited from their father, but they had walled it straight in half, and every possession they owned, down to the last match, was divided equally between them. This tense and tenuous state of affairs persisted until 1963, when the Timarzga River (a tributary of the Upper Nkur) flooded and washed away not only their house but most of the others in Aith Yusif and Tazirand. The elder brother then moved across the tribal border into the Igzinnayen, settling with affinal kinsmen in Ikhuwanen, while the younger brother rebuilt in a less vulnerable spot not far away from the original home.

This is an extreme example; but at the other end of the scale, that of indivision, very few cases can be cited, at least in the Jbil Hmam mountains. In the Aith Turirth as of 1954–55 there were only two instances of indivision: one of these involved the sons of the late 'Aisa Muhammadi n-Bu Tahar of the community of Ignan, who had been the *jari* or headman of the wider community of Bulma (encompassing Bulma itself, Ignan and l-'Ass). When he died in 1956, his several (four or five) sons all divided up his inheritance, although they continued to live together in the same house. The other case, that of the sons of the late Muh n-'Amar w-'Aisa in the community of l-'Ass, was the only one remaining as of 1965. In the Timarzga section, the heirs of the late 'Abssram n-'Ari 'Amarush of the community of Asrafil had not yet divided as of 1965, but there were indications that division would soon occur.

Division usually happens only rarely while the father is still alive, although two instances can again be cited for the Aith Turirth, in both of which the father himself opted for division when he had reached a very advanced age. One was the aforementioned Fqir Azzugwagh who founded a new branch of the Imjjat lineage and settled in l-'Ass after he fled north from the Igzinnayen. The Imjjat, as personified by the Fqir's sons and grandsons, rose to become one of the two strongest lineage groups in the Aith Turirth section and would have remained so had a fearful fratricidal vendetta not intervened among them to wreck lineage unity. The other case was a very old man of the Yinn 'Aisa w-'Amar sublineage of the Aith Uswir, residing in Ignan. In the first case, division occurred some five or six years before the Fqir Azzugwagh's death; in the second, interestingly, although the sons had received their shares by 1967, while their father was still alive, none of the daughters had received theirs. It should be stressed that according to the Shari'a, daughters theoretically inherit half of what sons inherit, with the shares of two daughters therefore equalling that of one son; but although the implications inherent in this situation would form the subject-matter of another article, it should also be noted that if there are any sons, Berber practice tends in fact toward exclusion of daughters from inheritance – unless, of course, there are only daughters.

Regarding the absolute size of *r-murk* holdings, unpublished Spanish Protectorate figures for the Nkur Qa'idate (which included the very large section of the Aith Bu 'Ayyash and the three smaller ones in the Jbil Hmam, the Aith 'Arus, Aith Turirth and Timarzga) for 1952 are revealing (Rodriguez Erola 1952): 676 individuals owned less than one hectare of land, 1,286 owned one–three hectares, 25 owned from seven–12 hectares, and one man, unidentified but probably the then *qa'id* of the Aith Bu 'Ayyash, owned as much as 50 hectares. Thus holdings of less than three hectares predominated in the region.

The second basic category of real property, *r-mishra'* (lit. 'ford' or 'passage' from the collective land of one community to that of another) has been translated by several terms: collective land, common land and, more recently, 'commonage' (Reader 1966 p.68). It has also been called grazing land, pasture land and 'brushwood land', from *r-ghabth* (from Mor. Ar. *l-ghaba*, 'firewood, brushwood'), which indeed it generally is: the grazing land of a given community, located on just those same mountain slopes where the women go to collect scrub and brushwood (which in Aith Waryaghar territory generally consists of lentiscus, thuya and/or holly oak) for charcoal.

Despite this terminology, however, the real distinction between categories of land resides principally in the type of ownership or holding rather than in the use to which the land is put: this is a secondary consequence. *R-mishra'* land is owned by the *jma'th* (Mor. Ar. *jma'a*), the collective male membership of the local community, and for this reason it is also called *dhamurth nj-jma'th* or *'jama'a* land'. It is also the community that owns (1) the paths leading to such land and to other communities (and like the Aith Waryaghar houses themselves, these paths are often bordered by hedges of cactus, so that the livestock will not pass over cultivated land); (2) the cemetery; (3) the mosque or Qur'anic school and any associated saint's shrine; (4) any ponds from which the animals may drink; and (5) all irrigation ditches, although these may also be shared by other *jma'th*-s, or other local communities, of the same order.

No community lands are cultivated collectively anywhere in Aith Waryaghar territory. Rather, if need be, the *jma'th* assigns plots to individual nuclear families for cultivation, either temporarily or permanently. Some of the holly oak trees (*quercus ilex*) in the highlands are collectively owned. These trees produce high quality acorns, and in the Timarzga as well as in another neighbouring tribe to the south-west, the Aith 'Ammarth, they are picked in *dhwiza* or working bee gatherings which last for a day. The produce is put into piles and these are then divided by drawing lots (*dhasgharth*), while a representative of each family or lineage is present. Again in the Jbil Hmam (as well as in parts of the Aith 'Ammarth and among the little Sinhaja Srir tribes in the highest mountains of the Rifian chain), drawing of lots is a feature of the 'intermittent cultivation' (Sanchez Perez 1951) practised on collectively owned hills or mountains. In this case the members of the *jma'th* either break up the ground on the mountain or burn it, and then cultivate the plots (determined again by lot-drawing) for two or three years. After this they abandon them to turn into *r-ghabth* or 'brushwood land' once again, and break up new plots, using the ashes from the burned areas as fertiliser.

Generally, *r-mishra'* land does not lose its common or collective character until after a considerable period of time. When the members of the *jma'th* decide to break up any collectively held lands, these are parcelled out by lot proportionately to the male agnatic members of each participating lineage. An individual from each nuclear family within the lineage deposits an object in a given place. When all these objects (pieces of wood, sticks, stones, etc.) have been put down, someone in the *jma'th* calls out to a passer-by or a stranger, who then picks up the objects one by one out of the pile. This order determines the orientation of the plots of land. When all the objects have been picked up and the land has all been parcelled out, the *qadi* or Muslim judge assisted by two notaries or *'adul* then draw up a document, in Arabic, indicating how the land has been assigned and giving details of ownership, including a specific statement that the land was previously collective. Usages, procedures and custom resorted to for settling disputes resulting from this type of parcelling out of common land to individuals, however, are not in any way codified. During the *Ripublik* (a term which refers particularly to the period 1898–1921, the two-plus decades of near-anarchy preceding the Rifian War with Spain and France (1921–26)), all complaints were submitted to the collective decision of the *jma'th*, but in

practice, as Sanchez Perez noted, the opinion of its strongest member
generally triumphed, 'usually after a long and terrible feud between the
constituent lineages, which could last for months or even years' (ibid.
pp.99–100).

Another practice, formerly very common in the Jbil Hmam, was for
individuals to plant trees in mountain land that had once been collective and
was later broken up into plots. These trees were then the private property of
the person who planted them, as was the space they occupied, the area they
shaded and the terrain covered by their roots. Lands such as former river or
stream beds, which have no owner and are hence considered 'dead', can be
reactivated and recultivated by any member of the *jma'th* or even by an
outsider. After ten years of usufruct, they become the private property of the
individual who cultivates them. This type of utilisation of collective land
was also very frequent in the Rif during the *Ripublik*. Also common in the
past, because of the prevalence of bloodfeuds, were solicitations of the
jma'th by individuals who wanted to remove their houses to a collectively
owned mountain.

Even in Spanish protectorate times (1912–56, although effectively, in
the Rif, 1926–56), many Rifians sought to establish themselves on such
mountains and had no trouble in obtaining the authorisation of the *jma'th*.
They built their houses quickly and planted fig trees and cactus hedges
around them – and thus private property was established without
complications, and a secondary method for staving off an ever-expanding
population pressure was discovered. These concessions for the use of
common land may also be given to outsiders who have had to leave their
own tribes, to *shurfa'* (descendants, whether real or alleged, of the Prophet
Muhammad) who have prestige in the region, and to the *fqih*-s or Qur'anic
schoolmasters in the mosques. In the two latter cases, it is customary for the
men of the *jma'th* to plough the land for these individuals in a *dhwiza* or
working bee of a day's duration. A *sharif* (sing. of *shurfa'*) or a *fqih* is then
obliged to solicit the usufruct of the land over successive years and to bow
to the decisions of the *jma'th* regarding it. However, it is also customary to
give the *fqih* the concession and to provide him with a *dhwiza* not in
collectively held land, but in *habus* land only, to which we now turn briefly.

If a man for any reason donates land to a mosque or a saint's shrine
(which is usually associated with a mosque), this land is automatically
classed as *habus*. Such property never has an individual owner, and the so-
called 'family *habus*' reported for the Anti-Atlas (André Adam, personal
communication, 1960; Lafond circa. 1948 pp.83–95) does not exist in the
Rif. It is also irrevocable: once someone turns land over to the mosque or to
a saint's tomb as *habus*, he must sign a paper that he has done so, and this
paper is kept in the mosque. Neither the *fqih* of a mosque nor the *mqaddim*

of a mosque or shrine, its caretaker who is simply nominated by the *jma'th*, receives any income from the *habus* property, although the *mqaddim* must act as its administrator. He may possibly receive some charitable offerings or *sadaqa* made in money, but it is never much. Among the Aith Waryaghar, *habus* property is near to minimal in extent: in the Jbil Hmam there are only 3.5 hectares of registered *habus* land, in the community of Tigzirin in the Aith Turirth, and possibly slightly more of undeclared *habus* land in that of Aith Yusif in the Timarzga (Hart 1976 pp.97–101).

After discussing the division of land (*battu n-tmurth*), we turn now to the rather more interesting issue of the division of water (*battu w-aman*). The principles which govern it are five in number: (1) water division ideally follows division of land in all respects, for the owner of a plot of land is also the owner of the subsoil, and water moving through the latter, as well as passing over the former, belongs to him; (2) rights of preference are for human beings, animals, land and turbine grain mills, in that order; (3) river water is collectively owned; (4) upstream people have a prior claim over downstream people (a self-evident premise); and (5) the less irrigation water is available, the more elabourate are the rules governing its distribution, which is again more evident in the northern plain. The fourth principle represents no grave problems, except insofar as the course of the river itself is subject to modification – by rains, for instance; but although the first principle is adhered to by all groups that irrigate from the upper course of the Ghis River (lit. 'muddy river', the second river in Waryagharland, west of and less important than the Nkur), it is not adhered to by those groups that irrigate from the lower Ghis, below the point where it reaches the Plain of al-Husayma. In this last case, to be discussed later, water rights and land rights are quite distinct and may be sold separately.

We start, therefore, with the relatively simple division of irrigation water in the Jbil Hmam, water originating for the most part from the Upper Nkur and its tributaries, and then move down to the greater complexities of the plain. But first some observations about irrigation ditch terminology. Any ditch is called *dharga* (pl. *dhargiwin*), and it may emanate either from a river (*dharga ughzar*) or from a spring (*dharga nj-'unsar*). The distinction between these is based both on the volume and on the use of the water concerned: water from river ditches is not divided on the basis of 'turns' (*nubth* (pl. *nubath*), from Mor. Ar. *nuba*, also used to refer to an elementary or nuclear family, the economic unit of production), since there is always enough for everyone concerned; but water from spring ditches is so divided because most springs in the region provide only a trickle. The 'turn' concept as applied to the division of irrigation water is crucially important, and hence Emilio Blanco Izaga's characterisation of the Aith Waryaghar as a 'turn-based society' (*una sociedad turnante*) is very much to the point (Hart and Blanco Izaga 1975 Vol. I p.102; 1995 p.116).

The point of origin of any ditch – the point at which the river water actually enters the ditch – is called *uggug n-targa*. The point further along where the water is channelled off from the ditch in order to irrigate a specific field (*agra* (pl. *igran*)) or plot of land is called *anqssar*, while *dhasarsth* (pl. *dhisuras*) is the hollowed-out log or tree-trunk acting as a conductor of the water over points where it would otherwise be lost or wasted. These hollowed-out logs are a major feature of the irrigation ecology of the Aith Turirth and Timarzga sections. The total surface area of any garden, orchard or field under irrigation, and thus falling into the category of *dhamurth w-aman*, is called *dhaghzwith* (pl. *dhighza*). In the local community of l-'Ass in the Aith Turirth, the total amount of land under irrigation is therefore termed *dhaghzwith nj-'Ass*.

A given plot or terrace of irrigated land, the maximal segment, so to speak, of a *dhaghzwith*, is known as *dhaqqirat* (pl. *dhiqqiradhin*); and in l-'Ass, to continue with the example just given, there are about 140–50 such *dhiqqiradhin*. Each of these is subdivided into smaller segments called *dhathutsh* (pl. *dhithura*); and each of these is yet again subdivided into minimal segments called *r-hawdh* (pl. *r-ahwadh*). The walls between terraces or plots of any or all of the three above categories are termed *dhsunda* (pl. *dhisundawin*), and boundaries between plots or subplots are called *agmir* (pl. *igmiren*). Every single unit or subunit of land under irrigation subdivision thus has its corresponding designation.

But even though the Fqir Azzugwagh and his friend 'Amar w-'Aisa from the Aith Turirth community of Aith 'Aru Musa originally went halves over the purchase and division, in about 1870, of both land and irrigation water in l-'Ass, the descendants of the latter, the Dharwa n-'Amar w-'Aisa, remained undivided even in the 1960s as they felt no need to divide, whereas the sons of the Fqir Azzugwagh divided up even before his death. The present unequal water distribution in l-'Ass is, like the land distribution, owing to unequal lineage proliferation over time; and this inequality persists even though there is enough water to go around. The land through which it flows is steep and craggy: the upper part was bought from the small lineage of the Ihammuthen, and the lower from the much larger one of the Yinn Hand w-'Abdallah (which had earlier, in 1853, provided a wife for the Fqir Azzugwagh). These two lineages are both genuine Aith Turirth ones, but it seems that they themselves had previously bought the land from the people of Ikhuwanen in the tribe of the Igzinnayen, who were the original owners not only of this land but also of the adjoining lands of the present Aith Turirth communities of Bulma and Ignan, which again had come into the hands of the expanding Aith Turirth through purchase at the end of the eighteenth century (Hart 1976 pp.110 n.23, 507). It is perhaps ironic that in the l-'Ass case, half the land reverted through repurchase to a man from the Igzinnayen, the Fqir Azzugwagh, but he and his sons were to become Aith Waryaghar in fact if not in name. Documents in Arabic held by the family speak of him and his descendants as *l-Gzinnayi aslan wa l- Waryaghli daran* ('of Igzinnayen origin but of Aith Waryaghar residence'), indicating clearly that from a long-term point of view, fixity of residence or domicile among Rifians takes precedence over tribal origins (Hart, in preparation).

As with the land, so with the water: in the 1960s, as at the time of purchase about a century earlier, both were divided in half (or more accurately into eight shares – four for the Dharwa ('sons of') 'Amar w-'Aisa and four for the Dharwa Ufqir Azzugwagh). The latter were then divided into shares for their constituent sublineages: one for the Dharwa n-'Amar Uzzugwagh, one for the Dharwa n-Muh Akkuh Uzzugwagh, and two for the Dharwa n-Mzzyan Uzzugwagh combined with the now extinct sublineage of the Dharwa n-Muh Uzzugwagh.

It is worth noting that the Saru nj-'Ass, the l-'Ass River, another tributary of the upper Nkur, trickles out of a spring, the Mizab nj-'Ass, in the rocks. Legend has it that this spring gushed forth when one of the saints or *shurfa'* of the holy lineage of the Dharwa n- Sidi Hand u-Musa of the Igzinnayen, finding no water on the spot with which to perform his pre-prayer ablutions, tapped the rock with his stick. His tapping produced a miraculous trickle, which gradually developed into the deep gorge cut by the l-'Ass river. Even though the water here is relatively abundant, there are nonetheless *nubath* or 'turns' of irrigation, which begin every evening at sunset and continue for the next 24 hours.

The irrigation turns in l-'Ass are divided in the same way as the land. Four days or 96 hours were allotted to the whole lineage of the Dharwa Ufqir Azzugwagh, which in 1955 were subdivided as follows: one 24-hour day for the five *nubath* or elementary families of the Dharwa n-'Amar Uzzugwagh; a second 24-hour day for Muh Akkuh Uzzugwagh and his married son, thus two *nubath*; and two days or 48 hours for the three *nubath* of the Dharwa n-Mzzyan Uzzugwagh, of which one, as well as one of the Dharwa n-'Amar Uzzugwagh, consisted of a young unmarried man and his widowed mother. After the death in 1956 of old Muh Akkuh Uzzugwagh and the marriage of his second eldest son, as well as the formation of a *nubth* by yet a still younger son, half-brother to the other two, with his widowed mother, one *nubth* was lost and two were gained. The other four days or 96 hours were allotted to the three *nubath* of the Dharwa n-'Amar w-'Aisa, again including an unmarried son and his widowed mother. By 1959 the Dharwa n-'Amar w-'Aisa had been reduced to only two *nubath* by the death of one of their members, whose widow was then remarried to the unmarried brother just mentioned, as widow inheritance is standard practice in the Rif.

These instances of the proliferation and attrition of *nubath* within a given lineage are mentioned here to show that despite such fluctuations over time, the rules governing both ownership of land and of its irrigation water are absolutely ironclad. Since the land and the water rights in l-'Ass were originally bought by two men who had become great friends, all the descendants of both of them continue to observe the original distribution into halves. This distribution also applies to olive oil, for the Fqir Azzugwagh and 'Amar w-'Aisa jointly built an olive press as well. One result is that the Dharwa Ufqir Azzugwagh, who are numerous and live on the upper slope, have all long since divided their land and water, while the Dharwa n-'Amar w-'Aisa, who are few and live down below, were still in indivision at the time we left the field. It is perhaps ironic that when the savage vendetta broke out that was to ravage l-'Ass for the first two decades of the present century, it was not at all between these two lineages of very unequal size but between the full brothers 'Amar and Mzzyan Uzzugwagh and their sons, with the Dharwa n-'Amar w-'Aisa taking the side of the former and Muh Akkuh Uzzugwagh taking that of the latter, as the final brother Muh Uzzugwagh, who had no sons, had already been killed in the Igzinnayen over another matter entirely. (For full details, cf. Hart 1976 pp.325–38, recapitulated in Hart, in preparation).

Like all natural features, all irrigation ditches are named. The mere existence of secondary and tertiary ditches in the plain, which lead to those that irrigate individual plots, is already an indication of the considerably greater complexity of water rights there than in the Jbil Hmam, where the l-'Ass case is fairly representative. This kind of ditch subdivision exists in the Jbil Hmam, to be sure, but not to the same degree as in the plain, where not only was there less water available – for much of it was lost through filtration – but where the population density is very much higher (166 per square kilometre in the former as opposed to only 38 per square kilometre in the latter, as taken from the 1960 Moroccan census: cf. Hart 1976 p.18). Furthermore, it was only after the *pax hispanica* that the Nkur River, along its middle and lower courses, became the *de jure* tribal border between the Aith Waryaghar on the west and the Axt Tuzin and, further north, the Thimsaman on the east. Even at the time of fieldwork there were still some overlaps on both sides of the river (i.e. minor extensions of Aith Waryaghar territory into those of the Axt Tuzin and the Thimsaman, and vice versa). Some general observations on water utilisation among the Aith Waryaghar serve to bring these points into greater relief.

As noted elsewhere (Hart 1958 pp.208 ff.; 1976 p.111), all water usage, both at the collective and at the individual levels, was subject to agreements between the users. (We employ the past tense here simply because it is our understanding that after the completion of the Nkur River dam, appropriately called Sidd Muhammad bin 'Abd al-Krim al-Khattabi, above Bni Bu 'Ayyash in 1987, most of the river water goes directly to the provincial capital of al-Husayma and the local cultivators now receive only a fraction of it.) Such agreements, particularly for the lower Nkur and the plain, were at the time of fieldwork generally made at the beginning of the summer and applied especially to sources that had only an intermittent flow or one of short duration. They dealt with the whole range of dams, networks of ditches, repairs to ditches effected on a *dhwiza* basis, irrigations and turns, and infractions and sanctions. The last category was usually concerned with the appropriation of turns out of order, and the resultant quarrels which were generally settled by the local *aquwwam* or specialist in customary law pertaining to agriculture or irrigation.

One obstacle to such agreements, however, might have lain in the path of the ditch itself rather than in the distribution of the flow (which is or was calculated in as equitable a manner as possible) because it was necessary to obtain the prior consent of each property owner over whose land the ditch would pass. Any owner would of course have raised strenuous objections if he were not provided with a turn, and in any event he generally made it understood that the ditch was not to cross his land at all but to follow the boundaries around it.

Under these circumstances, the division of irrigation water posed no major problems, and during the *Ripublik* natural means were used to calculate the time – usually, though not always, on a 24-hour basis. The actual time of day, before the wristwatch was introduced, was calculated by measuring the length of a man's shadow and pacing this length off with one foot just in front of the other.

Once the number of turns was decided upon, the duration of each and its order of occurrence were then established. This generally took place at the point of origin of the ditch and was done by drawing lots (usually straws, pieces of wood or stones). In the Jbil Hmam, in communities such as l-'Ass where water is plentiful, the order of turns was fixed once and for all. But this was not necessarily the case in the plain: for the Dharga n-Tfirasin from the lower Ghis, for example, lots were redrawn at any time the users deemed it necessary, such as when a ditch was washed out by rain or, at the other extreme, when there was a complete lack of water in summer. Once the necessary repairs were made, redrawing took place, under the aegis of the *aquwwam*.

It is noted earlier that a major and self-evident premise underlying the Aith Waryaghar irrigation system is that upstream people have priority over downstream people. To this a corollary must now be added: the fact that jurisdiction of the riverain people does or did not extend to the middle of the river bed. The basic reason for this lies in the torrential regimen of the rivers themselves: they may be short in overall distance, but they have rapid currents, they become flooded easily during storms, and as a result they give rise to new and diverse channels that constantly vary and modify their banks. This is particularly true of the Nkur, and this fact of hydrography gives rise to a multiplicity of incidents and to frequent modifications of agreement, 'all of which are contrary to the essentially conservative and traditionalist character of the Rifian' (Blanco Izaga 1939 pp.103–4; Hart and Blanco Izaga 1975 Vol. II p.354, 1995 pp.393–4). Even more important is the role of the Nkur River as a somewhat fluctuating tribal boundary, as the following story graphically illustrates.

Sidi Mhand u-Musa, the founder of the Iziqqiwen lineage of that Aith Waryaghar tribal section made up of *shurfa'* who are known collectively as Imrabdhen, who died about 1838–39 and is buried in the 'Hillock of the Saints' in Aith Hishim, and who is not be confused with Sidi Hand u-Musa of the Igzinnayen, is generally recognised as the foremost saint among the Aith Waryaghar lowlanders. Not only did he have, so legend has it, the ability to be in two places at once, but he is also credited with having mounted the Aith Waryaghar guard on the mainland (at the Burj al-Mujahidin in Ajdir, which was much later to become bin 'Abd al-Krim's capital and which is today the main administrative centre in Aith Waryaghar territory) against the Spanish who since 1673 had occupied al-Husayma Island in the middle of the bay of the same name. (Sanchez Perez even says that this tribal guard was mounted as a reaction to the Spanish occupation of the island and their declaration of it as a *plaza de soberania*, and that the guard on the mainland lasted until 1926, for 253 years: cf. Sanchez Perez 1952 p.42). The most spectacular achievement of Sidi Mhand u-Musa, however, was, through a miracle, to cause heavy rain to re-route the course of the Nkur River in favour of the Aith Waryaghar and at the expense of the Axt Tuzin, whose own saint, Sidi Bu Jiddayn, was held to have been bested in this hagiolatrical contest. The incident is mentioned here in order to indicate the advantages (or disadvantages, depending on the point of view) of a 'fluid boundary'.

This augmentation of already existing points of friction has made a virtue of necessity. The organisation of Aith Waryaghar society has deeply conditioned its members' attitudes toward ownership of land and water, so that any possible demands or threats voiced by downstream groups for a transfer of even a minimal portion of the flow are useless. This may sound like belabouring the obvious, but the principle is very well suited to Rifian rivers because in normally dry river beds water rises up only in certain parts; these narrow fissures seem to be independent of each other, and each, by means of an improvised dam (*uggug*) feeds a series of successive ditches. Furthermore, the nature of these streams, with their irregular flow and occasional devastating overflow, have convinced the Rifian farmer that he cannot profitably cultivate any land beyond what is necessary for his own subsistence. In any case, further cultivation would attract the attention and envy of neighbours or even strangers, which would, in turn, lead to blows.

Here another factor emerges in the mountains of the Jbil Hmam: only a very small part of the water in the upper courses of the rivers needs to be used for irrigation, since in general water is overabundant while land is lacking. As Blanco Izaga very appropriately observed, this has provided an excellent reason for preventing Aith Waryaghar highlanders from ever thinking in terms of large-scale irrigation developments. As of 1967, the Moroccan government planned to build a dam, that referred to above, on the Nkur River above Bni Bu 'Ayyash and to turn the whole plain into a sugar-cane plantation, although as of 20 years later, only the former objective had been achieved. Blanco went on to observe (as of 1939) that since the Rifians had been in no way favoured by nature, it was up to the then protectorate power, Spain, to help them; but he then realistically recalled that there had been nothing but prejudices and injuries in the case of the irrigation turn that the Aith Waryaghar lowlanders had to cede to the rather abortive Spanish experimental farm at Imzuren. There the land appropriated by the farm looked like 'minute green islets among the calculated holdings of the natives, whose ill will and caustic comments are just, logical and in no way flattering: *nubth nj-makhzan*, "the turn of the government", as they said, which means that a squad of *mkhazni*-s has to be stationed on the spot to see to it that no poverty-stricken *akhammas* (sharecropper who receives a fifth of the harvest) tries, in the middle of the night, to get water out of turn' (Blanco Izaga 1939 pp.105–6; Hart and Blanco Izaga 1975 Vol. II pp.355–6,1995 pp.395–6).

In the plain, water is or was divided on a 24-hour basis in the major ditches, but in the smaller segments of these, people resort to division on the basis of a 'hoe' (*ayarzim*), a 'yoke' (*dhiyuga*), a 'half-yoke' (*azgin n-tyuga*) or of 'days of ploughing' (*r-iyyam n-tyarza*). The 'hoe' basis refers to the number of regular users of the ditch who turn up, hoe in hand, to irrigate; and division is made in proportion to the land owners. 'Hoe' also refers to the proportion in which each landholder contributes to the number of workers in the maintenance and construction of the ditch. The 'yoke' basis means that those who have two draft animals (usually cows), which constitute a yoke, receive a full turn, while those with only one animal, and hence a 'half-yoke', only receive half a turn (Rodriguez Erola 1952). In the upper Nkur, where water is abundant, only the 24-hour principle exists, while the other methods of water distribution are geared for those regions where water is scarce.

Irrigation turns can thus be traded or swapped, but if anyone forgets his turn or fails to show up for it, he forfeits it. During the *Ripublik*, when ditches needed repair after heavy rains, for example, an announcement was made in the evening at the mosque, and any persons who failed to show up the next day to take care of the repairs were fined 2.50 duros hasani apiece (in Spanish times (1954–55) 16 pesetas, the then standard daily wage). The proceeds were used to buy food for those who did turn up. In Tazurakhth in the upper Aith Bu 'Ayyash section, anyone who refused to pay had to forfeit a rifle (which was returned to him on payment).

During the *Ripublik* the members of the *jma'th* handled all irrigation matters themselves but in Spanish times an *aquwwam* or irrigation supervisor was appointed in each section by the *qa'id* in order to regulate, on the spot if possible, all disputes and quarrels over land, water and animals. The independent Moroccan administration has continued to retain the *aquwwam* as a minor tribal functionary, and he is still appointed by the *qa'id*. He exacts fines according to the extent of damages caused and he must turn in a statement of damage to the *qadi*, who forces the guilty party to pay up. However, in this same connection there are two points of custom that are known to everyone: if a river in flood lifts up bodily a portion of A's property, for example, and places it on top of that of B, the lands in question now belongs to B rather than to A because it is B's land that now gives it its *asr* (Mor. Ar. *asl*, 'roots'). However, should the river place the land in question beside but not on top of that of B, it still belongs to A.

In the plain the usage of irrigation water from both the lower Nkur and the lower Ghis rivers has always been the subject of agreements, usually verbal for the Nkur and usually written for the Ghis. In this region the flow of water, even though highly variable, permits a regular distribution through permanent ditches, a distribution sanctioned by tradition and known to all. These ditches contain water all year round and because their utilisation has been regulated and stabilised, incidents do or did not often occur in the plain. However, to what extent this traditional distribution has been changed as a result of the construction of the Bin 'Abd al-Krim Dam we do not know, but the change has no doubt been great.

As suggested earlier, the irrigation system of the Aith Waryaghar not only parallels the lineage and territorial systems very closely, but it is also, wherever and whenever possible, based upon them and might even be considered as one mode of the latter. Where this is not the case, sales of individual property or of the property of minimal lineage branches have generally been the cause. Such sales have occurred most frequently in the plain, where the presence of the Spanish model farm at Imzuren further complicated the precolonial irrigation picture, even though it was grudgingly integrated into the lowland irrigational structure.

In the river beds there are certain points known to the Aith Waryaghar where water always rises up; and dams are made at these points for the source of the ditches as well as partitions for the water on both sides. After a dam has been built, holding as much water as possible, it is converted into a ditch-head in which the necessary outlets are made, and it serves as the point of origin of the primary ditches of permanent flow, usually two or three in number. The Aith Waryaghar say that the water going through these outlets is well distributed, by halves or thirds or whatever the case may be. Although this is what occurs in theory, in practice the distribution is far from perfect, as account is not taken of either the width or the depth of the outlets, which are improvised and variable. The primary ditches are divided, where necessary, into secondary branches, and it is in these branches that the irrigation turns are initiated, each one taking up water for 24 hours. The secondary branches are again divided into tertiary branches, also of periodic flow, which take up water either only during the day, or only at night; and these in turn give rise to the individual irrigation furrows that receive water only at certain hours, generally determined by those of the daily prayers.

The primary ditches tend to serve local communities (*dshar* (pl. *dshur*)); the secondary ditches with flows of 24-hour duration serve the *dharfiqin* (sing. *dharfiqth*) or lineage groups resident within them; the tertiary ones serve the *ijujga* (sing. *jajgu*) or lineage branches encapsulated within these *dharfiqin*. The distribution of water is sealed by instructions from the owners of the tertiary ditches so that if any of these ditches receives water during the day in one irrigation turn, it will do so at night in the following one, while the first man in one turn will be the last in the next. The two classes of turns making up this order of irrigation are usually set up for the full sequence and are, again, settled by drawing lots. At this level the transfer of irrigation turns may be effected at any time, and for the lower Ghis, as noted, the sale of such turns is entirely independent of the sale of property. The reason for this is lack of water. River water is supplemented here to some extent by the existence of wells, but not enough to make an appreciable difference. Disputes are resolved by the standard processes of arbitration, evaluation of damages, or indemnification.

In pre-Spanish times any stranger coming to that part of the Aith Waryaghar lowlands irrigated by the Ghis river in order to buy property and build a house had no right to the water from the irrigation ditch in his community until he bought and paid for his irrigation turn. To this end he had to have a document duly notarised by two *'adul* and signed by the *qadi*, proving the legitimacy of his purchase. Erola observed that in the lower Ghis one may as a result encounter individuals who own water rights but no land, whereas this is never the case in the upper Ghis (Rodriguez Erola

1953). In any case, in the upper Ghis none of the ditches are of any real importance and there is in fact little irrigation; it was only along the lower Ghis that they were important at the time of fieldwork. The Ghis may be the longest river in the Central Rif, but its only significant ditches, three in number, lead off from its lower course, in the plain: Dharga nd-Bzimma on the west bank and Dharga nd-Bu r-Ma'iz and Dharga n-Tfadhna on the east bank. Dharga nd-Bzimma had a five-day turn, distributed among the various lineages of the large local community of Ajdir; in 1938 it provided the water to turn one gristmill, and by 1953 there were several more such mills. Dharga nd-Bu r-Ma'iz had a three-day turn, split up between the various lineage groups included in Imhawren, r-Hujjaj and Tifirasin (each of which was then split into its own component segments for irrigation purposes), as well as moving three mills in 1938 and several more by 1953. We now focus upon Emilio Blanco Izaga's treatment of the flow from this particular ditch.

The most important principle emerging from Blanco's material on the Dharga nd-Bu r-Ma'iz ditch is the existence of what he neatly termed intermittent irrigation rights (Blanco Izaga 1939 pp.113–18; Hart and Blanco Izaga 1975 Vol. II pp.363–7, 1995 pp.403–8). By 1953, when we first began fieldwork in the Rif, the lineage of the Aith Bu Dhimmus which had been granted such rights had been fully absorbed and integrated into the normal user pattern for the ditch. Yet these 'intermittent' rights as originally discussed by Blanco in 1939 are of considerable structural interest and merit description: for they were not in any sense randomly intermittent but had a very precise pattern of rotation, a point that Blanco himself did not make sufficiently clear.

In the Imhawren turn from the Dharga nd-Bu r-Ma'iz ditch, the Aith Bu Dhimmus lineage (of the section of the Aith Yusif w-'Ari) figured as an outside element but only when water was scarce, for this lineage normally had its own turn in the Dharga n-Tfadhna (which had its own secondary ditch of Upper Tafadhna or Tafadhna n-Dara). Its structural insertion into the Imhawren turn thus assured its members of water that in hard times they might not otherwise have received. Hence the members of this lineage were given intermittent rights with the idea that their inclusion would not interrupt the general irrigation schedule. The pattern of this insertion and inclusion was regarded both by Blanco and the present writer is an excellent explanation of the fact that in the plain of al-Husayma there were very few incidents regarding irrigation turns other than those created by the unwanted presence of Spanish irrigators at the Imzuren experimental farm. It is worth spelling out this pattern of accommodation in greater detail.

On the first day, under normal circumstances, the Imhawren irrigated, and their turn was utilised by one of their three component lineages, the Aith 'Aru Hmid, the Aith 'Abdallah u-Hmid and the Aith Muhand u-Hmid (all descended from the sons of a common agnatic ancestor Hmid, and all of the Aith 'Ari section). The fourth and outside element, the Aith Bu Dhimmus, we leave aside for the time being. The second day was the turn of one of the two Tifirasin lineages, the Aith Mhand u-Yihya and the Im'arwen (both of the Aith Yusif w-'Ari section). On the third day (24 hours) the turn of r-Hujjaj was taken by one of its three constituent lineages, the Aith r-'Arbi, the Dharwa nd-Hajj Si 'Ari Ubarru and the I'arhuthen (all, again, of the Aith 'Ari section).

Thus, over a nine-day period, there was, under ordinary circumstances, the following arrangement:

TABLE 1
ORIGINAL IRRIGATION AGREEMENT: IMHAWREN, TIFIRASIN AND R-HUJJAJ

Day	Sequence	Turn
1	Imhawren	Aith 'Aru Hmid
2	Tifirasin	Aith Mhand u-Yihya
3	r-Hujjaj	Aith r-'Arbi
4	Imhawren	Aith 'Abdallah u-Hmid
5	Tifirasin	Im'arwen
6	r-Hujjaj	Dharwa nd-Hajj Si 'Ari Ubarru
7	Imhawren	Aith Muhand u-Hmid
8	Tifirasin	Aith Mhand u-Yihya
9	r-Hujjaj	I'arhuthen

Then the sequence was repeated. In the ordinary normal sequence each lineage of Tifirasin irrigated once every six days, while each lineage of Imhawren and r-Hujjaj only irrigated once every nine days. Now, if we intercalate the Aith Bu Dhimmus into the picture, we see that each Tifirasin lineage continued to irrigate every six days, and each r-Hujjaj lineage every nine, on the same day as before; but the Imhawren lineages, to which the newly intercalated Aith Bu Dhimmus lineage was appended, underwent a shift. As a result four out of every five turns of each Imhawren lineage fell as usual nine days apart, and the remaining turn involved a gap of 18 days, with the newcomers irrigating regularly every 12 days. Thus without altering the general sequence of the turns and without detriment to the other two remaining lineage-cum-irrigation units, located slightly further away, the thirst of the Aith Bu Dhimmus was quenched while this lineage rotated around the Imhawren turns as indicated schematically in Table 2. Since the turns of the Tifirasin and r-Hujjaj lineages remained exactly as shown in Table 1, only the Imhawren turns are shown here.

As of 1953, the Aith Bu Dhimmus lineage had been fully integrated into the irrigation turn structure of the Tafadhna n-Dara secondary ditch of the Dharga nd-Bu r-Ma'iz while still retaining their original rights in the

TABLE 2
MODIFICATIONS TO TABLE 1 THROUGH INTERCALATION OF EXTRA LINEAGE
(AITH BU DHIMMUS) INTO IMHAWREN SEQUENCE

Day	Imhawren turn
1	Aith Bu Dhimmus – took the turn of Aith 'Aru Hmid
4	Aith 'Abdallah u-Hmid
7	Aith Muhand u-Hmid
10	Aith 'Aru Hmid – recuperated their own turn
13	Aith Bu Dhimmus – took the turn of Aith 'Abdallah u-Hmid
16	Aith Muhand u-Hmid
19	Aith 'Aru Hmid
22	Aith 'Abdallah u-Hmid – recuperated their own turn
25	Aith Bu Dhimmus – took the turn of Aith Muhand u-Hmid
28	Aith 'Aru Hmid

Tafadhna primary ditch. There is no question but that this integration had occurred through the outright purchase of an irrigation turn.

The Tafadhna ditch, to take a less complicated example, had a three-day turn. In 1938 it moved four mills and by 1953 there were several more. The distribution of its water was as follows: on the first day the Imrabdhen lineage of the Yinn Si 'Amar Umrabit; on the second day the Aith Bu Dhimmus (Ajdir) (12 hours), the Andrusen (or 'Andalusians') lineage (two hours 40 minutes), and the Aith Bu Dhimmus (nine hours 20 minutes); and on the third day the Imhawren (Aith Aru Hmid, Aith 'Abdallah u-Hmid and Aith Muhand u-Hmid). Here the situation as we found it in 1953 was substantially the same as Blanco had described it in 1939.

We now make some general remarks on the ditches emanating from the lower Nkur. The Nkur contains many more ditch outlets of importance than does the Ghis, but, as Blanco pointed out, its irrigation regimen is less exact, both because it has more water, and because there is no need for compensating wells. Written agreements regarding distribution of Nkur River water are few and relatively recent. As noted, the river acts as the *ad hoc* boundary between the Axt Tuzin and the Thimsaman on the east and the Aith Waryaghar on the west, and in its fast-moving upper course there is always more than enough water and irrigation turns are a simple matter. Even in the middle Nkur there is still plenty of water to irrigate meanders such as those of Dhaghzwith n-Dasa, in the Axt Tuzin, and Tazurakhth. But in the lower Nkur, north of the Thanda Hawa lagoon, the complexity of irrigation turns approaches that of the lower Ghis.

Again, a much greater population density, water filtration and subsequent loss are the reasons. The various accounts do not all correspond, a fact which is in itself significant. One document, probably drawn up in 1954–55 by the then *aquwwam* of the Aith Bu 'Ayyash, on the distribution of irrigation water from the Dharga n-Tufrasht ditch on the west bank of the Nkur, between the communities of Izakiren and Ighmiren, in the Aith Bu 'Ayyash section, stated that those of Ighmiren would receive three parts and those of Izakiren, five parts, but in the enumeration for the latter six parts are actually listed. Perhaps this is an indication how clerical errors in the drawing up of documents can lead to structural ambiguities. Another example is the Dharga n-Dahar, again on the west bank. According to Blanco's reckoning it moved two mills in 1938 and had two turns of 24 hours each, one for the Aith Bu 'Ayyash and the second for the Aith 'Ari. The latter turn was split up into two-thirds for the community of Aith Musa w-'Amar and one-third for that of Imzuren (Blanco Izaga 1939 p.124; Hart and Blanco Izaga 1975 Vol. II p.370, 1995 p.416). Blanco's representation for this distribution was as follows:

1st day:	Aith Bu 'Ayyash
2nd day:	Aith 'Ari (Aith Musa w-'Amar)
3rd day:	Aith Bu 'Ayyash
4th day:	Aith 'Ari (Aith Musa w-'Amar)
5th day:	Aith Bu 'Ayyash
6th day:	Aith 'Ari (Imzuren)

Our own information, from one source, agreed with this in that it gave half to the Aith Bu 'Ayyash and half to the Aith 'Ari, although it did not break the latter down into constituent user elements. But another interpretation gave primacy to the Aith Bu 'Ayyash, who received five out of eight turns while the Aith 'Ari only received the other three (Rodriguez Erola 1953). The distribution of lower Ghis water was indeed complex, because land and water were considered as two discrete entities. But because it was properly codified it was not ambiguous. Distribution of the lower Nkur water, however, tends or tended to be ambiguous in practice if not in theory.

The distribution of irrigation water from the upper courses of both rivers is a far simpler matter than in the plain of al-Husayma, where lineage discontinuity has created a veritable territorial jumble. The progression of the Aith Waryaghar from their original home in the Jbil Hmam down to the plain was very gradual, but in terms of sectional and lineage discontinuity and replication, which in the plain is extremely great, it can hardly be considered orderly. The sale of both land and irrigation rights created something of a patchwork quilt of sections, which were infiltrated by numerous strangers and stranger lineages as well, most probably by escapees from feuds at home. Prior to 1889–90, when the very first house was built in the plain itself rather than merely overlooking it, the plain had been used only for cultivation by irrigation, with the cultivators living in their communities in the surrounding low hills. But owing to the agricultural stake that several Aith Waryaghar sections already had in the plain, and owing to the patchwork nature of sectional and lineage distribution, irrigation ditches even at that time were already cutting across community and even across sectional and tribal holdings, as the above evidence makes clear (i.e. the ditches on the east bank of the lower-middle Nkur which irrigate not only for the Aith Waryaghar but for the Axt Tuzin and the Thimsaman as well). The plain has long been a maze of irrigation ditches, ranging from concrete-reinforced primary ditches to mere furrows, and after the establishment of the *pax hispanica* and, even more, after Moroccan independence, it became a virtual maze of local communities as well. There is not enough land or enough water for all, both because of the proliferation of autochthonous lineage groups and the accretion and growth of others from outside (Hart 1976 pp.107–15).

The Aith Waryaghar would hardly seem to qualify as a 'hydraulic society' in Wittfogel's sense – and they are disqualified entirely on political grounds, for Wittfogel's thesis is that centralised despotism arose in precisely those parts of both the Near and Far East where major irrigation works could be and were undertaken. Nonetheless, irrigation is or was of extreme importance to them, such that, at least in part, they may, to use Gray's terminology, be considered to be 'irrigation-based' (Wittfogel 1957; Gray 1960). More recently Gilman Guillen has justifiably included them in a survey of acephalous societies in which internal conflict is also often 'irrigation-based' (Gilman Guillen 1987 pp.68–9) – or rather, as having been irrigation-based in the very recent past, because since 1960 and particularly since 1970 they have ever increasingly turned into migrant industrial workers in certain EU member countries (Holland, Belgium and France in particular). These same observations, to a lesser extent – even the final one about labour migration in Europe – can also be applied to the Ait 'Atta of the Moroccan South, to whom we now turn.

＊　＊　＊　＊　＊

To the best of our knowledge, no Ait 'Atta land deeds or documents have yet been found, and the only one, from the Saghru, which does deal with the subject in part is unfortunately undated (or at least the copy of it that we were permitted to photograph in 1961 was undated: cf. Hart 1966, 1981 pp.219–27). In theory, however, the Ait 'Atta recognise four types of land tenure: (1) the *igudlan* (sing. *agudal*), or collective pasturelands, with fixed opening and closing dates, mostly in the Central Atlas and generally at some distance from the houses or communities of the tribal sections that use them; (2) pasturelands designated as *l-khla* (Mor. Ar. 'empty countryside'), *akal n-ijamma'm* or *tamazirt n-l-jma't* (lit. *'jma'a* land, collectively owned land'), belonging to the *taqbilt* or section in a residential sense, land which is located just beyond areas of cultivation and without opening and closing restrictions; (3) *bil-khayr* cultivated land, mostly in the Saghru, derived from 'the law of the first occupant' (de Monts de Savasse 1951), from lot-drawing or arbitration and devolving through inheritance to filial heirs; and (4) individual property holdings (Mor. Ar. *l-mulk*), known to the Ait 'Atta generally as *aharmil* ('pure property') or *aidda* ('patrimony').

In practice these four categories are generally reduced to three, as the second is not common in the Saghru or is assimilated to the first, while the third is assimilated to the second. *Habus*, however, forms a fifth category, one which, in Ait 'Atta territory as elsewhere in Morocco, refers, as noted, primarily to religious endowments, land donated in an inalienable fashion to a mosque, to which its income reverts. All Ait 'Atta communities possess mosques and most possess some *habus* land. 'Private *habus*' is simply another name for remaining in indivision. As de Ligniville has noted, the head of a tent or a family cannot set up a *habus* for any one member of his family, but only for his heirs collectively; and this procedure was often used in precolonial times (i.e. before the Ait 'Atta were finally 'pacified' by the French in the bloody Battle of Bu Gafr in the Saghru in 1933) to protect objects of value, such as guns (de Ligniville 1937).

In general, however, the proportion of individual holdings throughout Ait 'Atta territory is small compared to collective property. Not only does this stand in direct contrast to the situation prevailing among the Aith Waryaghar, but, as de Monts de Savasse has so correctly observed, Ait 'Atta land tenure is designed to keep strangers out (de Monts de Savasse 1951). Again in contrast to the Aith Waryaghar, the Ait 'Atta in general attain the extraordinarily high figure of 85 per cent for resident males who are agnatic members of the lineage groups associated with any given territory (Hart 1981 pp.121–2), whereas in the same context the Aith Waryaghar percentage is down to 58 per cent (Hart 1976 pp.235–7). This exclusion of strangers creates the prevailing trend toward property indivision, known to the Ait 'Atta as *ur ibdi*, *tishshurka* or *mann*.

This ideal is still adhered to remarkably strongly, especially for all *igudlan* and certainly for all uncultivated land. Even at Usikis, a largely sedentarised Ait 'Atta settlement on the south slope of the Central Atlas, where cultivation under irrigation is extensive, informants held the neighbouring and previously hostile tribes of the Ait Murghad, the Ait Hadiddu and the Ait Siddrat in no little contempt because of their tendency toward *bdan*, to divide such land. Transhumance is still held to be the ideal, although sedentarisation is in fact becoming accentuated everywhere under the effect of the inevitable division of the land.

Ait 'Atta land division systems were first described by de Monts de Savasse in the principal valleys of the Saghru, where the archetype is that used in the Wad Ragg (de Monts de Savasse 1951). Each Ait 'Atta *khums* or 'fifth' (of which, as among the Aith Waryaghar, there were five, but employed in each case toward different ends: toward the division of fines for murder among the latter and toward the annual election of the top chief among the latter: cf. Hart (1967) 1984) took its plots, and then certain sections or *tiqbilin* (pl. of *taqbilt*) within these 'fifths', either immediately or later, proceeded in turn to divide the land among their subsections and only then did the latter do so among their constituent lineages. The Ait Y'azza of the middle Ragg and the Ait Wallal of the upper Ragg, upstream from the administrative post at Ikniwn, now have individual holdings as a result of this process.

This system was based on the 'law of the first occupant', on lot-drawing (*grat illan*) or on arbitration. Through inheritance these lands passed to the sons and patrilineal descendants of the original owners, who then divided them up in turn. Development of land for agriculture in this way is what the Ait 'Atta of the Saghru mean by the term *bil-khayr* (Mor. Ar. 'with the good' (i.e. without hindrance)). This, de Monts de Savasse notes, corresponds with our notion of possession but not of property, which as noted is *mulk* in Arabic and *aharmil* to the Ait 'Atta. No business transaction of any sort is possible on *bil-khayr* land, no sale, no purchase, no exchange and no mortgaging. Right of possession ceases if the land is abandoned for a period, variable from one section to another and from zone to zone, but generally from two to ten years. Any litigation over contested land is handled by the sectional *ajmu'* or council, for, as also noted, there are no written deeds.

The right of peaceful occupation of collective land is also admitted, but the tenant knows that if the owning group decides to divide it he must abandon his plot and his house, taking only the beams and doors with him, as wood is precious in southern Morocco and virtually absent in the Saghru. Although he is not reimbursed, the group must either wait until harvest time or give him the seed. Hence, after several centuries of peaceful occupation an w-'Atta (sing. of Ait 'Atta) can be expelled for the good of the collectivity, his only compensation being the benefits he derived therefrom for many years. In fact *bil-khayr* cultivation has permitted tribesmen, in those sections where the *ajmu'* is opposed to division, an extra agricultural base in order to avoid complete dependence on the outside world.

After the initial division, the fifths established well-defined zones of good sheltered pastureland, often watered by springs, by a river along the main axes or by a subterranean sheet of water capable of being used for a well or a *khattara* (an underground irrigation ditch). Such a complex is the normal *agudal* of the Ait 'Atta of the Saghru. As the Saghru is exclusively Ait 'Atta territory, rigid opening and closing dates, as manifested in the *igudlan* of the Central Atlas, have been replaced by division between the constituent sections of each fifth. We discuss those of the Saghru first.

The *igudlan* of the Saghru are small, and their axial sections also contain small zones of *bil-khayr* cultivation such as those at Anu n-Izim ('well of the lion') and Tagudilt. In the Central Atlas they are much bigger and, aside from the controversial Agudal n-Tlmast (discussed below), they function purely for festival sheep transhumance. An *agudal* is the property of the section and has both its general statutes and particular clauses, *shrut* (sing. *shart*). Its limits are known to all, particularly to members of other sections, while the opening and closing dates, where appropriate, as well as proscriptions on numbers of livestock and zones of *bil-khayr* cultivation, are established by the constituent sectional councils in order to protect the grass. Custom decreed that no part of an *agudal* may be divided in its totality should the arriving section want to sell all or part of it and if the *ajmu'* gives its consent. Interestingly, de Monts de Savasse also notes that in 1936, after an arrangement between the Ait Wallal and the saints of the Ihansalen, of Zawiya Ahansal, one which involved the swearing of a collective Berber oath by the former, the Agudal n-Ait Wallal became the exclusive property of the Ihansalen; and the Ait 'Atta no longer had any real rights to it. However, as the Ait Wallal had previously admitted *bil-khayr* cultivation, the Ihansalen let them build houses and dig wells. But when a conflict broke out, the Ait Wallal could not produce their title deeds, which had been either lost or, more likely, confiscated by the *igurramen* or saints of Zawiya Ahansal; and the Ait Wallal lost the case (cf. de Monts de Savasse 1951; Hart 1981 pp.104–6, 128–9.)

The *igudlan* in the Central Atlas are a major feature of Ait 'Atta transhumance as well as of that of other tribes in the region. Not only do they have rigid opening and closing dates, but in some cases even a limitation is placed on the number of sheep which may be pastured there. Two or more sections generally share one of these special areas of common pasture, and trespassing by outsiders or even by individuals entitled to use the *agudal* at any time when it is officially closed is strictly forbidden, as it may lead to extremely heavy fines and often even to fighting. At the Agudal n-Ilimshan, just south of the Tizi n-Ilisi pass, which is reserved for the Ilimshan section (of the Ait Wahlim fifth) alone, no such problem arises; but the situation at the Agudal n-Tlmast, beside the Tizi n-Ilisi, is very different. Here there is an annual brawl which occurs as regularly as clockwork, one which neither the French nor the Moroccans, since Independence in 1956, have been able to resolve; and although one Moroccan administrator at Usikis thought in 1986 that he had just done so, subsequent events evidently proved him wrong.

The annual sheep-and-grass mêlée at Talmast occurs between two different subsections of the large Ait Bu Iknifen section (of the Ait Wahlim fifth), those who are resident at Talmast and their southern or *iqibliyen* 'cousins' who come up annually not only from the Usikis-Msimrir area, but from Imidar and at least six other points further south and east where Ait Bu Iknifen settlements are also to be found. The conflict allegedly stems from the insolubility of a local legend: for when Dadda ('Grandfather') 'Atta, the eponymous lay tribal ancestor of the Ait 'Atta, assisted by his 40 grandsons, chased two other tribal groups out of the Central Atlas at the behest of Sidi Sa'id Ahansal, all he asked in return was sufficient grass for his sheep. Neither he nor Sidi Sa'id, of course, had any inkling about the extent to which the Ait 'Atta and their sheep would proliferate in future. What this came to mean was that even in late precolonial times, the sheep of the southerners had already started to overrun the area of common pastureland which the northern residents had, by common consent, marked out for their own use and which, by 1936, they had even begun to cultivate (Hart 1981 pp.5–7, 11–14).

Individual *mulk* holdings (Ait 'Atta *aharmil* (pl. *iharmal*)) in the ancestral land in the Saghru resulted from a cascade of successive divisions from fifths down to lineage groups and the family level. But *mulk* holdings are not yet widespread for the simple reason that most groups, unlike the situation prevailing among the Aith Waryaghar, have yet to push their land tenure to its logical limits. These are determined in the following manner: both among the Ait 'Atta and other Berber tribes in the Central Atlas, in order to ascertain the limits of arable land belonging to any particular house, its owner performs an act called *tyukta n-umazir*, 'the limits of the land'. He gets up on the roof, takes off his silham or cloak, puts his foot on one part of it and holds the other end (the hood, for instance) in his teeth. While doing this he then throws a stone as far as he can. The point where the stone lands marks the limit of the house, and nobody may drive or pasture his sheep beside it, while the tree nearest the house is then referred to as *tamatart*, becomes holy and is never cut (Hart 1981 pp.106, 129).

As noted, the Ait 'Atta have not as yet had to push their land to its limits, and indeed they guard against it. *Mulk* land is found among the Ait Wallal of the upper Ragg near Ikniwn, among the Ait Y'azza of the middle-lower Ragg, and in the *hurm* or inviolate territory of the Tafrawt n-Ait 'Atta, containing the former tribal capital of Igharm Amazdar, where until 1933 the top chief or *amghar n-ufilla* of the supertribe was annually elected. In this last instance it is linked to peculiarities proper to this zone, while in other parts of the Saghru it remains in the hands of sections which have inherited land acquired originally through the law of the first occupant. However, some sections have bought land and converted it to *mulk* – for example, the Mkibbi and l-'Azib n-Zakir regions under the Ilimshan section and that of Aghriz under the Ait Bu Dawud (both of the Ait Wahlim fifth).

In addition, most of the valleys bordering the Saghru and the oases conquered from riverain people or bought from other tribes are pure *mulk* in terms of category. Here a given group would buy land and divided it into parts known as *taggurt* (pl. *tiggura*) – analogous to the shares of participants or partners in an industrial enterprise. The participants transmitted these 'shares' to their descendants as an integral and exclusive property right.

In French times, a sectional division of an *agudal* or a cultivated area into *tiggura* accorded with the rights which the constituent lineages of the section had originally acquired within the collectivity and which were generally proportional to the size of the lineage groups concerned. Thus within the overall Ait Bu Iknifen section its constituent lineage proportions were as follows: Ait Brahim u-Yusif, three-tenths, Ait 'Ali u-Sa'id, three-tenths, Ait Sa'id u-Dawud, three-tenths, and Ait Brahim u-Ya'qub, one-tenth. The Ait Brahim u-Ya'qub took their smaller share 'off the top' (de Monts de Savasse 1951) and the other three then divided the rest equally. Within the sections their respective councils argue long and hard about the rights of each lineage, and then they designate experts, those of the Tudgha oasis region being particularly well reputed. After this they divide the valley into a variable number of zones along the river bed, sometimes two but generally three – an upstream zone, an intermediate zone and a downstream zone.

If, for example, 60 *tiggura* are to be created, each of these zones would be divided into 60 fields. A *taggurt* owner will thus have three fields, one in each zone. The disposition of each field is generally from the steep bank of the river, perpendicular to its axis, to the outside valley, being bounded both on left and right by fields of owners of neighbouring *tiggura*. The field includes low-lying lands irrigated by a first ditch, then other lands above irrigated by other ditches, and finally extends over the first slopes or plateau situated 'above' the water, an area which the Ait 'Atta call *amardul*. It is on the *amardul* that the tent and the threshing floor, and eventually the house, are set up. The field thus extends from the river to the mountains, from whence the vivid local expression establishing the right of a landowner *zig isilman ar udaden* ('from the fish to the mouflons'). Fields are assigned by lot, but nonetheless sometimes on the intervention of a notable, the section agrees to let a family retain a previous *bil-khayr* and thus avoid building a new house.

By this process each section is cannoned in each zone in a given portion and proportion. Sectional notables retain an accurate knowledge of the original allotment and hence litigation over land tenure is rare among the Ait 'Atta. The legitimate presence of a stranger who claims to hold land within a group must be proven by duly constituted deed of purchase. Otherwise he will be treated as an intruder or a dishonest *akhammas* or sharecropper.

Land is divided down to the level of the *tashat*, the elementary family, and it represents an extreme degree of parcellation: each plot is measured out on the ground in the presence of the *ajmu'*. Ditches permit everyone to obtain irrigation water, and each field is surrounded by a mound of earth called *tagmunt*. Certain wider mounds permit the passage of animals and hence become 'roads' (*ibriden* (sing. *abrid*)). This extreme division within the upstream, downstream and intermediate zones, within an unlimited space left on the *amardul* side, is highly logical in terms of equalising everyone's chances of benefiting from the very variable factor of water – the essence of life in southern Morocco (Hart 1981 pp.106–8).

Water rights and water division correspond numerically to land rights and land division, but even if boundary disputes are infrequent, those over the division of water are constant, provoking violent and often sanguinary quarrels. Irrigation is a continuous process, taking place day and night, and is calculated in months, days, hours and minutes, as we have seen it to be among the Aith Waryaghar lowlanders who irrigate from the lower Ghis river. Each sector and often each *igharm* (Tamazight) or *qsar* (Mor. Ar.) – the striking several-storeyed 'apartment' dwelling of adobe and stone which is the norm almost everywhere in Morocco south of the Atlas – has its own system which might appear complex to outsiders but not to its practitioners. As always, the rules are invariably more complex the lesser the water supply. Equitable water division is a major responsibility of the sectional *amghar* or chief, whose normally annual election by a process known as 'rotation and complementarity' among constituent subsections had no counterpart in the Rif. Sometimes its importance warrants the presence of a special *amghar n-w-aman*, *mukallif n-w-aman* or *amghar n-tirugwin* (water chief, water representative or irrigation ditch chief), who is assisted by the headmen of the section's consituent lineages. Irrigation follows the order of these lineages, but as properties extend over several zones, water must be circulated over considerable distances in order to irrigate the fields of a given section. This occasions water losses, and herein lies the inconvenience of the system.

Water rights, most of the time, are linked to rights in land, as in the Rif: when land is sold, the associated water right is also sold. But in less wealthy sections, poor people may sell part of their water rights to richer neighbours and hence reduce the value of the land.

The logic of this system of land and water division is clear from a consideration of the annual activities of a *taggurt* owner. His upstream zone, even in meager years, is completely devoted to the double cultivation of wheat in winter and maize in summer. In a good year, he can put the whole of the winter crop and half of the summer crop in the central zone. Finally, should the lower zone become very dry, no ploughing will be done, but in a

year with heavy rain he may extend it considerably. Now, if the section
should decide to bring water from an upstream point, the new network of
ditches, now irrigating a wider area, means that the owner can create a new
plot beside his *taggurt*, thereby pushing the outer edge of his field toward
the *amardul*. Often, especially in the Saghru and the southern oases, the
owner will dig a well in his field. He does not, however, lose his rights to
irrigation water, but has now an additional and independent source of water
for crops which particularly need it.

Thus by these processes an Ait 'Atta family can acquire property in a
sector of the overall supertribal territory which comprises several fields
with possibilities of lateral extension and of extension of its lower parts.
This property renders the family master of the soil, with corresponding
water rights and, with only a few exceptions, total *ius utendi et abutendi* –
rights of sale, purchase, mortgage and exchange.

A division effected among members of a section which is scattered
territorially throughout the supertribe (as indeed almost all Ait 'Atta
sections are) may also affect individuals who are far removed from each
other spatially. For distance does not affect rights, while absence is an
integral guarantee of them as they are upheld by agnates or next-of-kin.
When the Ait Isful section divided land in the Tagunit region of the Dra
River valley in about 1950, members of the same section living in the lower
Tudgha region sold their *tiggura* to their 'brethren' established in the lower
Dra, as they no longer wanted to have the burden of property far away from
their own area of residence. The play of sales and exchanges after division
is usually very active and permits plots to be regrouped, but it has a
disruptive effect on sectional ties. Here certain Ait Isful in the
Tinghir/Tudgha region lost the justification for maintaining socioeconomic
relations with their 'brethren' in the Dra. As de Monts de Savasse very
tellingly remarks, sedentarisation is accentuated by the division of land (de
Monts de Savasse 1951; Hart 1981 pp.108–9).

The same author has also cogently suggested that as the establishment of
Igharm Amazdar as the Ait 'Atta tribal capital in the Saghru occurred
relatively late and only well after the consolidation of Ait 'Atta power (i.e.
circa. 1890), the original function of their five fifths or *khams khmas* may
have originally been quite different from what it was to become later,
namely, the annual election or selection of the top chief or *amghar n-ufilla*
of the supertribe by the twin processes of rotation and complementarity,
which we have described at length elsewhere (Hart 1981 pp.19–98). It was,
rather, that of dividing the agricultural and irrigable land in the Saghru into
five parts through the drawing of lots (*grat illan*). Hence it would seem clear
that the institution of five fifths already had an economic function before it
acquired its later political one. This economic function also had clear

repercussions in terms of the transhumance of Ait 'Atta sections to the Central Atlas (cf. de Monts de Savasse 1951).

De Monts de Savasse posits that first of all, the *khums* or fifth constituted by the two section-aggregates of the Ait Wallal and the Ait Unir took or were allotted one share (for the Ait Wallal are generally regarded as the oldest or senior 'Atta section), and the remainder was then redivided into five. Now a second *khums*, made up of two more section-aggregates, the Ait Isful and the Ait 'Alwan, were allotted their share, and the remaining four-fifths were again redivided into five. At this juncture a third *khums*, that of the Ait Unibgi, took two shares, while the remaining three-fifths were now allotted to the remaining two fifths of the Ait Wahlim and the Ait 'Aisa Mzin (this last including the Ait Y'azza and three other much smaller sections, the Ait Khalifa, Ait l-Firsi and Ait Khardi), in the respective proportions of three to the former and two to the latter.

De Monts de Savasse calculated thereby that a whole unit of 625 plots of land in the Saghru was divided up as follows:

> 125 for the *khums* of the Ait Wallal-Ait Unir
> 100 for the *khums* of the Ait Isful-Ait 'Alwan
> 160 for the *khums* of the Ait Unibgi
> 144 for the *khums* of the Ait Wahlim
> 96 for the *khums* of the Ait 'Aisa Mzin

These figures are also quite accurate indicators of the numerical strength of each fifth. After each *khums* received its share of the relatively rich *igudlan* of the Saghru, the people of the inviolate region of the Tafrawt n-Igharm Amazdar (or Tafrawt n-Ait 'Atta) were ratified in their rights to the land irrigated by the *khattara* canals which had been dug, while those individuals from the first Ait 'Atta lineages were confirmed in their possession of the water points they had developed (e.g. Tanut n- Haddu w-Ishshu, 'the little well of Haddu w-Ishshu', named for the man who dug it originally). At this point, according to de Monts de Savasse, all the rest of the Saghru was recognised as the collective land of the whole supertribe. None of its member sections nor fifths had the right to take over or monopolise any part of this land. No clauses or rules limited the use of the land for transhumance, and if certain zones were more particularly and more habitually occupied by certain sections at certain times of year, this did not give them any individual rights to the land in question. De Monts de Savasse even opined that this fact, sometimes lost from sight by his own former *Affaires Indigènes* colleagues in the Central Atlas, is what is really at the bottom of the annual pasturage brawl at Talmast between resident and southern Ait Bu Iknifen (de Monts de Savasse 1951; Hart 1981 pp.31, 65).

As Lefebure has indicated, there are four broad territorial bands

belonging to four out of the five Ait 'Atta fifths (the exception, not
mentioned by Lefebure, being that of the Ait Isful-Ait 'Alwan) which run in
a north–south direction and are oriented toward the northern and north-
western pasturelands of the Central Atlas, on which they tend to converge
(Lefebure circa. 1976). This too is of interest as having very possibly
represented an original situation; but subsequently, with the extreme
discontinuity and replication of sections which gradually came about, its
qualitative aspects have become considerably more attenuated. A better
case could in fact be made for the participation, in this historical north-
western push of the Ait 'Atta (and other Berber) transhumants from the late
sixteenth to the early twentieth centuries (cf. Hart 1993), of all five fifths
based on toponymy: for there are a very few northern and discontinuous
splinter groups of Ait Isful, such as the small handful of nuclear families of
this section resident at Usikis (which is otherwise inhabited by the Ait Bu
Iknifen, Ait Yazza and Ait Unibgi), as well as a very northern Ait 'Alwan
lineage among the Ait 'Atta n-Umalu (the Ait 'Atta 'of the Shade') at
Wawizakht, which is just south of the Middle Atlas divide. Then, once this
happened, the Ait Isful-Ait 'Alwan *khums* would presumably have been
squeezed out by the pressure of the others or, perhaps more likely, would
have fallen into more lucrative patronage situations in the Dra Valley which
claimed the bulk of their attention (Hart 1981 p.32).

   The fact of sedentarisation being accentuated by the division of land is
strikingly apparent among the Ait 'Atta of Usikis, whose high valley on the
south slope of the Central Atlas, above the Dadss River gorges, generally
has abundant irrigation water. At Usikis the water is divided into four parts:
one for the Ait Bu Iknifen lineage groups residing in Igharm n-Ta'dadat,
another for the equally Ait Bu Iknifen lineages residing in the original
Igharm n-Ait Bu Iknifen, and two for the Ait Y'azza and the Ait Unibgi
jointly, who then split their share in half. In precolonial times, informants
said, the Ait Y'azza had more land than anyone else and the Ait Unibgi had
more water; and hence they joined forces for irrigation. This may not have
been literally true, for as of 1961–62 and our most intensive fieldwork, the
two Ait Bu Iknifen *igharman* at Usikis were twice the size of those of the
other two sections and had correspondingly more land. But the lands of the
Ait Y'azza and the Ait Unibgi are both located further upstream along the
Aqqa n-Usikis or Usikis river, with corresponding advantages. The Ait
Unibgi are closest to the point where the river enters the valley and hence
have in fact the most water. In any event, the major part of the land in the
valley is under cultivation, irrigation being used only for grains (although
when we revisited the region in 1986, apple orchards and potato fields had
both been introduced to produce cash crops, and were doing very well). The
concept of *mulli*, an individual irrigation turn belonging to a *tashat* or

elementary family, applies only to grainfields and not to anything else simply because there is almost always enough water.

On the rare occasions that there is little water, two ponds or *uggugen* (sing. *uggug*) located just above the Usikis valley are used. They are filled by the Usikis River, the water being used for a three- to six-day period according to the pattern described above. Irrigation normally takes place both during the day and at night, but only in the daytime if water should be scarce. In times of plenty, water is so abundant that there is no need to divide it.

The situation among the Ait Usikis may be contrasted with that prevailing among the Ait l-Firsi (of the Ait 'Aisa Mzin fifth, comprising the Ait Y'azza, Ait Khalifa, Ait l-Firsi and Ait Khardi) in the Saghru, who are probably the poorest of all Ait 'Atta sections and among whom water is very scarce indeed. In order to divide it equitably, they use a waterclock to measure out the contents of their pond or deposit. The time piece is a small bowl with tiny perforations: it is put into the deposit, and exactly one hour elapses before the holes fill up and the bowl sinks. Then they pour the water back into the deposit and repeat the process. Our informant said that once in French times one man sold his water turn to another, and they both went to the French post at Tinghir to sign a statement to this effect. The French AI officer maintained that it was impossible to measure water in such a way, so the men asked him to come and have a look to see how it worked. He did so and then, astonished, wrote out the deed of sale.

A totally different, far more precise and far more complex situation from that at Usikis (where the *taggurt* system is not specifically invoked) or even among the Ait l-Firsi prevails further south, among the Ait Isful of the Ktawa district around Tagunit. Niclausse's unpublished account of this case (1954) is a fascinating if incomplete jigsaw puzzle which, when completed, sheds very interesting light indeed on the whole concept of division and indivision among the Ait 'Atta. The whole question of the protective patronage–clientage relationship between the Ait 'Atta sections in this area and its autochthonous Haratin population of sedentary black oasis cultivators is the nodal point of Niclausse's analysis; but here interest centres on the designation of Ait 'Atta protectors, or *ra'yan* (Mor. Ar. sing. *ra'i*, 'shepherd, herder') to police the *tiggura* belonging to the Haratin or Drawa, to which they are assigned. In this southern oasis area the *taggurt* is never completely divorced from the context of the *qta* (Mor. Ar. properly *qat'a*, 'cut, piece, section'), the common land of each *qsar*. The irrigable portion of each *qta* is made up of a variable number of *tiggura*, and the precision in division and allotment arises both from the multiplicity of social relationships in the region and the scarcity of water and of cultivable land.

The designation of *ra'yan* takes place twice a year, in January and in August. The August designation is the more important, as dates are by far the biggest source of revenue in the region. Hence the redistribution must be made before the harvest is in, as the *ra'yan* have to be paid. Before the meeting starts, everyone marks out propitious sites as well as ones held to be not as good. At the meeting itself, Niclausse recounted that the Ait Isful *amghar* or *shaykh* plus two representatives for each of its four constituent subsections, all crouching in a circle after having rapidly invoked God's aid, began to establish the count of *tiggura* family by family, with the help of fine thongs cut from palm fronds: '*Ti-n, Mhand u-Hsayn; ti-n, Mbark u-Yusif; ti-n, Barka u-Khiyi*'. The *shaykh*, 'about whom one does not know whether to admire more his astonishing memory or his profound knowledge of his section' (ibid.), enumerated almost without omission the 359 *tiggura* of the Ait Isful, while watched over by the sectional notables. Women who are nuclear family heads have a right to only half a share, while a few *shurfa*' and strangers are admitted in very reduced numbers. Any w-Isful who has been absent for a long time and has not left anyone to represent him in the Ktawa is ineligible and forfeits his right to a share.

The details of the count were not established on a subsectional basis but on the somewhat different one of *qsur* (pl. of *qsar*) settlements, in conformity with the inscription that the transhumants evidently requested on the French tax rolls. Niclausse inferred from this, almost certainly correctly, that the subsections were losing their former importance, for the *tiggura* in question were divided into six local *qsur*, as follows:

Ait Isful of Qsar Blida	62 *tiggura*
Ait Isful of Qsar Ulad Yusif	65.5 *tiggura*
Ait Isful of Qsar Ait Gizzu	55 *tiggura*
Ait Isful of Qsar Ait Bu Udad	46.5 *tiggura*
Ait Isful of Qsar Qsibt Ait Isful	100 *tiggura*
Ait Isful of Qsar Guruggir	30 *tiggura*
Total	**359 *tiggura***

The next operation was the highly arithmetical division of the *tiggura* into thirds (*le-tlat* (sing. *tilt*)), each third containing 120 *tiggura*, except for the final third with only 119, and of the interested Ait Isful communities into three appropriate teams, as follows:

Team A:

Ait Gizzu	55 *tiggura*
Ait Bu Udad	6.5 *tiggura*
Ait Guruggir	30 *tiggura*
Total: 131.5 *tiggura*, minus 11.5 *tiggura*	**120 *tiggura***

Team B:

Blida	62 *tiggura*
Ulad Yusif	65.5 *tiggura*
Total: 127.5 *tiggura* minus 7.5 *tiggura*	**120 *tiggura***

Team C:

Qsibt Ait Isful — 100 *tiggura*, plus 11.5 *tiggura* from first third and 7.5 *tiggura* from second third = **119 *tiggura***

The extra 19 *tiggura* added to the final third (i.e. 11.5 subtracted from the first and 7.5 from the second) were those which any inhabitants took if they wanted to establish themselves outside their own sector of domicile. In the event that there were no takers, they were attributed *ex officio* to absentees.

Clearly in this case the division had nothing to do with the subsectional structure of the Ait Isful. However, at the point when the area was divided into thirds, the tone of the discussion, hitherto quiet, became louder, although only some five or six notables seemed to have the right to speak. The problem was now one of location of the *tiggura*. Was each group going to be attributed the sector surrounding its *qsar* or was the *qta* of each *qsar* to be divided among all the subsections taking part? Some people were afraid that the decision recorded by the *Affaires Indigènes bureau* at Tagunit would then become immutable so the principle of the freedom of arbitration of the *ajmuʿ* was to be adopted:

1. To achieve this the first third was made up of the areas comprised by the *qsur* Qsibt ar-Ramla, Knazda and Nsrat. The remainder, ultimately to form the second and third thirds and comprising the whole left bank of the Dra from the *qsar* of Bni Simgin to that of Qsar l-Kbir, were not yet divided. Finally, a further sector, comprising the large *qsur* of Bni Hayyun and Khaswan and remaining in indivision, was to be divided among the three thirds.

2. The first third was allotted to Team C, that of Qsibt Ait Isful, whose *qsar* is located on the *qta* belonging to Nsrat.

3. Teams A and B then divided the remainder into sectors of identical value in terms of date harvest revenue: Sector 1 – the northern area except for Bni Simgin; Sector 2 – Bni Simgin and Blida; and Sector 3 – the southern area.

4. Each of these was again divided and finally a definitive division emerged.

5. The function of the original *ajmuʿ* was now complete. In the internal sectional distributions, Team B may be regarded as typical of the

division pattern. Here the Ait Isful of Blida and those of Ulad Yusif came to a rapid agreement to allot Sectors 2 and 3 to the Blida group and Sector 1 to that of Ulad Yusif, with the area of indivision still remaining so among them. In this way each person would stay near his own sector of domicile.

6. The next sector was that internal to the Ait Isful of Blida, where the lineage segments themselves continued to subsegment. The owners of *tiggura* there, each speaking for his agnates, began to divide their own allotment into three thirds, as follows:

Sector A: Qsar l-Kbir, one-half of the one-sixth of Blida
Sector B: One-half of Blida, one-half of the one-sixth of Bni Hayyun
Sector C: One-half of Blida, l-'Ansar

7. The subsection total of the Ait Isful of Blida was originally estimated at 62 *tiggura*, but two *tiggura* had to be handed over to the Qsibt Ait Isful, in Team C, leaving 60 *tiggura*. On a further recount it was found that one had been omitted. This previously unaccounted-for *taggurt* was allotted to the best team, which, as everyone unanimously agreed, was Team A. The constituent lineages of the Ait Isful of Blida were thus grouped into lots of 20 *tiggura*, and now account was taken of their subsections of origin, as follows:

Team A:	Ait Brahim u-Hammi	20 *tiggura* plus 1 (the extra *taggurt* allotted to them)
Team B:	Iqban	17 *tiggura*
	Ait Bab Ighf	3 *tiggura*
	Total:	**20 *tiggura***
Team C:	Ait Ishshu	11 *tiggura*
	Ait Umnasf	9 *tiggura*
	Total:	**20 *tiggura***

The two *tiggura* handed over to Team C came from the Ait Bab Ighf lineage. Now lot-drawing, once again with palm frond thongs, yielded the following distribution of allotments: Team A – Sector 3; Team B – Sector 1; and Team C – Sector 2.

8. Within this framework the analysis centres on the allotment of Team C. Those involved decided that of the 20 *tiggura*, six would be at Blida, the other half of the Blida sector belonging to the Ait Isful, and 14 on the half of Bni Hayyun. The allotment was to take place by mutual understanding, if not by lot-drawing. This turn of 20 *tiggura* was divided as follows: 16 *ra'yan* (guardians) who would then take on the guardianship of the land themselves; and two *tiggura* of men who were

unable (such as *mkhazni*-s in French military service) or unwilling to participate in the guardianship. One of their kinsmen joined them to his own, forming a sector of three *tiggura*. The *ra'aya* of these *tiggura* was halved between the owner and the *ra'i*. Finally, the two remaining *tiggura*, belonging to four women who were elementary family heads, each one counting for a half share, were taken over by their cousin.

This proportion of *ra'yan* to *tiggura* did not reflect the general appearance of the Ait Isful subsection at Blida, for here sedentarisation is more advanced and true transhumance is rare. Yet in one Ulad Yusif team, there were eight *ra'yan* for a total of 17 *tiggura*, and in the other Ulad Yusif team, only 17 out of a total of 43.

A detailed description of the other remaining divisions would provide no more information. At the end of the allotment session, which lasted six hours, the time limit for the installation of the *ra'yan* on the allotted *tiggura* was fixed at eight days for all those present, and at 13 days for those still on transhumance. After this period was over, the responsibility of the *ra'yan* would begin for all those involved.

Elsewhere, as Niclausse points out (ibid.), land division differs. Among the Ait Inzaren (Ait 'Alwan) at the *qsar* of Tiraf n-Ait 'Alwan, the process was not only less elaborate than among the Ait Isful but also differed in that it was not the *tiggura* which were at the base of the division but the resident lineage groups. The area was divided into four equal parts, with the constituent lineages aiming to obtain mutually equal plots. Each lineage established its sector through lot-drawing among the *ra'yan*. The number of *ra'yan* per lineage – as only the lineage members and no Haratin were involved – might have differed enormously, but each *taggurt* owner had a right to half the share of the *ra'yan*, the other half going to the guardian. At the *qsur* of Zawiya Sidi Salah and Ait Hassu (Ait Wahlim), the required number of *ra'yan* was established jointly by resident sedentaries (*shurfa'* and Haratin) and Ait 'Atta according to the date harvest. The area was divided into two equal parts: one for the Ait 'Ali u-Hassu (Ait Wahlim) and the Ait Khardi (of the Ait 'Aisa Mzin fifth) of Rgabi, near Mhamid l-Ghuzlan, and the other for the Ait Khardi of the Ktawa. Here only poor men acted as guardians, and thus from the whole *ra'aya* levied at harvest time, the sedentaries took the value of four *tiggura* for their own expenses. At the *qsur* of Bni Sbih and Ait r-Rba', the *ra'aya* was taken over by the Ait Bu Dawud (Ait Wahlim), who arranged division by mutual agreement, while Ait r-Rba' levied half the dues turned over to the guardians.

In the Mhamid l-Ghuzlan area, however, Niclausse reported that frequent quarrels which led to draconian measures. Here the number of *ra'yan* was as follows: *qsar* of Rgabi – four, from the Ait Hassu (Ait

Wahlim); *qsar* of Ulad Dris – four, from the Ait 'Alwan; *qsar* of Bunu –
eight, from the Ait 'Alwan; *qsar* of Talha Bni Mhammad – four–ten, from
the Bni Mhammad Arabs (Ait 'Atta clients); *qsar* of Talha Shurfa' – five,
from the *shurfa'* themselves; *qsar* of Ulad Yusif – four, from the Arabs of
the 'Arib (also Ait 'Atta clients), *qsar* of Mhamid (l-Ghuzlan) – eight, from
the 'Arib (although both these last two were raised to 16 in 1952, by mutual
consent, because of the date harvest); and *qsur* of Ulad Yihya and Znaga –
six, from the 'Arib (again, raised to eight in 1952 by mutual consent because
of the date harvest). Given this limited total of *ra'yan* (47 before 1952, and
73 afterward), infinitesimal for the extent of the area, the apportionment of
ra'yan created no difficulties for the sections or groups concerned. Each
section designated one of its members who was replaced every six months.
As there was no question of *tiggura* in this region, the *ra'yan* kept all the
dues incurred for themselves. In this respect their situation was an envious
one and they were constrained to do their job impeccably, which meant in
particular that they should not increase their 'personal' flocks unduly
(Niclausse 1954; Hart 1981 pp.110–16).

As de Monts de Savasse (1951) noted, the Ait 'Atta *taggurt* is one part
land and one part water. It is of variable dimensions and volume, depending
on its location, annual rainfall and the amount of work needed to develop
the land. Its origin differs according to whether it may have resulted from
the division of ancestral lands, as in the Saghru, or from that of newly
acquired ones, as in the Ktawa.

In the first instance, *tiggura* were distributed according to the principles
involved in the original parcelling-out, and they now represent a retention of
form and structure after the loss of the original function. The present owners
occupy this patrimony through inheritance, modified by later transactions. In
the second instance, a group bought and developed the land, expenses
incurred being shouldered by those involved, either on a pro-rata basis of their
previous rights or in terms of the sums they agreed to pay. Their lineages or
families transmitted the shares thus acquired to their descendants.

De Monts de Savasse also noted (ibid.) that as of 1950, among those Ait
'Atta sections dependent on the AI *bureau* of Tinghir, the average extent of
a *taggurt* oscillated between two and seven *'aishar* (an obvious derivative
of the Ar. root *'-sh-r*, as in *'ashra* ('ten') or *'ashur* ('tithe')). The *'aishar*,
also known to *qsur*-dwelling Ait 'Atta, is a surface measure employed by
the Haratin of the Tudgha oasis (the Ait Tadghut or Ahl Tudgha) equalling
16 square metres or one-fortieth of a hectare. Even the smallest landowners
have one-half, one-third, one-fourth or one-eighth of a *taggurt* of irrigated
land in any one sector; and some have as many as ten *tiggura*.

The owner of a *taggurt* may treat his possessions just like shares: he may
negotiate, he may stipulate the size of the *taggurt* he sells and he may also

sell *tiggura* resulting from his inherited ancestral lands. In the latter case he loses any future advantages which may result from collective work done on the land in question, such as an extension, as among the Ait Bu Iknifen of Waklim in the Imidar area, which increased *taggurt* surface area by almost one-third (Hart 1981 pp.116–19).

We now consider certain features of Ait 'Atta collective oath with respect to property rights. This is in order to emphasise the fact that the fundamental consideration in Ait 'Atta land tenure is the exclusion of strangers.

Until Independence in 1956, a defendant in a land dispute had to furnish ten co-jurors (*imgillan* or *ait 'ashra*, 'people of ten') from among his own agnates (*imyisaten* (sing. *amyisa*)) in order to affirm his property rights. In fact this meant the defendant himself plus nine of his agnatic lineage mates. The number was the same for litigation over fields larger than one handspan (*tardazt*). According to de Monts de Savasse (ibid.), Ait Atta custom regarding real property has never admitted testimonial proof (i.e. accusing witnesses rather than denying co-jurors). This seems too extreme, although ten co-jurors were also required for intersectional or interlineage litigation over collective property. Indeed, any w-'Atta accused of converting collective land into *mulk* (or *aharmil*) for his own profit had to furnish ten *nuqqran* oaths – himself and nine other co-jurors or *imgillan* from his lineage, but designated by the plaintiff.

In fact, *mulk* property is conceived quite relatively, for it is sometimes in the hands of a large group, and often whole lineages stay in indivision. In such a case only the lineage headman handles property transactions, but even so Berber individualism may assert itself. Any adolescent male old enough to fast (during the month of Ramadan), to bear arms or to marry (16–17 years) may ask to set up his own tent apart and claim his share of his father's inheritance. Indivision provided common lineage property but also emphasised common risks and responsibilities over bloodwealth (*d-diyit*, from Ar. *diya*) for murder and the bloodfeud (*tamaddiyt*). Hence a father rarely refused to accord his sons the benefits of division if so requested.

Division procedures prescribe one part for the father, one part for each living male child and one-half part for each living female child, as dictated by the Shari'a. As the father is both guardian (*a'asib*, from the Ar. root '-s-b*, and hence related to Ibn Khaldun's famous concept of *'asabiya* or 'agnation in action') and tutor of his daughters, he will legally gain two shares plus the administration of his daughter's half. Any man may also transfer to his male grandchildren of a deceased father the share that the latter would have received. He also has the option of maintaining one-third of his possessions; and even if division has not occurred he can provide for his grandchildren in writing by willing them their deceased father's share.

Indeed, this is the only will or testament that is admitted, for the Ait 'Atta say that 'a dead man must no longer concern himself with the things of this world'.

A father is also the guardian of his under-age children. Once division has occurred, he handles their property until they attain majority. Later his children may request accounts of this guardianship, but in indivision the father is the sole judge. Prior to independence, division of property occurred in front of the father and his nine oldest agnates or *ait 'ashra*, whose presence was the essential prerequisite for the validity of any property division. If any of the *ait 'ashra* were absent when division occurred, they were replaced by the next nearest kinsmen from the same lineage or another closely related to it patrilaterally. If agreement did not exist between those involved over the way in which division was to occur, particularly in the case of absentees, the *ait 'ashra* themselves either undertook the actual division or made sure that the rights of the absentee were respected. Absentees included those who had disappeared. As de Monts de Savasse notes (ibid.), although departure from the supertribal territory and the relinquishment of rights were sufficient, in precolonial times, to render a man an *imishki* (a tribeless individual) and to constitute his 'legal death', a simple disappearance meant that the share of the man concerned had to be put aside and could not be sold. After 'pacification' in 1933, customary notions of 'legal death' had to be revised, and the existence of new ties and links of all sorts had to be taken into account.

The central theme of de Monts de Savasse's excellent though unpublished study (ibid.) is, if anything, that land tenure among the Ait 'Atta is the basis of law and custom. However, an equally good argument could also possibly be made to show that land tenure is simply one major medium through which Ait 'Atta social organisation works and functions (for an analogous line of reasoning, cf. Fortes 1969 p.289). Exclusion of strangers is the keynote of Ait 'Atta notions of real property, and the preservation of the patrimony of the group concerned, at each and every level of subdivision or segmentation, was watched over at all times by the vigilant judges and keepers of Ait 'Atta customary law, the *ti'aqqidin* of the *istinaf* or tribal supreme court of appeal at Igharm Amazdar.

A stranger could practically never acquire land in the Saghru, and an w- 'Atta of one section could only do so with great difficulty in that of another, as an analysis of stranger land tenure incidence shows. As mentioned earlier, 85 per cent of all Ait 'Atta men are resident agnatic members of the lineage with which their territory is associated. This figure is extraordinarily high by global standards, even though for the Ait 'Atta themselves it may in fact be somewhat conservative. Among the Ait 'Atta of Usikis, for example, it rises to 88 per cent. Strangers here included admitted strangers, both stranger Ait 'Atta and even non-Ait 'Atta who were resident at Usikis as of the 1960 census. If, however, only the non-Ait 'Atta residents are excluded and incipient lineages of Ait 'Atta strangers who have come in from outside *are* included, this figure rises to 97 per cent. An analysis of the whole of Ait 'Atta territory suggests that the Usikis case is not atypical, although Fifth III (below) appears surprisingly low.

TABLE 3
INFERRED AGNATIC LINEAGE MEMBERS RESIDENT IN TERRITORIES OF ALL
FIVE FIFTHS AND IN AIT 'ATTA-LAND AS A WHOLE

Fifth I	Ait Wahlim	88.59 per cent
Fifth II	Ait Wallal – Ait Unir	97.60 per cent
Fifth III	Ait Isful – Ait 'Alwan	50.00 per cent
Fifth IV	Ait Unibgi	89.60 per cent
Fifth V	Ait 'Aisa Mzin	97.50 per cent
	Average	88.50 per cent
	Ait 'Atta n-Umalu	84.66 per cent
	Average	86.05 per cent
	Average of both averages	85.35 per cent

It need only be added that the Ait 'Atta figure of 85 per cent beats the record of the Tiv in Nigeria, in this domain, of 83 per cent (Bohannan 1957 p.1) – whereas the Aith Waryaghar figure of only 58 per cent is not much higher than that of the Central Rifian tribes as a whole, estimated at 49 per cent (Hart 1976 pp.235–7), and is hence closer to that of the Nuer in the Nilotic Sudan at only 45 per cent, slightly less than half. The association of agnatic members of all Ait 'Atta lineages within the territory occupied by the corresponding lineages is extraordinarily high, even in territory gained through conquest. Strangers are thus effectively excluded both from political participation and land ownership (Hart 1981 pp.119–21), although there were further and ancillary considerations which helped to maintain this situation. We now look briefly at some of them.

The first was the total absence among the Ait 'Atta of the highly permissive institution of *amhars* – a form of son-in-law adoption through agricultural contract still found among many Middle Atlas tribes such as the Zimmur, the Iziyyan, the Ishqiren and the Ait Mgild. *Amhars* allows a poor man, usually an Arab, to move into the mountains in a lean year and obtain work as a sharecropper for a wealthier Berber. The contract agreed upon must last a minimum of two years, and the sharecropper may provisionally marry his patron's daughter. Only at the end of the contract, when a true brideprice or *s-sdaq*, also unknown among the Ait 'Atta, is paid, does the marriage become definitive. Should he decide to depart or to ask for divorce before the end of the contract, his provisional wife, his patron's daughter, retains custody of any children. After definitive marriage, of course, this no longer applies (Denat 1951). To the Ait 'Atta, however, he would still be an encroaching stranger and strangers move into 'Atta-land only at express Ait 'Atta invitation.

Alienation of property cannot occur through marriage, as an ut-'Atta, an Ait 'Atta woman, may not bring any real property from her inheritance to a stranger husband or their children simply because she only receives the money equivalent of her inheritance. In any case, she is still under the very strict tutelage of her nearest male agnate, her *a'asib*, who also acts as her guardian. In addition, property alienation cannot result from the aftermath of division because it is carefully watched over by the *ait 'ashra* and donation is only made to the male children of a deceased son. Nor can it result from sale, as agnatic priority rights of *shfa'a* (or, in Tamazight, *tashfa't* ('pre-emption')) permitted all close agnates to buy back family lands up for sale. Finally, alienation cannot result from dishonest expropriation because of the essential inadmissibility of testimonial proof over matters concerning land. This was certainly the case before 1956.

In this web of contexts two key concepts stand out: *shfa'a* – the more important – and *rahn*. *Shfa'a* among the Ait 'Atta refers to pre-emptive or priority rights of agnates both over land and over women in marriage. Under *shfa'a*, if any man should object to a projected sale of land by one of his agnatic kinsmen or to the exogamously arranged marriage of one of his agnatic kinsmen, neither the transaction nor the marriage could be completed.

The latitude given to the institution of *shfa'a* in Berber Customary Law was very much wider than in Muslim Law, where it does not extend to all the agnatic lineage mates of the objector (Marcy (1939) 1954 p.144). In 1956 it was rescinded by an independent Moroccan administration as part and parcel of the customary law associated with the French-promulgated Berber Dahir or Decree of 1930.

In Ait 'Atta Custom any sale of land had to be made public precisely so that the right of *shfa'a* could be exercised by a kinsman who might be far away on transhumance; and three auctions, each of a week's duration, were held in order that an absentee could return home to make his *shfa'a* claim. In practice, any outsider wanting to buy land belonging to a given lineage or to any of its members would offer a price. Any lineage member could in turn make a counter-offer of half that price, or slightly more. This would ensure that the land in question remained in lineage hands, for a lineage member's word and price automatically overrode those of a stranger. Should anyone want to marry a woman of a lineage not his own (and father's brother's daughter marriage among the Ait 'Atta is a cultural and structural desideratum), he would offer the members of that lineage a certain sum. If the father's brother's son of the girl in question wanted her for himself, he would, again, offer half that sum or slightly more; and this again was sufficient to put any stranger out of the running. A young man, however, had to make his *shfa'a* claim to his father's brother's daughter public as soon as he heard that her father was thinking of marrying her off.

The whole issue revolved around agnatic priority and in this respect land and women were treated in exactly the same way. The reasoning was that no one wants to sell, even at a high price, his land or his sisters or daughters to an outsider. Throughout the whole Tamazight-speaking area of the Central Atlas it was very rare that any immediate monetary considerations should override *shfa'a* restrictions. Thus agnatic members of the property-owning and women-holding lineage retained their *de facto* as well as their *de jure* priority.

Rahn was also abolished in 1956 as its implications in Berber and Ait 'Atta Custom were far wider than in the Shari'a. As Marcy pointed out (1954 p.144), the essence of *rahn* revolved around the pawning and pledging of real estate, although it might also involve movable property. In Muslim Law *rahn* consists either of a loan for use bearing on a piece of real property or of a pure and simple pledging or pawning contract, in which the creditor does not enjoy the benefits. In Customary Law, as Marcy saw it, *rahn* was a commutative contract. One person lent another land for a determined period, with the enjoyment of its benefits in exchange for the loan of a stipulated sum of money, seldom more than half the value of the property. According to the Shari'a, this is illicit (ibid. p.144; Hart 1981 pp.122–4).

For de Monts de Savasse, however, (1951) the institution derives from the Berber tendency to live for the present, and hence to be chronically short of money. He even noted that some of his informants in the Saghru told him that the institution had its origins in the religious practice and duty of the pilgrimage, observing in the same context that this, if true, is curious, as the number of Ait 'Atta who prior to 'pacification' had made the *hajj* to Mecca was infinitesimal (ibid.; Hart 1981 p.131).

In any case, the way it worked was as follows. The owner of a field might 'sell' it to another for either a fixed or an indeterminate period, and for this he took a sum of money, not necessarily related to the value of the land, from him in exchange. Here the land was simply a guarantee. However, the transaction was then made public, as in a definitive sale, so that close agnates could exercise *shfa'a*, and a document was then drawn up to be remitted to the creditor.

As the *rahn* was the object of a document, there could be no argument except over its authenticity, which was sworn to by five co-jurors, including the owner. No transactions over the land involved could be made until the loan period was over. Nonetheless, if the section concerned wanted collective work done on the land, the debtor-owner was consulted and did not have to share expenses. If the tenant engaged this work to be done, it was at his own risk and he had to pay for maintenance. In case of decease, the obligations incurred passed to the heirs. A *rahn* could be prolonged if both parties agreed, with or without a fixed time period, provided that the occupant turned money over to the owner. This new transaction was then made public for the free play of *shfa'a* rights, and entered on the document. At the end of the period fixed, if it was fixed, and at the owner's pleasure, he could recuperate his property if he reimbursed his tenant all the money registered on the act. During the colonial period, furthermore, there were only two admissible forms by which acts of sale could be declared to be lost: either through fire or through the combats sustained during the 'pacification', especially at the bloody final battle at Bu Gafr in the Saghru in February–March 1933 (for details, cf. Hart 1977; 1984 pp.159–94).

In colonial times, *rahn* became less and less common, except in the Saghru and particularly in the Tafrawt n-Ait 'Atta, where *mulk* sales were not allowed and where until independence *rahn* remained the only possible property mutation. Even in the precolonial period the *rahn* was difficult to tolerate and was abused by setting up interminable extension periods. *Shfa'a* rights were impeded by applying enormous sums to insignificant plots of land. Prior to pacification, too, *rahn* was never made public.

It is not difficult to see how this system could be abused. By the 1950s, in the case of any *rahn* which did stipulate a fixed period, the eventual pre-emptor had to wait until the end of it. The maximum time limit then admitted for a *rahn* was ten years. As with a sale, after the three weeks' delay, the *shfa'a* right was foreclosed for all *ruhun* (pl. of *rahn*) contracted since the late 1940s; and insofar as the exercise of *shfa'a* rights was concerned, the *rahn* itself was little different from a sale. This fact in itself made the abolition of the *rahn* easier when the Berber Dahir was rescinded.

It is appropriate here to mention two ancillary concepts, those of *rtal* and *tila'*. The first is lending without interest for no stipulated period. If sufficient time passes, it is thought that a certain amount of *baraka* accrues to the lender. In some respects today *rtal* is more important than either *shfa'a* or *rahn*. However, if the lender is the local government, making loans of seed, the loan must be repaid at harvest time, even if a good many people sell one-fourth or even one-third of their crop before harvesting it. The second is lending at interest, and this could be as much as 50 per cent in precolonial times if a man desperately needed money. But usury is strictly forbidden in Islamic Law, and *tila'* was yet another practice expunged in 1956, the watershed year of Moroccan independence (Hart 1981 pp.122–5).

It should now be obvious that the predilection of the Ait 'Atta for their land to remain in indivision is as strong as that of the Aith Waryaghar for theirs to be divided. But this pull in technically opposite directions, if viewed comparatively, nonetheless brings them neatly together when we look through the prism of turns, shares and parts of a whole. This fact in itself relegates to secondary rank and status the fact of whether the whole in question is composed of dry-farmed land, land under irrigation or a combination of both. Indivision and division are, in effect, two sides of a coin, and different modes of the same thing. Division may begin simply but, as amply demonstrated here, it can also develop ramifications which become incredibly complex.

But what is perhaps the most curious fact of all, as well as that most worthy of being placed on record, is that impeccable ethnographies on this whole subject may be found in the unpublished reports from the early 1950s at the CHEAM (Centre des Hautes Etudes de l'Afrique et l'Asie Modernes) in Paris of two French army captains, R. de Monts de Savasse and Marcel Niclausse, for the Ait 'Atta. For the Aith Waryaghar, of a decade or more earlier, we should signal the studies by two Spanish army colonels, Emilio Blanco Izaga and Andres Sanchez Perez, and then again, and also unpublished, in the 1950s of another Spanish army captain, José Rodriguez Erola – who was assigned the administration of the Aith Waryaghar while still holding only a captain's rank, as normally it was regarded as a job for a major. But the calibre of all these reports, published or not, is first-class. We feel strongly that the quality of the ethnography of these French and Spanish army officers turned tribal administrators, far from being diminished by the demise of colonialism (whose servants, admittedly, they were), has, to the contrary, grown over the years, for they are models of ethnographic and reportorial accuracy. We take this opportunity to pay tribute to the excellent work done by all of them on Berber land tenure and division of irrigation water both in precolonial as in colonial Morocco.

BIBLIOGRAPHY

Berque, Jacques, *Maghreb: Histoire et Sociétés* (Algiers: Société Nationale d'Edition et de Diffusion (SNED); Gembloux, Belgium: Duculot 1974).
Blanco Izaga, Col. Emilio, 'Conferencia sobre Derecho Consuetudinario Rifeño', ms. (1935).
——, *El Rif (2a. Parte) – La Ley Rifeña – II: Los Canones Rifeños Comentados* (Ceuta: Imprenta Imperio 1939).
Bohannan, Paul, *Judgment and Justice among the Tiv* (London, New York and Toronto: Oxford University Press and International African Institute 1957).
de Ligniville, Capt., 'La Coutume Privée des Ait Atta du Sahara', ms., CHEAM Report No.551, 1937 (available for consultation at the Centre des Hautes Etudes de l'Afrique et l'Asie Modernes (CHEAM), Rue du Four, Paris).
de Monts de Savasse, Capt. R., 'Le Régime Foncier des Ait Atta du Sahara', ms., CHEAM

Report No.1815, 1951 (available for consultation at CHEAM, Paris – see above).

Denat, Capt., 'Droit Coutumier Berbère Ichkern: Contrat de "Amhars"', *Revue Marocaine de Droit* 7 (1951) pp.293–9.

Fortes, Meyer, *Kinship and the Social Order: The Legacy of Lewis Henry Morgan* (Chicago IL: Aldine Publishing Co. 1969).

Gilman Guillen, Antonio, 'Regadio y Conflicto en Sociedades Acefalas', *Seminario de Estudios de Arte y Arqueologia* (Consejo Superior de Investiogaciones Cientificas, Universidad de Valladolid 1987) pp.59–72.

Gray, Robert F., *The Sonjo of Tanganyika* (Oxford: Oxford University Press and International African Institute 1960).

Hart, David M., 'Emilio Blanco Izaga and the Berbers of the Central Rif', *Tamuda, Revista de Investigaciones Marroquies* VI/2 (1958) pp.171–237.

——, 'A Customary Law Document from the Ait 'Atta of the Jbil Saghru', *Revue de l'Occident Musulman et de la Méditerranée (ROMM)* I/1 (1966) pp.91–112.

——, 'Segmentary Systems and the Role of "Five Fifths" in Tribal Morocco' (1967), in Akbar S. Ahmed, and David M. Hart (eds.), *Islam in Tribal Societies From the Atlas to the Indus* (London: Routledge and Kegan Paul 1984) pp.66–105.

——, *The Aith Waryaghar of the Moroccan Rif: An Ethnography and History.* Viking Fund Publications in Anthropology, No.55 (Tucson: University of Arizona Press 1976).

——, '"Assu u-Ba Slam (1890–1960): De la Resistance à la "Pacification" au Maroc (Essai d'Anthropologie Sociale)', in Charles-André Julien, Magali Morsy, Cathetrine Cocquery-Vidrovitch and Yves Person (eds.), *Les Africains*, Vol. 5 (Paris: Editions Jeune Afrique 1975) pp.75–105.

——, *Dadda 'Atta and His Forty Grandsons: The Socio-Political Organisation of the Ait 'Atta of Southern Morocco* (Wisbech, Cambridgeshire: MENAS Press 1981).

——, *The Ait 'Atta of Southern Morocco: Daily Life and Recent History* (Wisbech, Cambridgeshire: MENAS Press 1984).

——, 'Rejoinder to Henry Munson, Jr., "On the Irrelevance of the Segmentary Lineage Model in the Moroccan Rif"', *American Anthropologist* 91/3 (1989) pp.765–9.

——, 'Four Centuries of History on the Hoof: The Northwest Passage of Berber Sheep Tranhumants Across the Moroccan Atlas, 1550–1912', *Morocco: Journal of the Society for Moroccan Studies* 3 (1993) pp.21–55.

——, *Documents from the Moroccan Rif* (Wisbech, Cambridgeshire: MENAS Press; Tetouan: Université Abdelmalek Saadi, in preparation).

—— (ed. and transl.), and Blanco Izaga, *Emilio Blanco Izaga: Colonel in the Rif.* Ethnography Series, HRAfLEX Books MX3-001 (2 vols., New Haven: Human Relations Area Files 1975).

——, *Emilio Blanco Izaga: Coronel en el Rif.* Biblioteca de Melilla No.8 (Melilla: Auyuntamiento Municipal de Melilla/Fundacion Municipal Sociovcultural/UNED-VCentro Asiociado de Melilla 1995).

Lafond, J., *Les Sources du Droit Coutumier dans le Souss: Le Statut Personnel et Successorial* (Agadir: Editions du Souss circa. 1948).

Lefebure, Claude, 'Des Poissons aux Mouflons (seg Iselmane ar Oudaden): La Vie Pastorale des Ayt Atta du Maroc Presaharien', in *L'Elevage en Méditerranée Occidentale* (Paris: Centre National de la Recherche Scientifique (CNRS) 1977) pp.195–205.

Marcy, Georges, 'Le Problème du Droit Coutumier Berbère' (1939), *Revue Algérienne, Tunisienne et Marocaine de Legislation et de Jurisprudence* (1954) pp.127–70.

Munson, Henry, Jr., 'On the Irrelevance of the Segmentary Lineage Model in the Moroccan Rif', *American Anthropologist* 91/2 (1989) pp.386–400.

Niclausse, Capt. Marcel, 'Rapports entre Nomades et Sédentaires dans le Coude du Dra: la Raia', ms., CHEAM Report No.2306, 1954 (available for consultation at CHEAM, Paris – see above).

Reader, D.H., *Zulu Tribe in Transition* (Manchester: Manchester University Press 1966).

Rodriguez Erola, Capt. José, *Caidato del Nekor, Comarcal de Beni Uarioaguel, Territorio del Rif*, ms. (1952).

——, *El Caidato del Alto Guis: Estudio Economico-Social*, ms. (1953).

Sanchez Perez, Col. Andres, 'Aprovechamientos Comunales y Formas de Cooperacion en el Rif', *Seleccion de Conferencias Pronunciadas en la Academia de Interventores Durante el Curso 1950–51* (Tetuan: Alta Comisaria de España en Marruecos/Delegacion de Asuntos Indigenas 1951) pp.95–104.

——, 'Datos Historicos sobre Ciudades Rifeñas', *Seleccion de Conferencias y Trabajos Realizados Durante el Curso de Interventores 1951–52* (Tetuan: Alta Comisaria de España en Marruecos/Delegacion de Asuntos Indigenas 1952) pp.29–47.

Wittfogel, Karl, *Oriental Despotism* (New Haven: Yale University Press 1957).

Index

Books of Related Interest

Technology, Tradition and Survival
Aspects of Material Culture in the Middle East and Central Asia

Richard Tapper, *SOAS, University of London* and **Keith McLachlan**, *formerly of SOAS, University of London*

Seeking to promote a wider knowledge of traditional technologies in the Middle East and Central Asia, the contributors address three related themes: the history, originality, variety and sophistication of traditional science, technology and material culture in these regions; their influence on the history of Europe and the West; and the threat posed by modern Western technologies to the survival of traditional technologies which have continuing value according to late-twentieth-century standards of sustainability and appropriateness to local cultural, social and ecological conditions. There is a clear need for conservation of some artefacts that are under current threat of extinction.

Individual chapters focus on specific aspects of technology and material culture: science and medicine; water technologies; vernacular architecture, both fixed buildings and the mobile tents of nomads; looms and weaving; and the structure of bazaars.

224 pages illus, map 2001
0 7146 4927 9 cloth
0 7146 4487 0 paper
History and Society in the Islamic World

Tribalism and Rural Society in the Islamic World
David M Hart

An anthropological study of tribal society in the islamic world with particular reference to Morocco and a comparison between Morocco and Pakistan/Afghanistan. All the societies considered are Muslim in nature and the approach taken is from the structural-functionalist perspective.

170 pages 2001
0 7146 4928 7 cloth
History and Society in the Islamic World

FRANK CASS PUBLISHERS
Newbury House, 900 Eastern Avenue, Ilford, Essex, IG2 7HH
Tel: +44 (0)20 8599 8866 Fax: +44 (0)20 8599 0984 E-mail: info@frankcass.com
NORTH AMERICA
5804 NE Hassalo Street, Portland, OR 97213 3644, USA
Tel: 800 944 6190 Fax: 503 280 8832 E-mail: cass@isbs.com
Website: www.frankcass.com

French Military Rule in Morocco

Colonialism and its Consequences

Moshe Gershovich, *Massachusetts Institute of Technology*

On 14 August 1844, French and Moroccan armies collided at the Battle of Isly which marked the beginning of Morocco's incorporation within the rising orbit of European imperialism. A hundred years later, French and Moroccan soldiers fought side by side for the liberation of France. When resisting foreign domination, Moroccans demonstrated the same endurance they had shown when serving the cause of the colonial power which had gained control over them. The French conquest of Morocco was one of the longest and toughest in the annals of European colonialism. However, once occupied, Morocco became one of the sources of France's finest colonial troops.

Both sides of this equation form the substance of this book. It presents a comprehensive analysis of French colonial ideology and delineates the manner in which the French army sought to conquer Morocco and control its inhabitants. It further examines the manner in which France recruited and utilized Moroccan combatants, highlighting their contribution to France's national security and imperial expansion. In conclusion, the book explores the Franco-Moroccan military symbiosis during the early years of Moroccan independence and assesses the impact of French rule on the shaping of Morocco's post-colonial national character.

256 pages illus, maps 2000
0 7146 4949 X cloth
History and Society in the Islamic World

FRANK CASS PUBLISHERS
Newbury House, 900 Eastern Avenue, Ilford, Essex, IG2 7HH
Tel: +44 (0)20 8599 8866 Fax: +44 (0)20 8599 0984 E-mail: info@frankcass.com
NORTH AMERICA
5804 NE Hassalo Street, Portland, OR 97213 3644, USA
Tel: 800 944 6190 Fax: 503 280 8832 E-mail: cass@isbs.com
Website: www.frankcass.com